Cross Encounters

Cross Encounters
A Decade of Gospel Conversations

Tony Miano

Solid Ground Christian Books
Birmingham, Alabama USA

Solid Ground Christian Books
PO Box 660132
Vestavia Hills AL 35266
205-443-0311
mike.sgcb@gmail.com
www.solid-ground-books.com

CROSS ENCOUNTERS
A DECADE OF GOSPEL CONVERSATIONS

TONY MIANO

First edition June 2016

ISBN: 978-159925-360-2

Cover design by Borgo Design in Tuscaloosa, Alabama.
Contact them at borgogirl@bellsouth.net

Cover Photo is of Tony Miano ministering on the street
with cover photo by Matt DeJesus
Used with permission.

Editor's Note: All of the Bible verses printed in this book are from the New American Standard Version, unless they were quoted from a different version during a transcribed conversation (e.g. English Standard Version) or in an appendix written by a different author (e.g. New King James Version).

Table of Contents

Dedication

I love to invest in the spiritual lives of younger men. Discipling men who are young enough to be my sons (and whom I love as sons) brings me great joy. I count each opportunity to offer younger men even a moment of encouragement, correction, or instruction as an undeserved privilege. And for these opportunities, of which I have had many over the years, I am thankful to the Lord.

This book is dedicated to all the young men in whose lives I have been grateful to play a small role—young men like Joey Cusenza, Jimmy Revelino, Warner Aldridge, and Donnie Johnson.

Preface

Loving God and loving people (Matthew 22:34-40): for the Christian, these are the only two prerequisites for evangelistic engagement. Every Christian lives under the command of God to make Jesus Christ known to lost people bound for hell (John 17:20-21; Acts 1:8; Jude 20-22) and to disciple those God causes to be born again to a living hope (Matthew 28:18-20; 1 Peter 1:3). Though still imperfect people, those who love Jesus love to obey Jesus (John 3:36; 14:21).

When it comes to evangelism, Christians do not lack training. It is not another plan, scheme, or method they need. Those who are truly born again know the gospel, for one cannot be saved by a gospel they do not know. What most Christians lack is enough love for Jesus and for the lost.

Did you just wince?

In order to prove my point, I ask you to take a few moments before continuing and make a list of all the reasons why you are apprehensive about striking up a gospel conversation with a stranger. You will likely find that none of the reasons on your list have anything to do with the eternal fate of lost people. Instead, *you* are the common denominator.

"I don't want to say the wrong thing." "What if I'm asked a question I can't answer?" "What if I push a person further away from Jesus?" "I need to develop a relationship with a person before I can talk to them about Jesus." "If I just come out and tell my friends what I believe, I might lose my friends and lose the opportunity to talk to them about Jesus in the future." "If I stand up to my professor and tell him I believe God created everything, I can kiss a good grade in that class goodbye." "I'm just a month away from being eligible for a promotion and a raise. I'll wait until after I get the new position to share the gospel with my coworkers."

"I," "me," and "my" are the best friends of many professing Christians, friends with whom they cannot bear to part. The symptoms of idolatry of self are hard to miss.

For many professing Christians, self-love relegates love for the lost and love for Jesus to the shadows of self-preservation. Their love for Jesus comes out of the shadows on Sunday morning and during the mid-week home fellowship—safe places of expression. Sadly, their love for the lost rarely, if ever, makes it out of the shadows. So, in order to appease their consciences, they adopt man-centered, non-evangelistic methodologies like "friendship evangelism," which are geared more toward protecting the Christian from American Evangelical-level persecutions like a lack of popularity or a loss of self-esteem than reaching the lost with the gospel.

While I believe readers will learn much about evangelism in this book, this book is not a training manual. It is not a "how to" book, even though there are several chapters in the book that provide practical help for your evangelism efforts. It is a "what happens" book. This book is a collection of real stories about real conversations with real people who really need Christ. The stories in this book, drawn from a decade on the streets and in other places around the world, are examples of what happens when a Christian swallows his fears, takes risks, tries to put shoe leather to his faith, and communicates the gospel to strangers.

My hope is that this book will serve as both a source of edification to my brothers and sisters in Christ and as an evangelism tool in their hands. My hope is that Christians will read this book and be encouraged, emboldened, and equipped to communicate the gospel with people *out there*. My hope is that Christians, once they've read this book, will put it into the hands of their unsaved friends, family members, relatives, coworkers, fellow students, professors, or anyone else who needs to come to repentance and faith in the Lord Jesus Christ.

The stories are not laid out in chronological order. Each chapter is a complete story, with no attachment to the previous or following chapters, although they have been grouped according to theme or location. This book is designed to be read either from start to finish or chapter by chapter.

The book begins with "The Burglar," a short, fictitious story—a parable, really—that illustrates the law and the gospel. I wrote "The Burglar" as an evangelistic booklet. I decided to include it as the first chapter in this book because I want everyone who reads *Cross Encounters* to understand that the gospel is most important. This book is not about me. It's not about my experiences. It's about Jesus Christ.

The power of God for salvation to all who believe is not found in one's chosen evangelistic methodology. It is not found in a Christian's ability to make and maintain relationships with lost people. It is not found in the street preacher's oratory skills, the apologist's ability to dismantle the worldview of his opponent, or the eye-popping design of a gospel tract. The power of God for salvation to all who believe is *the gospel* (Romans 1:16), and Christians should unapologetically and unashamedly believe it and communicate it.

The gospel is a message that can only be communicated with words (Romans 10:14-17), whether in spoken or written form. The gospel can be faithfully and effectively communicated through preaching, debate, conversation, the distribution of literature (paper missionaries), and many other ways. However, the power of the message is not in the form of communication, but rather in the message itself.

Most chapters in this book contain a full presentation of the gospel. Some do not. Because this book contains so many gospel presentations, I am concerned the reader may see it as redundant. Please don't. To see the presentation of the gospel as redundant would be irreverent. Please don't gloss over the gospel, and please don't skip it all together. While I hope you find each story in this book compelling, my prayer is that you will find the gospel of Jesus Christ more so.

If every person who picks up this book reads only the gospel before putting it down or tossing it aside, with this I will be content. However, I encourage you to read on.

For some readers, footnotes can be a distraction that takes away from the flow of the book. I've tried to keep the footnotes to a minimum, limiting them to definitions of terms and the occasional evangelism "quick tip." My goal is that they would add, not detract, from the reader's experience.

Interspersed among some of my favorite personal evangelism stories are chapters written to help Christians step out of their "comfort zones." It was important to me in writing this book that I not only encourage readers with stories of evangelism, but also encourage readers to engage in evangelism. It would not be fair for me to light a fire under you (so to speak) and not assist you in directing the flame. With that in mind, this book includes several "how to" chapters and appendices: how to navigate contact with law enforcement or private security, how to establish a sidewalk ministry outside an abortion clinic, how to get permission to conduct evangelism at your local mall, and how to engage in "friendship evangelism" and actually be evangelistic.

Most of the stories in this book have positive endings. While every story does not end with a person coming to repentance and faith in Jesus Christ, the reader will likely be left as I was at the end of the conversations: hopeful that the man or woman with whom I spoke would receive the free gift of eternal life. Choosing mostly positive stories was, of course, intentional. I want you to finish this book feeling not only encouraged in your own walk with Jesus Christ, but also motivated, even challenged, to go love God and love people through biblical evangelism.

I have a short list of books, after the Bible, that have significantly impacted my life. The list includes *The Gospel According to Jesus*, by John MacArthur; *Holiness*, by J.C. Ryle, and *A Pastor's Sketches: Conversations with Anxious Souls Concerning the Way of Salvation*[1], by Ichabod Spencer (1798-1854), who pastored Second Presbyterian Congregation of Brooklyn for 22 years.

MacArthur's work introduced me to the lordship of Christ and the Doctrines of Grace. Ryle's work is a continual source of conviction in my life—the conviction to pursue holiness, with the desire to be conformed to the image of Christ. Spencer's work is more than just a book. It is a faithful companion. *A Pastor's Sketches* is often my book of choice when I travel. Every chapter is a beautiful example of the practical fulfillment of the two greatest commandments: to love God and love people. Reading *A Pastor's Sketches* is like accompanying a great man of God as he engages in door-to-door evangelism or pastoral

---

[1] A wonderful, single-volume edition of this work is available through Solid Ground Christian Books (http://www.solid-ground-books.com/detail_58.asp). You can read contemporary reviews of this classic work at the link provided.

visitation. A pastoral student can learn much in seminary. But the experience of serving side-by-side with a pastor is invaluable. *A Pastor's Sketches* provides the reader with this kind of experience in written form. I have been asked by people over the last several years to write this book. Reading *A Pastor's Sketches* gave me the motivation I needed to start the project.

In addition to Pastor Spencer, there are many other people to whom I owe a debt of thanks, such as Margaret Gill and Steven Holley. Margaret transcribed several audio recordings of conversations in this book. Steven transcribed the hour-long conversation with Mohammed (Section VI).

This marks the second book Allison Pari has edited for me, the first being *Should She Preach? – Biblical Evangelism for Women.* Allison is an amazing writer and a skilled grammarian. Not only did her editorial work greatly improve the book, but her insights and suggestions took the book to a level I could not take it on my own. She is also my lovely niece.

Jerry Dorris created the front and back cover designs and did the layout for the book. Jerry's work took what I hope you will find to be memorable stories and made them easy on the eyes.

Michael Gaydosh, with Solid Ground Books, did not take long to decide to publish this book when I first came to him with the idea. Michael's patience and encouragement throughout the publication process was a great source of encouragement. It is an honor, privilege, and blessing to have a title in the Solid Ground Books catalog.

Last, but certainly not least, I owe a debt of gratitude to a group of men and women I call my Peer Review Team. Once the manuscript had weathered the editorial process and was ready for publication, a group of friends read the manuscript. They provided wonderful feedback, encouragement, and counsel. The members of the Peer Review Team were: Pastor Geoffrey Kirkland (who also graciously agreed to write the Foreword), Donna Hebert, Kevin St. John, Tim Schiller, Bobby McCreery, Joey Cusenza, Pastor Mike Reid, Warner Aldridge, Richard Story, Chris Fisher, Jeff Rose, and Jimmy Revelino.

With that, join me now as I share some of my favorite cross encounters—stories from a decade of evangelism on the streets and elsewhere.

Foreword

It was over a hundred and fifty years ago that Ichabod Spencer wrote his excellent work, *A Pastor's Sketches*, which traced his conversations with many people about the state of their souls and the way of salvation. God has designed the gospel to spread through the verbal proclamation. It is a valuable exercise to recount how God has worked in various situations and how God's people have guided anxious souls to the cross, unveiled the way of salvation in Christ, and urged the hearers to repent and trust in Christ. It proves to benefit those who observe how faithful Christians have compassionately led people to Calvary. One cannot read through the Book of Acts and miss how frequently the apostles went back to the people of God to report to them all that God did through them as they proclaimed the gospel publicly and from house to house. We can only imagine how encouraging, stimulating, and exciting those accounts must have been for the believers to hear.

When the gospel goes forth, God moves. God always works through His Word. It happens just as the Lord promised Jeremiah: "I am watching over my word to perform it" (1:12). Never does a person proclaim the gospel of saving grace without any effect. In conversations with lost and blinded souls, believers need to courageously expose their sin, confidently point to God's only provision for salvation in Christ, and singularly urge them to turn from sin and trust in Jesus Christ alone for deliverance from divine wrath. How encouraging it is to learn from others who have engaged in such conversations! Furthermore, how instructive it is to have many of these conversations transcribed so we can grow in our courageous and patient proclamation of God's grace in Christ to the lost. Several benefits come about through reading such accounts. I will elucidate five of them.

1. *A strong motivation to grow in proclaiming Christ and His gospel.* Reading about the accounts of others and how God uses the verbal communication of His gospel at different times and in different venues produces in the believer a fiery passion

to do likewise. In a sanctified and provocative way, it refocuses the believer's mind on that which truly defines God's purpose for us, namely, to proclaim Christ and His gospel.

2. *A growth in understanding how faithful saints have proclaimed Christ and His gospel in various settings and with people of multifaceted backgrounds.* Accounts such as this demonstrate to us how faithful people of God have responded to the most hostile of rebels and to professing Christians who do not, in fact, possess Christ. Observing how evangelists respond in such cases provides insight for responding biblically and courageously in various settings.

3. *A thrilling wonder at the supernatural power of the message of the gospel that powerfully converts sinners.* Observing how God has worked causes the sanctified soul to soar in the heavenly places with wonder, amazement, and worship because our God uses a proclaimed message—the ultimate message—to save and sanctify, to convert and change, to deliver from divine wrath and drive people to the divine Savior! Reading such accounts proves to be thrilling, not simply because of the evangelist or his responses, but because of the unstoppable power of the gospel and of the unshakeable sovereignty of God!

4. *A renewed humility that God chooses to use weak vessels as His instruments in presenting the gospel and trusting Him for growth.* It should humble believers to know that God used a donkey of old as part of His purposes in delivering sacred truth. Believers remember the power to save resides not in the Christian or his tactics but solely in the faithfulness of presenting His Word without reservation. Hearts become humbled when considering the awesome wonder that God uses weak vessels as His vehicles to speak His Word to lost souls so as to deliver them from God's eternal wrath.

5. *A powerful exhortation to remind us that the believer's primary duty in life is to proclaim the excellencies of Him who called us out of darkness and into His marvelous light.* Quite simply, reading such gospel encounters exhorts and reminds us that the preeminent reason for our existence as Christians on earth is to

be both worshipers of God and announcers of His great salvation. A volume like this has a convicting and a challenging effect. It convicts us of the need to proclaim our Savior more and challenges us to increase our evangelism efforts through fervent, faithful, and frequent gospel conversations, by the strength of the Spirit, for God's glory.

A resource such as *Cross Encounters: A Decade of Gospel Conversations*, where conversations are transcribed, proves to instruct, humble, and stir us up to zealous evangelism. Let God's people read this volume with gospel-believing gladness and with humble delight in observing how God uses faithful witnesses to speak His gospel to the lost so that the Spirit of grace may grant new birth!

The Word of God tells us that Jesus went about "doing good" (Acts 10:38) and we also know from Scripture that Jesus relentlessly devoted Himself to preaching all over Israel (Luke 4:44; 9:6). May we read *Cross Encounters* with a prayerful heart, a captivated spirit, a lowly gladness, and a renewed resolve, all shrouded with an indomitable confidence in the absolute sovereignty of God to save sinners through the faithful telling of the gospel. And in the end, let us faithfully proclaim Christ and Him crucified (1 Corinthians 2:2) and fervently pray that the Word of the Lord will spread rapidly and be glorified (2 Thessalonians 3:1). To God be the glory!

Pastor Geoffrey Kirkland
Christ Fellowship Bible Church of St. Louis
December 24, 2015

The Burglar: A Parable of the Gospel

His life was one of petty crimes. Well known in the community as a self-righteous young man, he always had an explanation to justify his run-ins with the law. He was often in trouble, but he repeatedly managed to avoid appearing before the judge, choosing to accept plea bargains instead of taking responsibility for his actions. Ignorant of legal proceedings, he was unaware that the judge had to approve every plea bargain. Blinded by his self-righteousness, he did not realize that his freedom wasn't the result of his own ability to manipulate the system. His freedom was the result of the judge's patience—a patience that had limits.

He was always sorry when he got caught, but his remorse was nothing more than worldly sorrow.[1] It never amounted to true repentance.[2] Even before being released from jail for one of his myriad offenses, he was already planning his next effort to satisfy the ravenous desires of his darkened heart.

He was really no different than the other members of his community. He was simply more prone than others to act upon his sinful thoughts, although he wasn't very good at accomplishing his crimes. His sins always seemed to find him out.

Tired of being known in the community as a petty criminal, the man set his sights higher. He decided he would expand his criminal activity from bike thefts and shoplifting to burglary. He would enter someone's home and steal from the residents as they slept in their beds. He knew in exactly which home he would begin this seedier and more desperate work: the largest home in town.

---

[1] See 2 Corinthians 7:10. "Worldly sorrow" is any sorrow or grief that does not result from a heart conviction for sins committed against God.

[2] "Repentance" is a changing of mind about God and sin, which is brought about by the work of the Holy Spirit in a person's life. This changing of mind always leads to a changing of direction and action. A person who repents will begin to love the things God loves and hate the things God hates. Repentance, which is a gift from God (see Romans 2:4), will include placing one's faith and trust in Jesus Christ alone for salvation.

Late one night, after filling his stomach and liver with 40 ounces of malt liquor, the man decided to break into the home. He watched the place from a distance, waiting for the last light to be extinguished. Emboldened by liquid courage and thinking himself a crafty criminal, he waited a while longer for the residents to fall deep into sleep.

He hopped over the small picket fence surrounding the front yard of the home, causing it to creak. The neighborhood dogs began to bark, alerted to the fact that something was moving in the night. He hid himself in the darker shadows and waited for the dogs to quiet themselves.

He made his way to the back of the home, where he found the kitchen door. To his surprise, it was unlocked. He entered the house with a flashlight in his hand. He also had a knife in his pocket, just in case.

He slowly made his way through the dark kitchen and even darker hallway into the living room. He stood in the corner of the room and surveyed its contents with a flashlight. The light briefly drew his attention to several family pictures on the walls. A father and mother. Parents with what appeared to be an only son. He felt a smile form on his face as he wondered what it would be like to have a family, to have parents who loved him. The smile quickly turned to a grimace as he envied the framed testaments of relationships he saw on the walls.

He didn't stop there. His anger toward the family, a family he had never met, grew. He didn't believe he could ever have what they had, so he didn't think they should have it either. The burglar coveted. He was never content with what he had and always wanted more. He always wanted what someone else had.

The burglar realized he had already been too long in the home. He cleared his mind and returned to the task at hand. As he rummaged through the darkened room, opening and closing bookcases, end table drawers, and the like, he didn't realize how much noise he was making, that is, until he heard a sound coming from the back of the house.

Someone was awake.

He froze in his tracks as the sounds came closer and closer. Was it someone going for a midnight snack or had they heard him rummaging through their possessions? The footsteps got louder. Then the figure gasped loud enough to startle the burglar, who immediately turned and shined the flashlight on a young boy.

The boy screamed.

Acting impulsively and according to his nature, the burglar rushed toward the boy while pulling the knife out of his pocket. With an instinctive lunge, he plunged the knife into the boy's chest. The boy slumped forward but did not fall right away. He lifted his head and looked at the burglar as if to ask, "Why?" With a loud exhale, the boy cried, "Father!" He fell to the ground, holding the handle of the knife still in his chest.

He was dead.

With the boy's spattered blood on his clothes and face, the burglar stood silent, motionless. Then he heard the sound of feet running down the hall in his direction. He turned and rushed through the closed front door, almost ripping it from its hinges.

The burglar (now a murderer) ran. While he ran from the police who he knew would soon be on the scene, he also tried to run from his conscience, which, until this moment, had been seared by years of sinful behavior. But no matter how fast or how far he ran, he could not run from his thoughts. He could not run from the images and the sounds of a boy dying in front of him. He could not run from the thoughts of the burglary and murder he had just committed.

So lost was he in thought that he didn't see the patrol car coming toward him. It wasn't until he heard the siren that he looked up to see the flashing blue and red lights directly in front of him. He made no effort to evade arrest. He simply put his bloody hands on the hood of the patrol car and allowed the officers to take him into custody. He gave no resistance.

After being booked at the police station, he was interrogated by detectives. He confessed to his heinous crime and provided a written statement. This was a death penalty case. He would receive no plea bargains. His only hope was to plead not guilty and hope for the best in court. Maybe he could get off on a technicality. Maybe the confession would be thrown out.

Still no remorse. Still no repentance. Nothing more than a worldly sorrow. While he knew what he did was wrong, while he felt bad about it, and while he might even be able to convince some that he didn't intend to kill the boy, his thoughts were really only of himself and the consequences he would likely face.

The trial began early on a Friday morning. It was unusual to begin a trial on the last day of the work week. It didn't take long for the prosecution to make its case. Horrific crime scene photos brought both male and female jurors to tears. Compelling physical evidence including finger prints, DNA, and blood splatters on the burglar's clothing was presented to the jury.

And then there was the burglar's handwritten confession.

Throughout the morning, as he sat and listened to the testimony of the detectives and the district attorney's presentation of the physical evidence, the burglar could not shake the nagging thought, "I've seen the judge before. But where?"

His attorney made little noise, rarely objecting to the prosecution's line of questioning or introduction of evidence. He knew his client was guilty. His strategy was to do as little as possible to upset the judge and jury and then make a plea for his client, focusing on his client's poor upbringing and lack of opportunities in life.

To the amazement of all in the courtroom, the case was given to the jury for deliberation before the noon hour. Nobody left the courtroom. Something told them the jury would quickly return with a guilty verdict.

The burglar was led out of the courtroom and into a holding cell. There he sat. He wondered if he would die an old man in prison or strapped to a gurney with a sharp needle inserted into his arm. He saw no other options. He knew there were no other options.

And there was that nagging thought: "I've seen that judge before."

An officer came to his holding cell. "It's time," he said as he inserted the large brass key into the cell door. The officer led the burglar back to his seat at the defense table. His reappearance caused a low and mumbled buzz in the courtroom.

The people in the courtroom snapped back to attention when the judge reentered from his chambers. "All rise!" barked the bailiff. Everyone rose to their feet, standing quiet and still. Then the jury was led into the courtroom.

"You may be seated," said the judge. "Has the jury reached a verdict?" he asked.

The foreman of the jury stood, holding a folded piece of paper in his hands. "We have, your honor."

"Please hand the verdict to the bailiff," the judge ordered.

The jury foreman extended his hand to the bailiff, who received the written verdict and presented it to the judge at his bench. The judge slowly opened the piece of paper and read it silently.

"Oh no!" the burglar whispered to himself with a terrified tone. "Now I remember where I've seen the judge!"

His mind went back to that fateful night, to the living room where he murdered a boy in cold blood. He closed his eyes to replay the scene in his mind, and his mind's eye took him to the framed family portraits.

"He's the father!" he said to himself with a gasp. "I murdered the judge's son!"

The judge refolded the piece of paper and placed it on his bench in front of him. He turned his gaze to the defendant.

"Will the defendant please rise?" ordered the judge.

Both the burglar and his attorney rose to their feet.

"Mr. Foreman, how do you and the jury find the defendant in this case?" the judge asked.

"We, the jury, find the defendant in this case guilty of murder in the first degree."

The burglar's attorney asked, "Your honor, the defense requests that the court poll the jury."

One by one, the 12 jurors verbalized their decision. "Guilty. Guilty. Guilty…"

Once the jury had been polled, the judge thanked them for their service, released them, and had them escorted from the courtroom.

"Do the people have any objection to the court imposing sentence upon the defendant at this time?"

"No, your honor."

"Does the defense have any objection to the court imposing sentence upon the defendant at this time?"

The defense attorney turned and looked at his client, now shedding tears for maybe the first time in his life. The now convicted criminal shook his head.

"No, your honor."

The judge looked sternly into the murderer's eyes, holding his gaze for several silent moments. "Young man, having been found guilty of murder in the first degree, while in the commission of a felony burglary, you are sentenced to death. You are to be taken from this courtroom and into the execution chamber without delay for the immediate imposition of sentencing."

Now loudly sobbing, the murderer dropped his chin to his chest. The bailiff moved in between him and his attorney to lead the dead-man-walking from the courtroom to the last place he would ever see on earth—the execution chamber.

"Wait!" the judge ordered.

The bailiff stopped. All eyes in the courtroom turned from the man about to die to the man who sentenced him to death.

"Young man, you murdered my son. You broke into my home and, in cold blood, you murdered my only son. The sentence I have issued to you is just, according to the requirements of the law. You deserve to die for your crimes. You deserve to die for murdering my son."

What happened next had never before been seen in a courtroom and has not been seen since.

The judge rose from behind his bench—his sovereign, judicial place of authority. As he stepped down, he removed his robe—the symbol of his authority.

The judge made his way to his son's killer. Again, he looked him in the eye. "Yes, you deserve to die for your crimes. There is nothing good in you. You have no redeeming qualities. You are a wicked man. You are, after all, a man with a sin nature and a heart that is deceitful and desperately sick [Jeremiah 17:9]. Yes, you most certainly deserve to die."

Knowing his life would soon be over, knowing there was no hope, the murderous burglar forgot his worldly sorrow in hateful rage. "Get on with it! If you're going to execute me, then execute me! I'm tired of hearing that I killed your son! I know I killed your son! And you know what? I would probably do it again!"

"I know," the judge said.

"You know? That's it? I killed your son, I tell you I would probably do it again, and all you have to say is, 'I know?'"

"I have more to say," the judge replied. Again, several moments of silence filled the courtroom. "Yes, I have found you guilty and I've sentenced you to death. But I'm going to take your place."

Every jaw, including that of the murderous burglar, dropped.

The judge ordered the handcuffs removed from the convicted man and placed on himself.

"You are free to go. You are exonerated[3] of your crimes and your conviction is hereby expunged[4] from your record. What the law requires of you—death as the just punishment for your crimes—I am going to take upon myself. I'm doing this because I love you."

With those solemn and unbelievable words, the judge was escorted to the execution chamber where he allowed the executioner to strap him to a gurney and inject a chemical cocktail into the vein of his left arm.

Standing just outside the execution chamber was the man who moments earlier had been inexplicably set free. There he stood and watched as the judge died. He died a death he did not deserve in order to take upon himself the punishment the murderer rightly deserved for his crimes committed against the judge.

No one took the judge's life. He willingly laid down his life so his son's murderer could go free. The tears the murderer shed were different now. No longer did tears of self-pity flow from his eyes. The tears that now flowed were tears of love, contrition[5], brokenness, and repentance.

The wrath, anger, bitterness, and hate he had felt toward the judge were gone. He knew the pardon he received was undeserved and unmerited. He knew he had just been given a gift he could never

---

[3] "Exonerate": to declare someone free from blame or fault or wrongdoing, especially after a court proceeding.

[4] "Expunge": to erase or remove completely.

[5] "Contrition": the state of feeling remorseful.

repay. In an instant, by a supremely sacrificial act of love, the burglar's heart was changed. No longer was his desire to satisfy himself. He now had a new heart, with new desires to try to live up to so great a sacrifice, so great a gift. He knew he never could live up to it, but it would become his life's labor of love.

How do I know these things?

I am the burglar.

What you just read was a parable, a simple story used to illustrate a moral or spiritual lesson. While the story is not true, there is much to learn from it. Yes, I am the burglar, but so are you. We have all sinned. We have all broken God's law and fall short of His glory (Romans 3:23) every day of our lives.

What is sin?

All wrongdoing is sin (1 John 5:17). Everything and anything a person thinks, says, or does that does not proceed from faith in Jesus Christ is sin (Romans 14:23). Sin is to disobey, to break the law of God (Nehemiah 9:29). Sin is lawlessness[6] (1 John 3:4). It is important to note the Person against whom your offenses are committed. "For I know my transgressions, and my sin is ever before me. Against You, You only, I have sinned and done what is evil in Your sight, so that You are justified when You speak and blameless when You judge" (Psalm 51:3-4).

Every sin you have ever committed in thought, word, and deed is a crime against God, your Creator. The One you have sinned against is the One before whom you will stand to give an account for your life.

Like every other human being, you were created in the image of God. You are an image-bearer of your Creator. You know this is true for two reasons:

First, creation itself testifies to the reality of the Creator. For the wrath of God is revealed from heaven against all ungodliness and unrighteousness of men who suppress the

---

[6] "Lawlessness": a willful defiance of the known will and law of God (i.e. "don't lie;" "don't steal;" "don't take God's name in vain," etc.).

truth in unrighteousness, because that which is known about God is evident within them; for God made it evident to them. For since the creation of the world His invisible attributes, His eternal power and divine nature, have been clearly seen, being understood through what has been made, so that they are without excuse (Romans 1:18-20).

Second, God has given you a conscience. He has written His law on your heart. God has given you the ability to understand the difference between right and wrong, good and evil: "…in that they show the work of the Law written in their hearts, their conscience bearing witness and their thoughts alternately accusing or else defending them, on the day when, according to my gospel, God will judge the secrets of men through Christ Jesus" (Romans 2:15-16).

You know it is wrong to lie because you were created in the image of God, and God is not a liar. God is truth.

You know it is wrong to steal because you were created in the image of God, and God is not a thief. God is good.

You know it is wrong to engage in any form of sexual immorality because you were created in the image of God, and God is not a fornicator. He is not an adulterer. God is faithful.

You know it is wrong to harbor bitterness or resentment in your heart. You know it is wrong to be angry without cause. You know it is wrong to hate another human being, which God equates with murder (1 John 3:15), because you were created in the image of God, and God is not a murderer. God is love.

You know it is wrong to take God's name in vain, to use His name to express anger, surprise, disgust, or even joy. You know it's wrong to make His name common or a curse word, because you were created in the image of God, and God is not a blasphemer. God is holy.

But there is more.

Your sins are not only wrong thoughts, words, and actions against other people; your sins are against God. King David of Israel knew this well, as evidenced by his statement in Psalm 51 (referenced above).

So heinous are your sins in the mind of God that it is as if you broke into the Judge's house and murdered His Son, trampling through the Son's blood as you ran out the front door.

> For if we go on sinning willfully after receiving the knowledge of the truth, there no longer remains a sacrifice for sins, but a terrifying expectation of judgment and the fury of a fire which will consume the adversaries. Anyone who has set aside the Law of Moses dies without mercy on the testimony of two or three witnesses. How much severer punishment do you think he will deserve who has trampled under foot the Son of God, and has regarded as unclean the blood of the covenant by which he was sanctified, and has insulted the Spirit of grace? For we know Him who said, "Vengeance is Mine, I will repay." And again, "The Lord will judge His people." It is a terrifying thing to fall into the hands of the living God. (Hebrews 10:26-31).[7]

Like the burglar in the parable, you are without excuse (Romans 1:20). The soul that sins shall die (Ezekiel 18:4, 20). When you die and stand before the Judge (Hebrews 9:27), your Creator and

---

[7] In *Matthew Henry's Concise Commentary*, Matthew Henry (1662-1714), the British Nonconformist minister and theologian, explains Hebrews 10:26-31 this way (Matthew Henry, "Matthew Henry's Commentary: Hebrews 10," *Bible Hub*, accessed April 22, 2016, http://biblehub.com/commentaries/mhc/hebrews/10.htm.): "The exhortations against apostasy and to perseverance are urged by many strong reasons. The sin here mentioned is a total and final falling away, when men, with a full and fixed will and resolution, despise and reject Christ, the only Savior; despise and resist the Spirit, the only Sanctifier; and despise and renounce the gospel, the only way of salvation, and the words of eternal life. Of this destruction God gives some notorious sinners, while on earth, a fearful foreboding in their consciences, with despair of being able to endure or to escape it. But what punishment can be sorer than to die without mercy? We answer, to die by mercy, by the mercy and grace which they have despised. How dreadful is the case, when not only the justice of God, but his abused grace and mercy call for vengeance! All this does not in the least mean that any souls who sorrow for sin will be shut out from mercy, or that any will be refused the benefit of Christ's sacrifice, who are willing to accept these blessings. Him that cometh unto Christ, he will in no wise cast out."

God, you will not be able to claim either innocence or ignorance of violating God's Law. God, the good Judge who shows no partiality (Romans 2:11) and will not accept a bribe (Deuteronomy 10:17), will judge you according to the Law He has written on your heart. And contrary to what you may have heard, the Day of Judgment is not a court trial. It is a day of sentencing, and the punishment God has determined for all sin against Him is eternity in hell.

"The Father loves the Son and has given all things into His hand. He who believes in the Son has eternal life; but he who does not obey the Son will not see life, but the wrath of God abides on him" (John 3:35-36).

> Then I saw a great white throne and Him who sat upon it, from whose presence earth and heaven fled away, and no place was found for them. And I saw the dead, the great and the small, standing before the throne, and books were opened; and another book was opened, which is the book of life; and the dead were judged from the things which were written in the books, according to their deeds. And the sea gave up the dead which were in it, and death and Hades gave up the dead which were in them; and they were judged, every one of them according to their deeds. Then death and Hades were thrown into the lake of fire. This is the second death, the lake of fire. And if anyone's name was not found written in the book of life, he was thrown into the lake of fire (Revelation 20:11-15).

"The Son of Man will send forth His angels, and they will gather out of His kingdom all stumbling blocks, and those who commit lawlessness, and will throw them into the furnace of fire; in that place there will be weeping and gnashing of teeth" (Matthew 13:41-42).

"If your hand causes you to stumble, cut it off; it is better for you to enter life crippled, than, having your two hands, to go into hell, into the unquenchable fire" (Mark 9:43).

"But for the cowardly and unbelieving and abominable and murderers and immoral persons and sorcerers and idolaters and all liars, their part will be in the lake that burns with fire and brimstone, which is the second death" (Revelation 21:8).

In the parable, the burglar received the death penalty as the just sentence for his crimes. Likewise, the wages of sin is death (Romans 6:23). The just punishment for your sins against God is eternity in hell.

It is a remarkable, even shocking, scene in the parable when the judge, having sentenced the burglar to death, stepped down from his bench and took upon himself the punishment the burglar rightly deserved. Even more shocking than an unbelievable scene in that fictitious human courtroom, is the fact that God the Son, Jesus Christ, has actually done this. Jesus Christ has literally taken upon Himself the just punishment for a countless number of sinners.

> Being then the children of God, we ought not to think that the Divine Nature is like gold or silver or stone, an image formed by the art and thought of man. Therefore having overlooked the times of ignorance, God is now declaring to men that all people everywhere should repent, because He has fixed a day in which He will judge the world in righteousness through a Man whom He has appointed, having furnished proof to all men by raising Him from the dead (Acts 17:29-31).

And here is how He did it.

Some 2,000 years ago, God the Father sent His Son to earth in the person of Jesus Christ. He was born of a virgin, just as the prophet Isaiah declared He would be more than 700 years before His birth. "Therefore the Lord Himself will give you a sign: Behold, a virgin will be with child and bear a son, and she will call His name Immanuel" (Isaiah 7:14).

And:

> For a child will be born to us, a son will be given to us; and the government will rest on His shoulders; and His name will be called Wonderful Counselor, Mighty God, Eternal Father, Prince of Peace. There will be no end to the increase of His government or of peace, on the throne of David and over his kingdom, to establish it and to uphold it with justice and

righteousness from then on and forevermore. The zeal of the Lord of hosts will accomplish this (Isaiah 9:6-7).

Jesus, God the Son, humbled Himself and submitted Himself to the will of the Father, taking on the form of human flesh without setting aside His deity. Jesus did not regard equality with God the Father as something He had to hold onto, as if it were something He could lose or forfeit. Jesus was and is fully God and fully Man.

Have this attitude in yourselves which was also in Christ Jesus, who, although He existed in the form of God, did not regard equality with God a thing to be grasped, but emptied Himself, taking the form of a bond-servant, and being made in the likeness of men. Being found in appearance as a man, He humbled Himself by becoming obedient to the point of death, even death on a cross. For this reason also, God highly exalted Him, and bestowed on Him the name which is above every name, so that at the name of Jesus every knee will bow, of those who are in heaven and on earth and under the earth, and that every tongue will confess that Jesus Christ is Lord, to the glory of God the Father (Philippians 2:5-11).

Jesus, the God-Man, walked this earth for about 33 years. During that time, He obeyed the Father and His Law perfectly in thought, word, and deed. He knew no sin. He could not sin because He was, is, and always will be the sinless Lamb of God who came to take away the sins of the world. "For we do not have a high priest who cannot sympathize with our weaknesses, but One who has been tempted in all things as we are, yet without sin" (Hebrews 4:15). "The next day he [John the Baptist] saw Jesus coming to him and said, 'Behold, the Lamb of God who takes away the sin of the world!'" (John 1:29).

Yet, in spite of the fact that Jesus was the sinless God-Man, He voluntarily went to the cross. He suffered and died a horrific, bloody death He did not deserve.

When Pilate saw that he was accomplishing nothing, but rather that a riot was starting, he took water and washed his hands in front of the crowd, saying, "I am innocent of this Man's blood; see to that yourselves." And all the people said, "His blood shall be on us and on our children!" Then he released Barabbas for them; but after having Jesus scourged, he handed Him over to be crucified.

Then the soldiers of the governor took Jesus into the Praetorium and gathered the whole Roman cohort around Him. They stripped Him and put a scarlet robe on Him. And after twisting together a crown of thorns, they put it on His head, and a reed in His right hand; and they knelt down before Him and mocked Him, saying, "Hail, King of the Jews!" They spat on Him, and took the reed and began to beat Him on the head. After they had mocked Him, they took the scarlet robe off Him and put His own garments back on Him, and led Him away to crucify Him.

As they were coming out, they found a man of Cyrene named Simon, whom they pressed into service to bear His cross.

And when they came to a place called Golgotha, which means Place of a Skull, they gave Him wine to drink mixed with gall; and after tasting it, He was unwilling to drink.

And when they had crucified Him, they divided up His garments among themselves by casting lots. And sitting down, they *began* to keep watch over Him there. And above His head they put up the charge against Him which read, "THIS IS JESUS THE KING OF THE JEWS."

At that time two robbers were crucified with Him, one on the right and one on the left. And those passing by were hurling abuse at Him, wagging their heads and saying, "You who are going to destroy the temple and rebuild it in three days, save Yourself! If You are the Son of God, come down from the cross." In the same way the chief priests also, along with the scribes and elders, were mocking Him and saying, "He saved others; He cannot save Himself. He is the King of Israel; let Him now come down from the cross, and we will believe in Him. He trusts in God; let God rescue Him now, if He delights in Him; for He said, 'I am the

Son of God.'" The robbers who had been crucified with Him were also insulting Him with the same words.

"Now from the sixth hour darkness fell upon all the land until the ninth hour. About the ninth hour Jesus cried out with a loud voice, saying, "Eli, Eli, lama sabachthani?" that is, "My God, My God, why have You forsaken Me?" And some of those who were standing there, when they heard it, began saying, "This man is calling for Elijah." Immediately one of them ran, and taking a sponge, he filled it with sour wine and put it on a reed, and gave Him a drink. But the rest of them said, "Let us see whether Elijah will come to save Him." And Jesus cried out again with a loud voice, and yielded up His spirit. And behold, the veil of the temple was torn in two from top to bottom; and the earth shook and the rocks were split. The tombs were opened, and many bodies of the saints who had fallen asleep were raised; and coming out of the tombs after His resurrection they entered the holy city and appeared to many. Now the centurion, and those who were with him keeping guard over Jesus, when they saw the earthquake and the things that were happening, became very frightened and said, "Truly this was the Son of God!" (Matthew 27:24-54).

Jesus perfectly obeyed the Father in His life and in His death. In doing so, Jesus took upon Himself the punishment sinners rightly deserve for their sins against God. However, unlike the judge and the son in the parable, Jesus did not remain dead. After Jesus died on the cross and was buried, He rose from the grave, forever defeating sin and death.

Now I make known to you, brethren, the gospel which I preached to you, which also you received, in which also you stand, by which also you are saved, if you hold fast the word which I preached to you, unless you believed in vain.

For I delivered to you as of first importance what I also received, that Christ died for our sins according to the Scriptures, and that He was buried, and that He was raised on

> the third day according to the Scriptures, and that He appeared to Cephas, then to the twelve. After that He appeared to more than five hundred brethren at one time, most of whom remain until now, but some have fallen asleep; then He appeared to James, then to all the apostles; and last of all, as to one untimely born, He appeared to me also. (1 Corinthians 15:1-8).

Jesus sacrificially shed His innocent blood on the cross for those who would humble themselves, turn from their sins and turn toward God, and by faith receive Jesus Christ as their Lord and Savior.

> But He gives a greater grace. Therefore it says, "God is opposed to the proud, but gives grace to the humble." Submit therefore to God. Resist the devil and he will flee from you. Draw near to God and He will draw near to you. Cleanse your hands, you sinners; and purify your hearts, you double-minded. Be miserable and mourn and weep; let your laughter be turned into mourning and your joy to gloom. Humble yourselves in the presence of the Lord, and He will exalt you (James 4:6-10).

The burglar received mercy. He did not receive what he deserved—the just condemnation for his crimes. The burglar also received grace. He received what he did not deserve—a full pardon for his crimes. Justice was served. The burglar received the benefit of justice executed upon another on his behalf.

The God who created you and before whom you will one day stand is not capricious, arbitrary, or unjust like the false gods of Islam, Roman Catholicism, Mormonism, the Watchtower Society, or any other man-made religion. God is perfectly holy, righteous, and just. He must punish sin or else He would cease to be holy. At the same time, God is perfectly loving, merciful, gracious, and kind.

God's perfectly consistent character was beautifully displayed on the cross of Jesus Christ. At the cross, justice and mercy kissed, accomplishing full and free salvation for those who repent and believe the gospel.

But now apart from the Law the righteousness of God has been manifested, being witnessed by the Law and the Prophets, even the righteousness of God through faith in Jesus Christ for all those who believe; for there is no distinction; for all have sinned and fall short of the glory of God, being justified as a gift by His grace through the redemption which is in Christ Jesus; whom God displayed publicly as a propitiation in His blood through faith. This was to demonstrate His righteousness, because in the forbearance of God He passed over the sins previously committed; for the demonstration, I say, of His righteousness at the present time, so that He would be just and the justifier of the one who has faith in Jesus (Romans 3:21-26).

God will either be your Judge or your Father, your Executioner or your Savior. You must come to Him on His terms, for God does not negotiate with sinners.

...if you confess with your mouth Jesus as Lord, and believe in your heart that God raised Him from the dead, you will be saved; for with the heart a person believes, resulting in righteousness, and with the mouth he confesses, resulting in salvation. For the Scripture says, "Whoever believes in Him will not be disappointed." For there is no distinction between Jew and Greek; for the same Lord is Lord of all, abounding in riches for all who call on Him; for "Whoever will call on the name of the Lord will be saved" (Romans 10:9-13).

Repent. Believe the gospel. Turn to Christ and live. He will take your heart of stone that loves what is evil and hates what is good, and He will give you a heart of flesh that loves what God loves and hates what God hates. You will be reconciled to your Creator, not on the basis of anything you have done to earn or deserve it, but on the basis of God's mercy that appointed His Son to die on behalf of sinners.

But when the kindness of God our Savior and His love for mankind appeared, He saved us, not on the basis of deeds which we have done in righteousness, but according to His mercy, by the washing of regeneration and renewing by the Holy Spirit, whom He poured out upon us richly through Jesus Christ our Savior, so that being justified by His grace we would be made heirs according to the hope of eternal life (Titus 3:4-7).

Repent and believe the gospel, now, today, while you still have time. The Judge will show you mercy!

Section I:
Street Corner
Conversations

Evangelism Tip #1: 'Why Do You Carry a Cross?' *And Other Questions*

How It Began

"I am not a 'sign guy.'" That's what I used to say to myself. But two things happened many years ago that caused me to reconsider my position.

One day, while reading the local paper, I noticed a well-written and positive article about a man in my community named Willie Young. Willie Young was a "sign guy." For years I had seen him on various corners throughout our community, and when I saw him I would just smile and wave.

The following morning an evangelist by the name of David Cougle posted a video on Facebook. The video, which is just a few minutes in length, showed David and a couple of evangelists walking onto Bourbon Street. What drew my attention was the cross one of the evangelists was carrying. Because of the noise and chaos on Bourbon Street, the cross was used as a beacon to draw people to the evangelists, helping them to distribute tracts and engage people in conversation.

I am engaged in evangelism, in one form or another, almost every day of my life. Evangelism long ago stopped merely being something I do. It is a way of life for me; it is who Christ has called me to be through Him. I have learned that exceedingly great joy and an extraordinary sense of responsibility are two sides of the same coin that is God's will. But reading the article about Willie Young and then watching the video about David Cougle and his friends stirred my heart to the point of asking myself, "Can I do more? Am I doing enough to proclaim the gospel?"

Now, I readily admit that I am a workaholic. My tongue-in-cheek motto (though likely to be viewed as unhealthy by most) is "I can rest in heaven." I see every goal attained as an opportunity to set new, higher goals. When I shared on Facebook that I felt convicted to do more to further the gospel, I received the expected responses by some of those who know me: "You gotta be kidding me!"

Try to psychoanalyze me if you feel the need to do so. You can even question my motives if you want. But I genuinely believe that there is more I can and should do to spread the gospel of Jesus Christ to a lost and dying world.

So, with the aforementioned article and video in mind, I thought to myself, "Maybe it's time to reevaluate some of the forms of evangelism I've said I would never do."

Immediately, my thoughts turned to my office, which was located in our homeowners association clubhouse at the time. In my office, hanging on the south wall just above the air conditioner, was a four-foot wooden cross.

Several years ago, I pastored a small church plant that met in the HOA clubhouse. One of the young men in my church who was handy with tools built the cross to hang behind my pulpit during our times of corporate worship. When we closed the doors of the church for the last time, I kept the office in the clubhouse. I also kept the cross.

For seven years the cross hung on that wall, serving as little more than a memento and an ornament. I knew it was time to take that cross off the wall, but the thought scared me.

The Sunday morning I read the article about Willie Young, I walked to my office before we left for church. I took the cross down from the wall and placed it on my shoulder. It was heavy. The weight of it came from more than just its mere mass. When I shouldered that cross for the first time, I also felt the weight of what I knew I was going to do with it.

I felt a particular closeness to my Lord as I stood with the rest of my church family to worship that morning. After worship, Michelle (my eldest daughter) stood before the congregation to share her testimony. I was so very proud of her. Mahria was moved to tears as Michelle explained to the church the confident assurance she had that God would use the physical challenges she has faced throughout her life to allow her to minister to others.

Our pastor then stepped into his pulpit and began to preach. He continued his series of messages based on 2 Chronicles 7:11-22, focusing on verse 14 this particular morning. "If My people who are called by My name humble themselves…"

"Humble themselves."

My thoughts were taken far from the context of the passage to my little windowless office where, on a white-painted brick wall, hung a wooden cross. Among these thoughts was the idea of humility. Was a lack of that essential Christian character trait what discouraged me from carrying a sign? Would I let pride keep me from shouldering that wooden cross?

No sooner did I consider these things than Jesus' words consumed my thinking. "If anyone would come after Me, let him deny himself and take up his cross daily and follow Me" (Luke 9:23). While the verse has nothing to do with standing on a street corner and holding a wooden cross, it most certainly speaks of self-denial to the point of welcoming physical death in order to follow Christ.

"Humble themselves." "Deny himself."

As soon as we got home from church, I took Mahria to my office. I wanted her to look at the cross—one she had seen countless times over the last ten years—and help me decide what to write on the cross beam.

I thought of affixing the phrase "What If?" to the front of the cross. The phrase, displayed in other ways, has been useful in the past for soliciting and initiating spiritual conversations. But as I talked with Mahria, another phrase came to both our minds.

"Are You Ready?"

We agreed that would be the phrase placed on the front of the cross. Our hope was that unbelievers would see the cross, read the phrase, and ask themselves if they were ready to stand before Jesus Christ, face-to-face. We also hoped that believers would see the cross, read the phrase, and ask themselves if they were truly denying themselves and daily taking up their own crosses to follow Christ.

The decision made, I ran to a nearby craft store to pick up some vinyl lettering.

I drove around town hoping to find Willie Young on a street corner with his signs. My plan was to find him, introduce myself, and stand beside him holding my cross. It was 103°, even though it was 5:00 p.m. Willie wasn't at any of his usual locations.

I continued to drive around town. But now, instead of looking for Willie, I was praying for courage and trying to decide where I would stand and hold the cross. It didn't take me long to choose a location.

I drove through a quiet neighborhood until I reached the parking lot for their homeowners association clubhouse, at the corner of Avenida Entrana and Lyons Avenue. Lyons Avenue is a major street in Newhall, a community in my hometown of Santa Clarita.

After pulling into the small parking lot and parking my car, I sat for a few minutes questioning what I was about to do and wondering if there was any way out of it. I sent a text message to a small number of fellow evangelists, asking them to pray. Several quickly responded with words of encouragement. Understandably, a couple of the responses seemed hesitant, as if to say, "Tony, what are you doing and why?" I tried not to let those discourage me, recalling my own mindset less than 12 hours earlier. I would have been asking myself the same questions.

I got out of my car and looked at the four-foot cross in the back seat. "Lord, help me do this. I don't know what's going to happen," I prayed.

"If My people who are called by My name humble themselves…"

"Let him deny himself and take up his cross daily and follow Me."

I pulled the cross out of the back seat and leaned it against the car. I opened the trunk and removed my street evangelism box, which was filled with tracts and Bibles. I was determined that if anyone would stop long enough to engage me in conversation they would, at the very least, receive a tract.

With cross and box in hand, I made my way to the northwest corner of the intersection. Mature oak trees shrouded the north side of the street in much welcomed shade, providing a small reprieve from the 100° heat.

I set the box down behind me. "Well, here it goes," I said to myself with a sigh. As I picked up the cross and leaned it against my right shoulder, I immediately felt naked—the sense of being fully exposed with nowhere to hide.

I identify with Christ every time I hand someone a tract, engage someone in spiritual conversation, or step onto the box to open-air preach. Occasionally, with that identification comes a certain level of apprehension as I wonder what my identification with Christ might cost me. For me, up to that point, the cost had been minimal: rejection, mocking, insults, shunning by professing Christians, threats of violence, and one brief instance of very minor physical violence. But holding that cross on that street corner gave me the feeling that I was identifying with Christ to a greater extent than before. The feeling caused me to count the potential cost with a heightened level of sobriety.

Hundreds of people saw the cross and the words "Are You Ready" on the crossbeam. Some people waved. Some people gave a thumbs-up. Others shook their heads or laughed. A few people walked by on the opposite side of the street. Most did everything they could to ignore my presence.

However, when one young couple walked to the corner on my side of the street I was able to give them each a gospel tract. A short time later, they walked back from wherever they had been. When they got close enough for me to say something to them, I asked, "Could I have a couple minutes of your time?"

Their names were Joshua and Candace.

"Sure," answered Joshua.

"You've seen my cross. May I ask you, are you ready for eternity?"

"Yes we are. We are born-again Christians."

Joshua and Candace were new to the community and were trying to find a church to call home. Having lived in the community for more than 20 years, I was very familiar with most of the churches—the good, the bad, and the ugly. I gave them a couple of suggestions, which they appreciated.

A little while later, a small sedan stopped at the light. There were two young men in the car. The passenger leaned out the window and asked, "Ready for what?"

"Eternity."

"Oh. Is eternity coming?"

"Yeah, for everyone. We're all going to die someday, right?"

"That's true."

The driver leaned across his friend and exclaimed, "Hey! You're that cop!"

"Great," I thought. "I'm not going to be martyred for carrying a cross. I'm going to be killed for being a retired deputy sheriff."

"Well, I used to be," I answered. "I'm retired now. And, as you can see, I'm doing something different with my time."

The young man went on to explain that back in my days with the gang unit I had some, shall we say, professional contact with him and his friends.

The light turned green. The two young men smiled, waved, and went on their way.

Over time, the cross grew heavy. There is not a single rounded corner on the wooden beams. As my shoulders stiffened and the edges of the cross dug into my skin, I thought about how I could make it more comfortable. Those thoughts were quickly dashed by the thought of my Lord and Savior suffering and dying on His cross, which had no padding. It was made for torture, not comfort, and He endured it unto death, shedding His innocent, sinless blood for the remission of my sins against Him.

Even with the consistent noise of passing cars, it was peaceful on that shaded corner of Lyons Avenue. The sound of the breeze blowing through the trees (one of my favorite sounds, by the way) seemed more pronounced than the sound of vehicle traffic. Standing there alone with no one to talk to, I quietly prayed to my Lord and worshipped Him by humming hymns.

My thoughts and worship were interrupted by a phone call from Mahria to let me know that dinner was in 20 minutes. I took that as my cue to pack it up and call it a day.

While that hour spent on the corner of Avenida Entrana and Lyons Avenue on July 12, 2009 was for all intents and purposes uneventful, it was still a significant step outside my comfort zone. I liken the experience to my first time open-air preaching in 2005. In both cases, it would appear that our loving, gracious, and kind Lord allowed me to take these significant steps free from too much harassment from the world. It's hard to believe how many years have passed since that first outing. Harder still to believe is what the Lord has done for His glory, His people, and the furtherance of His gospel through the seemingly simple act of carrying a cross with three words written on the crossbeam.

Just as my experiences in open-air preaching have intensified since the first time I stepped onto the box, I fully expected the spiritual and physical warfare associated with carrying my cross to intensify as well. The Lord did not disappoint.

At this point, some readers might be asking themselves this question: "So, how does a wooden cross on a street corner communicate the gospel?" Holding a cross on the side of the road is not sharing the gospel. That being said, if holding a cross in public causes an unbelieving passerby to contemplate Jesus Christ and His work on the cross, if the question "Are You Ready?" causes an unbeliever to ponder whether or not he or she is ready to face the One who died on the cross and rose from the grave, then I think it can be a powerful tool. If seeing the cross on the side of the road causes someone to stop and contact me, giving me the opportunity to share the law and the gospel with them, of course that is all the better.

Furthermore, if a professing follower of Jesus Christ drives by and sees a "nobody from nowhere" like me standing on the side of the road holding a cross, and such a sight causes them to honestly consider what (if anything) they are doing for the cause of Christ, then it is worth the effort.

I'm still not a "sign guy" in the typical sense of the word. All too often, signs are used in inflammatory ways to call people names and to talk about sin without any context. You will never see me do that. But you just may see me someday in your community carrying a rugged wooden cross.

Some Common Questions

I would like to answer some of the most common "who, what, when, where, why, and how" questions I receive regarding carrying the "Are You Ready?" cross. Some questions are asked out of curiosity, others out of conviction. Some questions are asked out of skepticism, others with an arrogant air of pragmatic disapproval. Some questions are asked with unavoidable and long-held presuppositions in mind, others with a theological underpinning by those who are merely looking for a debate. And still other questions are asked in a passive-aggressive attempt to discourage.

Some of the most common questions, followed by my responses, appear here in no particular order.

Q: What do people typically say to you or ask you when they approach you with the cross?

A: "Ready for what?" This common response is why I decided to put these three simple words on the cross. What I hoped would happen has happened time and time again. People see the cross and the question and approach me to ask the most obvious question, "Ready for what?" My immediate answer is "Are you ready to stand before God and give an account for your life? Do you consider yourself to be a good person?"

Another question I am asked is "Are you ready?" Most often, this question is asked with a mocking tone by someone in a moving vehicle who has no intention of stopping and engaging in conversation. I call them "drive-by hecklers."

When false prophets like the now-deceased Harold Camping make false predictions about the judgment of the world, I am often asked, "Do you believe the world is going to end on this date?" My response: "Oh, please don't tell me you are one of those people who believe that nonsense." The look on people's faces when I answer this way is priceless. They approach me wrongly assuming that I claim to know when the world is going to end, and I immediately turn it back on them, making them squirm as they now have to explain that they are not part of Camping's group. Once I've dismantled the haughtiness with which the person asks this question, it is very easy to turn the conversation toward the law and the gospel.

Another question I am asked is, "Why are you doing this?" My answer: "I'm doing this so I can have conversations with folks like you, who stop to ask me why I am doing this."

Q: What are the typical things, positive and negative, that you have experienced? And what are your responses to them?

A: I have experienced so many things—good and bad—over the years as I've carried the cross throughout the greater Los Angeles County area.

The negative:

- I've had rocks thrown at me.
- I've received many one-finger waves.
- I've heard "Hail Satan" by motorists more times than I can count, and I've been called most of the names in the book (whatever book that is).
- I've been threatened with arrest by LAPD officers who tried to use an archaic city ordinance against over-sized picket signs to chase me off Hollywood Boulevard.
- I've been told by professing Christians that I am judgmental (even if I don't say anything). The mere presence of the cross is an offense to them.

The positive:

- I've had many wonderful one-on-one conversations with people because they were curious about the man carrying the cross.
- I know that at least a few people have come to repentance and faith in Jesus Christ because the Lord chose to use a conversation at the foot of the cross to plant seeds that would one day bear life-saving fruit.
- Several times Christians have stopped to encourage me. One lady brought me cookies. Another lady stopped to give me a bottle of water.

Untold thousands of people in my community alone have seen the cross. Some scoff and then buckle their seatbelts. Some are convicted. Some think back to times when others have shared the gospel with them. Some ask themselves if they are ready to stand before God.

Of course, there are also the positive things God has done that I will not come to know until I am with Him in heaven. I have faith, believing I will enjoy fellowship with people I never met on Earth who were impacted in one way or another by seeing a man on a street corner holding a cross. Soli Deo gloria!

Q: Do you usually stand on one corner or do you walk with the cross?

A: I've stood with the cross at every major intersection in my community, in addition to the following locations:

- In front of City Hall
- In front of an apostate church that ordained a lesbian to be the church's "pastor"
- At local political rallies
- At the scene of fatal traffic accidents (post event, of course)
- Near DUI checkpoints
- At large community events, such as "Concerts in the Park"

And, I've walked throughout my community with the cross, sometimes several miles during an outing.

Q: How do you begin? Do you pray? What do you pray? Do you read from the Bible? What scripture do you read?

A: My time out with the cross is usually impromptu. Because of the flexibility of my schedule, I go out with the cross whenever I have a mind to do so.

My prayer time related to "crosswalking" usually takes places while I'm out with the cross. I've spent some amazing times of solitary prayer and worship with the Lord while out on a street corner. I pray for the people who will see the cross. I ask God to bring people by my corner so I can put the gospel in their hand or share it with them in conversation. Whenever first responders (law enforcement, firefighters, paramedics, ambulances) roll "Code-3" (lights and sirens) through the intersection, I pray for their safety and I pray for those they are rushing to help.

Q: Do you go out alone?

A: Nine times out of ten, yes. Sometimes the only time of the day when I have any solitude is when I'm standing on a busy street corner with the cross. But occasionally Mahria and/or one or more of my daughters will come with me to keep me company and to hand out some tracts or snap some photos. I always welcome the fellowship of my family and other co-laborers for Christ.

Q: What times are best to stand on a street corner?

A: Any time, really. I've been out with the cross morning, noon, and night. The best time of day, however (and this is probably true in most communities), is during the evening commute. This is usually when traffic is the heaviest, giving more people the opportunity to see the cross.

Q: Aren't you concerned that an accident will happen because people rubberneck with or without slowing down to read your cross? Also, what if people stop in the middle of the road to ask you what "Are You Ready?" means but don't pull over or park? Should you encourage the people to park before you talk to them or shout back and forth and possibly hold up traffic?

A: To the first question, my answer is a resounding "no." First of all, during the years I have carried the cross, an accident has never happened in close proximity to where I was standing. In fact, people often slow down because of the cross, which can actually make the roadway safer.

Beyond that, I have no concern whatsoever about people "rubbernecking" to look at the cross. Have you looked at some of the billboards lately? Don't. So many of them are disgusting and sexually explicit. Or what about the "sign twirlers" who stand on street corners for minimum wage or less, providing cheap advertisement for local businesses? I would much prefer a motorist to get a stiff neck from looking at my cross than from looking at billboards or sign twirlers.

On occasion, when I've been on smaller residential streets, people have stopped at a light, rolled down their window, and asked, "Ready for what?" I answer the question as I usually do, and then I invite the person to pull over, park, and have a conversation. If they do not have the time or desire to do that, I ask them if I can give them something. If they agree, I hand them a gospel tract. I make it a point never to approach a car while carrying the cross. The person in the car does not know my intention, and I do not know theirs.

Q: From fellow "crosswalkers": Sometimes I wonder if standing on the corner with my cross is actually accomplishing anything. A lot of people see it, but there is little foot traffic, so I don't get many one-on-one conversations.

A: If you hand out tracts but you are rejected every time, is it still evangelism? If you go out and try to engage people in conversation but no one wants to talk to you, is it still evangelism? If you climb atop a box to open-air preach but you cannot draw a crowd, is it still evangelism? Yes! Too often, Christians define evangelism only by the results without giving a thought to the effort behind those results.

Carrying a cross produces an unknown amount of fruit. The "crosswalker" has no idea what is going on in the heart and mind of the motorist or vehicle passenger who sees the cross as they drive by. Instead of assuming that the cross has no effect unless the person stops to talk to you, why not hope that the person has heard the gospel from someone else and the cross is serving to water that spiritual seed? Why not trust that the Lord, in His infinite wisdom and power, can use a simple three-word question to cause the motorist or vehicle passenger to seriously consider their own mortality and then ask a Christian friend questions or maybe even open the Bible for themselves?

I'm not out on street corners with the cross because it "works" according to man's standards. I'm out on street corners with the cross because I believe by faith that the Lord will use it for His glory, regardless of what other Christians or unbelievers think about it. And, for me, carrying the cross is also an act of worship—not worship of a wooden cross, but worship of the One who gave His life for me on a cross.

Q: Should you carry the cross when the police tell you not to but you know that city ordinances say it is acceptable and you can prove it? Should you fight it with the police and take it to court or show them the law in writing? Are there laws about the size of a sign or cross that can be carried? I seem to remember someone having an issue with that. Do such laws only pertain to group "protest" type gatherings or any type of sign held?

A: Please refer to "It Happened for Jocelyn's Sake" and "Evangelism Tip #5: Hello Officer" for an in-depth answer to this question.

Q: I just had a conversation a few days ago with a brother in Christ who was talking to me about his concerns regarding the cross. He thinks that it will offend people before we even have a chance to talk to them about it. I explained why I carry it, agreed not to bring it to evangelism events that he leads, and everything is amiable. He was open but skeptical. Perhaps you can help answer that concern. He also mentioned that we will not have the chance to talk to most people who see the cross, so they will make assumptions about what it is saying, and we won't be able to explain it to them.

A: This is a simple question to answer. I would simply ask the skeptical Christian brother, "How do you know that?" His hesitation is based on conjecture. I would encourage him to pick up a cross and see if any of his assumptions are true as a result of his own experiences. He should encourage and edify his fellow evangelists for the effort they are making, instead of discouraging activity he has yet to experience to firsthand. Sadly, sometimes our contemporary Christian friends have too much in common with the friends of Job.

Q: I don't think carrying a cross is a good idea, because people might confuse you with bad street preachers, angry sign carriers, or discredited cross carriers like Arthur Blessitt.

A: For me, this last question/assertion is the most discouraging and frustrating of all. Sadly, I have heard it from Christian brethren and evangelists for whom I have a great deal of love and respect.

My response: Why give up the ground? Why concede to the enemy?

There are heretics who stand on top of boxes and preach false gospels. They men and women who are more concerned about creating the next confrontation with law enforcement and/or crowds of unbelievers than they are with anyone's eternal fate. Should biblical evangelists stop open-air preaching because there is a chance we might be wrongly associated with the false prophets and false teachers of our day who preach in the open air?

No!

There are false converts who stand on street corners and college campuses with disgusting signs that do nothing more than incite animosity, call people names, and speak only of God's wrath and judgment. Should biblical evangelists avoid carrying signs that have succinct, biblical messages and Scripture verses in proper context because there is a chance we might be wrongly associated with the false prophets and teachers of our day who carry signs?

No!

There are people out there like Arthur Blessitt, who is best-known for carrying a large cross around the world and who is also known for allegedly divorcing his wife because he "felt led" to do so, which allowed him to commit adultery with his now-second wife. Should biblical evangelists avoid carrying wooden crosses because there is a chance we might be associated with an adulterer who carries a cross?

No!

We should not stand aside and do nothing as people sully the name of Christ while standing on a box, while carrying a sign, or while carrying a cross. Shouldn't biblical evangelists use all these means and others to herald the gospel more loudly and more often than the heretics, false prophets, and charlatans? Yes. A hundred times, yes!

No, I will not give up the ground, nor should any other biblical evangelist!

Conclusion

Please pray for the many men and women around the world who are now carrying a cross. The Lord is using the "Are You Ready?" cross for His glory. People are hearing the gospel. People are receiving gospel tracts. People are contemplating their eternal destination as a result.

While carrying a cross might not be for everyone (and I do NOT fault any Christian who does not feel led to or comfortable with carrying a cross), it is the right thing to do for me and for many other godly, biblical evangelists around the world.

Gaia Defeated at the Cross

You and I cannot be useful if we want to be sweet as honey in the mouths of men. God will never bless us if we wish to please men, that they may think well of us. Are you willing to tell them what will break your own heart in the telling and break theirs in the hearing? If not, you are not fit to serve the Lord. You must be willing to go and speak for God, though you will be rejected.
Charles Spurgeon[1]

One afternoon I spent time with my cross on the corner of The Old Road and Constitution Avenue in Stevenson Ranch, California. As I walked from the nearby parking lot to the corner, I prayed that the Lord would allow me to hand out a few tracts and talk to at least one person.

Before I reached the corner, two teenage boys accepted tracts as they walked by me, and I thanked God for answering one of my prayers so quickly. I then prayed for all the motorists and pedestrians who would see the cross. I prayed that the Lord would use what some might call foolish, a man standing on the corner with a cross, to bring Himself glory.

About half an hour into my time on the corner, I saw a man walking toward me from the opposite side of Constitution Avenue. Even from a distance, I had a sense we were going to have a conversation. He had a smile and a look of curiosity on his face and his eyes were fixed on the cross.

The man crossed the street and stepped onto the sidewalk at my corner. I handed him a tract, which he accepted. Instead of walking away, as most people do, he began to pace in front of me.

---

[1] Each chapter in this book begins with an evangelistic quotation from the "prince of preachers," Charles Haddon Spurgeon. All of the Spurgeon quotes that appear in this book were taken from the Spurgeon.us website. Kerry James Allen, "Exploring the Mind and Heart of the Prince of Preachers," *Spurgeon.us: The Web's Largest Repository of Quotes by the Prince of Preachers*, accessed April 22, 2016, http://www.spurgeon.us/index.php.

The man (we'll call him Jim) pointed up at the cross and said, "This is really good, what you're doing."

"Thanks."

"So, I guess this is the year."

"The year for what?" I asked.

"It's 2012."

"And?"

"The Mayan calendar says…"

"No one knows the day or the time."

"No?"

"No. And anyone who says they do is a liar."

"Really?"

"Yep."

I introduced myself and extended my hand. Jim returned the gesture. "Jim, do you attend a church here locally?"

"No," he answered, with almost a sound of guilt in his voice.

"Do you believe God exists?"

"Oh, definitely. Actually, I kind of follow Gaia."

"Who's Gaia?"

"Mother Earth. Mother Nature."

"Do you believe in heaven and hell?" I asked.

"Yes, I do."

"Jim, what do you think a person has to do to go to hell?"

"Murder," he quickly answered.

I took Jim through several of the Ten Commandments. He admitted to being a liar, a thief, a blasphemer, and an adulterer-at-heart, and he was shocked to discover that God sees the hatred he had harbored toward others as murder (1 John 3:15). Jim understood that he had broken God's Law. He was concerned. He understood that if he died in his current sinful, spiritually-dead state God would send him to hell as his just punishment for his sins against Him. I asked Jim if he had any idea what God had done so that he would not have to spend eternity in Hell.

"He sent His Son to die on the cross."

"That's right. Do you know what that means?"

"I'm not sure."

"I appreciate your honesty."

As I do with so many others, I took Jim through a version of the "Courtroom Analogy." The more I shared with him, the more a look of concern filled Jim's eyes. Even through his sunglasses I could tell he was thinking deeply about what he was hearing.

"Would that be good news to you?"

"Yes."

"What would you think of the person who did that (paid his fine) for you?"

"I would be forever grateful."

"Well, let's see if you mean that, because what I just shared with you was a picture of what God actually did."

I proclaimed the gospel to Jim. His eyes never left mine and he seemed to hang on every word. "What God commands of you, Jim, is that you repent (turn from your sin and turn to God) and, by faith alone, receive Jesus Christ as your Lord and Savior. Does that make sense?"

"Yes, it does."

"Do you believe what I'm telling you is true?"

"I do believe."

I spent a few moments explaining to Jim that the worship of Gaia is idolatry, yet another sin for which he will be judged if God does not save him. "Jim, is there any reason why you wouldn't right now repent and put your trust in Christ alone for your salvation? Is there any sin in your life that you love so much you're willing to spend eternity in hell so you can continue to enjoy that sin in this life?"

"Wow. I need to give that some thought."

"Jim, the Bible says it's appointed once for a person to die and then judgment. I may never see you again, but I care about you. I don't want you to perish in your sins. I want to see you in heaven one day."

"I appreciate that. I think you will see me in heaven."

"I hope so. I really do. Do you have a Bible?"

"I do."

I gave Jim a copy of the Gospel of John and encouraged him to read it.

"I'm going to go home and read it right away."

"Can I pray for you before you go?"

"Please."

I put my hand on his shoulder and asked my Lord and Savior to save Jim, to bring him to repentance and faith and to give him the gift of eternal life. I shared information about my church with Jim and invited him to join us on Sunday. We shook hands, and Jim walked away.

I couldn't stop thanking and praising God. I do not know if Jim came to faith in Christ as I talked to him. I knew him for all of 20 minutes, so I certainly did not know his heart or mind. But what I saw in his expression, heard in his voice, and felt as we shook hands gave me every indication, fallible as it may have been, that I was watching the Lord save a soul right before my eyes. I believe and I trust God that this is true: on a street corner in Stevenson Ranch, the false god Gaia was defeated at the cross.

Russ and Chanelle: It Doesn't Take a Long Time

If you have not the time, God gave it to you, and you must have misspent it.
Charles Spurgeon

It had been a productive day at Living Waters. Among other things, I finalized the dates for the 2010 Ambassadors' Academy[1] season.

The drive home from the Living Waters Headquarters was uneventful, which is always a blessing when you drive more than 100 miles every day on Southern California freeways. Knowing I wouldn't have the time after dinner, I decided to stop at one of my favorite corners in town to carry my cross.

As I pulled my cross out of the trunk, I noticed a man (probably 10-15 years my senior) slowly walking across the street toward the corner where I planned to stand. His gait seemed to indicate that he had issues with either his knees or his back. He had paperwork in his hand and he was heading in the direction of a medical building.

I arrived at the corner just several seconds after he did. He looked at me, then at the cross, then at me again.

"Hi. How are you doing today?" I asked.

"Hi," he replied. "Fine."

Within moments, the light turned green and he slowly made his way across the street. As he walked away, I prayed for him and for my

---

[1] I served with Living Waters, an evangelistic ministry led by Ray Comfort, from 2008 to 2012. During that time, I developed and led a division of the ministry known as the Ambassadors' Academy. The Ambassadors' Academy was an intensive, three-day evangelistic training program. After an extensive application and interview process, fifty people from around the world were invited to come to Living Waters headquarters in Bellflower, California to participate in the Ambassadors' Academy. After a full day of classroom instruction, academy participants would be led in two days of street evangelism, which included open-air preaching, tract distribution, and one-on-one conversations. I had the honor and privilege of organizing and leading 20 sessions of the Ambassadors' Academy, during which we trained approximately 1,000 people to better engage in biblical evangelism.

time on the corner. Then I noticed that the man had stopped and sat down on a planter wall at the corner of the medical building across the street. I thought he might have been tired from walking and that he was just taking a breather, but I also noticed that he was watching me.

The man sat there for a minute or two. Then he stood up and pushed the crosswalk button, and when the light turned green, he slowly made his way back across the street. As the man stepped onto the sidewalk at my corner, he looked up at the cross.

"So, what church are you affiliated with?" he asked.

"I attend Granada Hills Community Church."

"Oh, so you live in Granada Hills and come up here?"

"No, I live here. I just attend church in the valley."

"Oh. So, why are you doing this?"

"I'm doing this hoping people like you will stop and ask me why I'm doing this."

The man chuckled.

"I'm asking people if they're ready—if they're ready to stand before Jesus Christ and give an account for their lives."

"I see."

"So, what do you think will happen to you when you die?"

"I don't think anyone knows."

"Really?"

"Yep. I'm a church-going man, but no one has ever come back to tell us what will happen to us after we die."

"You say that you're a church-going man. Do you believe the Bible is true?"

"I do. I believe the Bible."

"Well, the Bible makes it clear what happens after this life. The Bible says that it is appointed once for a person to die, and after that comes the judgment. And the Bible makes it clear that heaven and hell are real places. My name's Tony, by the way."

"Russ."

"Nice to meet you, Russ."

"Same here."

"Russ, we're all going to die someday. Ten out of ten people die."

"That's true."

"And when we die, we will stand before God and He will judge us according to the perfect moral standard of His law. If you've ever lied, He will see you as a liar. If you've ever stolen anything, He will see you as a thief. If you've ever taken His name in vain, He will see you as a blasphemer. If you've ever had a lustful thought about someone other than a spouse, then God will see you as an adulterer. If you've ever hated anyone, He will see you as a murderer. God is holy, righteous, just, and good. He must punish sin. And the punishment God has ascribed for sin is eternity in hell.

"But God provided a way of escape from His just and holy wrath. He provided a way for sinners to be forgiven. This is what God did. Two thousand years ago, God the Father sent His Son to earth in the person of Jesus Christ—fully God and fully Man and without sin. Unlike you and me, He never once violated the Law of God in thought, word, or deed. He was perfect in every respect. About 30 to 33 years into that earthly existence, He voluntarily went to the cross. He suffered and died, shedding His innocent blood, taking upon Himself the punishment you and I rightly deserve for our sins against God. Then, three days later, He rose from the dead, forever defeating sin and death. He is alive today and He will return at a time of the Father's choosing. What God requires of you, Russ, is that you repent. God commands that all people everywhere turn from their sin and by faith, and by faith alone, receive Jesus Christ as their Lord and Savior. He is your only hope."

As I shared the law and the gospel with Russ, he nodded his head and affirmed that salvation is by God's grace and not by works.

"Russ, the Apostle John wrote, 'I write these things to you who believe in the name of the Son of God that you may know that you have eternal life' [1 John 5:13]. Yes, if you know Jesus Christ as your Lord and Savior you most certainly can know that you have eternal life."

"Well, okay," Russ said.

I extended my hand to Russ and he gave it a firm shake. "Russ, thank you for talking to me."

"Thank you."

"God bless you, Russ. I will be praying for you."

"Thanks."

Russ smiled, turned, and walked away, but he didn't cross the street again toward the medical building. It was clear that he was heading somewhere when I first saw him. But now Russ walked back the way he had come, disappearing down a path in the distance. It was as if our conversation caused him to change his mind about what he was going to do and, instead, he headed back home.

I rejoiced in the Lord as I watched Russ walk away. I prayed that the Lord would draw Russ to Himself and give him the assurance of salvation that only the Lord can give. Within a minute or two of finishing my prayer, the Lord provided yet another opportunity to proclaim His gospel.

A white Ford Mustang stopped in front of me at the light. The tinted front passenger window rolled down. A young lady of Asian descent sat in the front passenger seat, a young man was driving, and another young man sat in the back seat. The young lady looked at me and smiled. "Ready for what?" she asked.

"Are you ready for eternity? Are you ready to stand before the Lord Jesus Christ and give an account for your life?"

"I'm ready," she said with a chuckle. "I'm a Christian."

"Really? What's your name?"

"Chanelle."

"Oh. Well, that's a pretty name."

"Thanks."

"My name's Tony."

"Hi."

I stooped down, lowered my cross, and leaned against it. I wanted to make sure I could look Chanelle in the eye. I also wanted to be able to keep an eye on the two guys in the car. (Sorry, it's the cop in me.)

"Chanelle, let me ask you, what if I wasn't a Christian and I only had three minutes to live? What would you tell me?"

"I don't know."

"Well, what's going to happen to me when I die if I don't know Jesus Christ?"

"I'm not sure." She looked down and remained silent for a moment. Then she said, "I'm not ready."

A car pulled up behind the car in which Chanelle sat. I waved to the driver, indicating that they would have to drive around the Mustang. I wasn't going to let this young lady go until I shared the gospel with her.

"Chanelle, this is what I would say to you: 'In just a few minutes you are going to stand before Almighty God, and He is going to judge you according to the perfect moral standard of His Law. If you've ever lied, He will see you as a liar. If you've ever stolen anything, He will see you as a thief. If you've ever taken His name in vain, He will see you as a blasphemer. If you've ever hated anyone, He will see you as a murderer. God is holy, righteous, just, and good. He must punish sin. And the punishment God has ascribed for sin is eternity in hell. And that's what you face in about two minutes unless God does something. This is your only hope. Two thousand years ago, God the Father sent His Son to earth in the person of Jesus Christ—fully God and fully Man and without sin. Unlike you and me, He never once violated the Law of God in thought, word, or deed. He was perfect in every respect. About 30 to 33 years into that earthly existence, He voluntarily went to the cross. He suffered and died, shedding His innocent blood—taking upon Himself the punishment you rightly deserve for your sins against God. Then, three days later, He rose from the dead, forever defeating sin and death. He is alive today and He will return at a time of the Father's choosing.

"'What God requires of you, Chanelle, is that you repent. God commands that you turn from your sin and by faith, and by faith alone, receive Jesus Christ as your Lord and Savior. He is your only hope. In just a minute or so you are going to stand before God. Unless He saves you, you are going to spend eternity in hell. My hope is that instead of receiving what you deserve for your sins against God, you will receive what you and I don't deserve, which is grace, mercy, and the free gift of eternal life. So please, repent and receive Jesus Christ as your Lord and Savior while He has given you time.' Does that make sense?"

She silently nodded her head. Another car pulled up behind us. As with the first car, I motioned to the driver to drive around the Mustang.

"Chanelle, is there any reason why you wouldn't repent and place your faith in Jesus Christ to save you?"

"No."

"Chanelle, there is nothing more important than where you are going to spend eternity."

"I know. My mom tells me that all the time."

"Your mom is right. Listen to her. Do you have a Bible?"

"Yes."

"As soon as you get home, read the Gospel of John."

"Okay."

"I bet your mom has been praying for you."

"She has been."

"I'm going to pray for you, too."

"Thanks."

"Thanks for talking to me, Chanelle."

"You're welcome."

I stood up and reached into my bag for some tracts. All three of the vehicle's occupants accepted the paper gifts. I picked up my cross and stepped back to my spot on the corner.

The driver of the Mustang had originally approached the corner intending to make a right turn. In California, you can make a right turn on a red light. But instead of proceeding through the intersection, the car didn't move. The driver inched forward and stopped again.

Chanelle leaned out the window and said, "Do you think the world is going to end in 2012?"

Recent false prophetic nonsense was getting some people excited about the notion that the ancient Mayan calendar had predicted the world would end in 2012.

"No, Chanelle. Jesus made it very clear that only the Father knows when Jesus will return and when the world, as we know it, will end. Anyone who tells you they know when those things will happen is lying to you. But the Bible makes it clear that we should live our lives as if we expect Jesus to return at any moment, because He could return at any moment."

"My mom says that, too."

"Listen to your mom."

And with that, the Mustang turned onto Lyons Avenue and drove out of sight. Once again, I prayed. I thanked God for another divine appointment and I prayed that He would graciously save Chanelle and her two friends.

I stood at the corner with my cross, but I'm not at all certain my feet were on the ground. I was thankful and blessed. I looked at my cell phone and saw that I had been on the corner for only 30 minutes. In less than 30 minutes' time, the Lord allowed me to share the gospel with four people who I probably never would have met had I not decided to stop on my way home from the office. It doesn't take a long time to share the gospel. All it takes is love and obedience. Don't you have 30 minutes to spare today? Who knows what the Lord will do to you and through you if you will just take the time.

Tricia's Trauma and False Hope

God does not need your strength: he has more than enough of power of his own. He asks your weakness: he has none of that himself, and he is longing, therefore, to take your weakness, and use it as the instrument in his own mighty hand. Will you not yield your weakness to him, and receive his strength?
Charles Spurgeon

One evening, I decided to take my cross to a new intersection: the corner of McBean Parkway and Creekside Road in Valencia, California. I was blessed to have my daughter Marissa with me. Having my daughters join me while I carry the cross is often an opportunity for us to catch up. This evening was no different.

Marissa and I stood on the southwest corner. In an hour's time, hundreds of motorists saw the cross. The response we received, positive and negative, was nothing out of the ordinary. At one point, our attention was drawn to two people cheering as they sat in a late-model convertible Corvette. When we turned and looked their way, the driver pumped his fists in the air and his female passenger made the sign of the cross with her fingers. They proceeded through the intersection and headed northbound on McBean Parkway when the light changed, but not long after that we noticed the same couple returning to the shopping center they had exited.

Marissa and I were chatting when we were approached by the man who had given us the fist pump. He introduced himself as Jeff. Upon closer inspection, his appearance did not match the Corvette he drove. His clothing was disheveled and his shirt was badly stained in several places. He looked tired. But he was very friendly.

"Are you homeless?" he asked. "Do you need something to eat?"

"Oh, no. We live here in Santa Clarita," I said.

"I told my wife that you didn't look homeless to me. We're from San Diego and there are homeless people on every corner. I told her, 'No. They love Jesus!' So why are you out here with the cross?"

"We're hoping to have conversations with people like you," I said.

"I'm a Jesus Freak!" he declared. "My wife loves Jesus, too, but she has a problem with alcohol. So, you're sure we can't buy you dinner or something?"

"No, really. Thank you for your kindness. We were planning to head home for dinner in just a few minutes."

"Well, my wife is probably buying you dinner right now."

We chuckled.

Jeff turned, looked up the sidewalk, and pointed. "And here she comes. See, I told you she was going to buy you something to eat."

Walking toward us was his wife, the woman we saw sitting in the passenger seat of the Corvette. Staggering is a better way to describe her gait. In her right hand she carried a plastic grocery bag.

When she arrived at the corner Jeff introduced her to us. Her name was Tricia. Like Jeff, her clothes were disheveled and dirty. Her hair was knotted and unkempt. The odor of an alcoholic beverage was heavy on her breath. Her eyes were bloodshot and watery, and her speech was slurred. One didn't have to be a trained observer like a police officer to conclude that Tricia was very intoxicated.

Jeff explained to Tricia that we were not homeless or in need of food. Tricia was unconvinced. I thanked her for her kindness and we accepted the grocery bag, which contained two large bags of chips. One was open and half-eaten. Jeff tried to convince Tricia it was time to leave, but when she refused, he simply walked away.

Then, Tricia began to tell me about her life—her very troubled life.

Tricia said she had served as a police officer in Salt Lake City and Chicago. She spent eight years with each department. To look at Tricia, you would not believe that she was once a law enforcement professional. But I believed in my heart I that was speaking to a sister behind the badge, one who had been broken by the profession.

"I don't know when it happened," she said. "But it just all started coming back. You know?"

I smiled and nodded my head.

"I had to kill two people. If I hadn't, my lieutenant would have been dead. I worked narcotics, undercover. It's just all coming back."

"I know, Tricia. I know."

"And then I started drinking. I hate it! I hate it!" Tears welled up in her eyes. "I love Jesus, but I just can't burden Him with all my stuff."

"But that's exactly what He wants you to do," I said. "There is nothing you've experienced that He does not understand. And there is no sin you've committed that He cannot forgive. Turn to Him."

"That's what I don't get."

"What do you mean?"

"I just don't understand why He would die for my sins. I can't dump my stuff on Him."

"Tricia, that's pride."

"It probably is."

"Until you let go of your pride, until you repent and truly turn to Him, there will be no freedom for you. Turn to Him, Tricia."

Tricia and I talked for about half an hour. I tried to gently reason with her, realizing that there was no way to know how much she could comprehend through the fog of her drunken state. My heart broke for her.

"Tricia, you and I have both had friends who have died in the line of duty. And their sacrifice always reminds me of something Jesus said. 'Greater love has no one than this, that one lay down his life for his friends' (John 15:13). And Christ's sacrifice on the cross is more than sufficient to cover your sins, your hurt, your pain. Turn to Him and live, Tricia."

I reached into my bag and removed a token I give only to police officers—a Ten-Four Ministries Challenge Coin.[1] "I want you to have this. I only give it to brothers and sisters behind the badge."

"What can I give you for this?"

"Nothing."

Jeff returned to the corner to once again, hoping to get Tricia to walk back to the car. Tricia staggered toward the street and I grabbed her arm to keep her from falling into traffic. Jeff put his arm around

---

[1] For a brief history of the tradition of the Challenge Coin: "The Challenge Coin Tradition," *Northwest Territorial Mint*, accessed April 22, 2016, http://custom.nwtmint.com/news_challengecoinhistory.php.

Tricia to steady her. "I love Jesus," he said. "And Tricia is born again, too."

"Jeff, Tricia doesn't believe that. She has yet to come to understand why Jesus died on the cross." In an effort to encourage and comfort Tricia, Jeff was trying to fill her mind with thoughts of hope she did not yet have and a Savior she did not yet know.

Tricia pulled away from Jeff and put her arms around me, thanking me for talking to her as she hugged me. She then put her arms around Marissa and held her tight. When Tricia let go of Marissa, I told her that I would be praying for her.

Jeff and Tricia walked back to their car.

"Let's go home," I said to Marissa.

"Are you all right?" she asked.

"Not really."

Tricia served two large cities for 16 years, probably giving more than a person should have to give to a community. It broke her. It broke her spirit. It broke her heart. And it left emotional and physical scars that only the Great Physician can heal.

Marissa and I walked back to our car. We spent some time in prayer for Tricia before heading home. Marissa held my hand most of the way.

Jared's Dinosaur Defense Dismissed

The law is also very useful, because it shows us our defections and stains. It is like the looking-glass which my lady holds up to her face, that she may see if there be any spot on it. But she cannot wash her face with the looking-glass. When the mirror has done its utmost, then there are the same stains. It cannot take away a single spot; it can only show where one is. And the law, though it reveals our sin, our shortcomings, our transgressions, it cannot remove the sin or the transgression. It is weak for that purpose, because it was never intended to accomplish such an end.
Charles Spurgeon

Amanda (the youngest of my three adult daughters) and I were spending some time with the cross on a local street and distributing tracts to pedestrians, when a young man with skateboard in hand walked to the corner on the opposite side of the street. As he pushed the crosswalk button and waited, he looked at me, looked across the street, and looked at me again. He dropped his head as if he was thinking about what he should do.

My phone rang. It was Mahria.

"Hi, honey."

"Twenty-five minutes until dinner."

"Okay. Got to go, honey. I think I'm about to have a conversation."

"Okay. Bye!" she said with an excited tone.

When the light turned green, the young man hopped on his skateboard and made his way to our side of the street. I handed him a gospel tract and asked, "Did you get one of these yet today?"

He took the tract from my hand and then walked behind me to the light pole, so I turned around to face him. His name was Jared.

Jared pointed up at my cross and said, "Is this about the Christian religion?"

"Well, it's about Christ, but it's not about religion. I'm asking people an important question. Are you ready to stand before Jesus Christ?"

"No, I'm not ready."

"Why do you say that?"

"Because of my youth."

"Oh. Are you not concerned because you think you have a long life ahead of you?"

"Yep."

"Do you have any idea when you're going to die?"

"No."

"Neither do I," I said. "So, what do you think is going to happen to you when you die? What's next after this life?"

"I'm not sure."

"Do you believe in God?"

"I believe someone created everything. But there's no mention of dinosaurs in the Bible. There are just so many questions about the Bible."

"Apparently you've never read the Book of Job. While it's true that the Bible doesn't contain the word 'dinosaur,' there are two creatures mentioned in Job that could very well be dinosaurs. 'Behemoth' [Job 40:15], while its exact identity is unknown, the word used in the Hebrew text indicates that it was a very large land animal that could have been a dinosaur. 'Leviathan' [Job 41:1], while its exact identity is unknown, the word used in the Hebrew text indicates that it was a very large sea creature that could have been a dinosaur of some kind."

"Really?"

"Really."

"Yeah, but there are so many inconsistencies in the Bible."

"Really? Can you tell me where they are?"

"Well, there is so much evidence in science."

"Are you referring to the science that up until 1492 believed the world was flat, when the Bible declared thousands of years earlier that the world is round [Isaiah 40:22]?"

"The Bible says that?"

"Yep. Or are you referring to the science that told people they should wash their hands in a bowl of standing water, when the Bible declared people should wash their hands in running water [Leviticus 15:13]?"

"The Bible says that?"

"Yep. Or are you referring to the science that taught that sick people should have their blood drained from their body, when the Bible teaches that blood is the source of life [Leviticus 17:11]."

"It says that, too?"

"Yep. Or are you trusting the science that up until a few years ago taught that there were nine planets in our solar system but now insists there are only eight?"

"Well, there are some flaws in science."

"Yes, there are," I said. "Seeing that you believe God exists, let's assume for the sake of argument that heaven and hell are real places. What do you think a person has to do to go to hell?"

"I don't know. Not believe in God, I guess."

"What do you think a person has to do to go to heaven?"

"Keep the Ten Commandments."

"So, how's that working out for you? Have you been able to keep them?"

"Well, nobody's perfect."

"You're right. I know I'm not."

Having quickly dealt with Jared's intellectual defense mechanisms, I now had an open door to deal with his conscience: "Jared, have you ever told a lie?"

"Yes."

"Me, too. If we tell lies, what does that make us?"

"Liars."

"Have you ever stolen anything?"

"Yes, I have."

"So have I. If we've stolen things, what does that make us?"

"Thieves."

"How old are you?"

"Twenty-two."

"Jared, let's say you started sinning (started breaking God's law) when you were 12 years old. You started much younger than that, but just to paint a picture, let's say you started breaking God's Law when you were 12. If you only sin three times a day in thought, word, or deed, in a year you will have broken God's Law 1,000 times. In 10 years, 10,000 times. In 20 years you will break God's law 20,000 times. Now, let's say you were standing before a judge, having broken the law, and the judge asks you what you have to say for yourself. You tell the judge, 'I'm sorry. I promise I will never do it again. So, I think you ought to let me go.' In response, the judge unrolls what looks like a giant roll of paper towels, which is your rap sheet, listing the 20,000 crimes you've committed. Do you think the judge is going to believe that you will never break the law again?"

"No."

"And you don't believe it either, do you?"

"No."

"So, if you were to die today and stand before God and He judged you according to the standard of His law, do you think He would find you innocent or guilty?"

"Guilty."

"And if God is a good and righteous Judge (and He is), what should He do with you? heaven or hell?"

"Hell."

"Does that concern you at all?"

"Yes, it does."

"Good. That means your conscience, which is a gift from God, is working. That's good. Do you have any idea what God did so that you might not have to spend eternity in hell?"

Jared looked up at the cross. "His Son died on the cross."

"That's right. Two thousand years ago, God the Father sent His Son to Earth in the person of Jesus Christ—fully God and fully Man but without sin. Unlike you and me, He never once violated the Law of God in thought, word, or deed. He couldn't. He was God in the flesh, the sinless Lamb of God. He was born of a virgin, just as the prophet said He would be, more than 700 years before His birth.

"Thirty to 33 years into that earthly existence, He voluntarily went to the cross. He suffered, shed His innocent blood, and died a horrific death. The Bible says that He was so badly beaten and mutilated that He could barely be recognized as human [Isaiah 52:14]. He suffered and died, taking upon Himself the punishment you and I rightly deserve for violating God's Law. Three days later, He rose from the dead and forever defeated death. Unlike the false gods of every other religion on the planet, Jesus Christ is alive and He will return at a time of the Father's choosing.

"What He commands of you is that you repent, that you turn away from and forsake your sin and receive Jesus Christ as your Lord and Savior. If God causes you to be born again, when you die and stand before Him, instead of receiving what you deserve for breaking God's Law (which is eternity in hell), you will receive what you don't deserve (which is grace and mercy and everlasting life in heaven with Jesus Christ). Isn't that good news?"

"It is."

"Will you give it some thought?"

"I will."

"Jared, I may not see you again. I care about you and I don't want you to go to hell. Please repent and believe the gospel while God has given you time. The Bible says that today is the day of salvation. The time to get right with God isn't when you are standing before Him waiting to be judged. That would be like standing before a judge in a courtroom and saying, 'Wait a minute, judge. I didn't think I would get caught. I didn't think the jury would find me guilty, and I didn't think you would punish me. So, I think you ought to just let me go and forget about the whole thing.'

A good judge is going to look at you and say, 'Jared, you should have thought about that before you broke the law. It's too late now.' I don't want that to happen to you, Jared."

"Me neither."

"Then get right with God while He's given you time."

The light turned green. It had turned green many times since Jared and I began our conversation. Jared and I shook hands and said goodbye.

Amanda and I packed up and went to the car. We drove about a quarter mile when the phone rang again. It was Mahria. "Five minutes until dinner."

"We're on the road. We'll be home in just a minute. God did it again, honey."

"Very cool!"

Yes, it was. It was very cool.

As a family, we prayed for Jared before enjoying the meal the Lord provided.

"Should I Still Honor My Father?"

I do not know how else we could care for some poor creatures, if it were not that Jesus teaches us to despise none and despair of none.
Charles Spurgeon

I made my way to the corner of 16th Street and Orchard Village Road in Valencia, California. It would be the first time I carried the cross at this intersection.

While en route to the intersection, I called Zack, one of my sons-in-the-faith. He wanted to talk about a recent witnessing encounter he had that raised objections from one of his Christian college classmates. We continued our conversation as I parked my car and made my way to the corner. After a few minutes, I saw a young lady walk toward me from across the street. I handed her an "Are You Ready?"[1] gospel tract as she stepped from the street onto the sidewalk.

She looked at the gospel tract and gasped. "These are my friends!"

"What? You know the kids in the picture?"

"Yes I do." She proceeded to point to each one as she stated their names. Then she looked up at me and said, "I see you everywhere. Do you have a job?"

She wasn't being sarcastic, which made what she said all the more humorous to me.

"Yes, I have a job. I serve with a ministry in Bellflower (at the time I was serving at Living Waters). I try to come out with the cross for an hour or so each day when I get home."

"How long have you been doing this?"

"About 2½ years."

"Why?"

"So I can have conversations with nice people like you."

---

[1] "Are You Ready?" is one of several gospel tracts I have written with Marv Plementosh of One Million Tracts. You will find all of my published tracts on the One Million Tracts website (http://www.onemilliontracts.com/Tracts-By-Tony_c31.htm).

She smiled and pointed up to the cross. "What does that mean?"

At the time, I had "John 14:6" on the back of my cross in large white letters. "John 14:6 says, 'Jesus said to him, "I am the way, and the truth, and the life. No one comes to the Father except through me,"'" I explained.

Because of the personal nature of what I am about to share, we will call the young lady "Karen."

I knew I still had Zack on my phone, but I also knew Zack would understand that I had to have a conversation with Karen. After a while, I heard the computerized voice of my Bluetooth say, "Call disconnected." I later learned that Zack's phone battery died. He texted me to say he was praying for Karen.

Karen told me she believed in God and believed in heaven and hell. She was 17 years old and had graduated early from an area high school. I learned she had lived in the community for a couple years but was originally from Moorpark, where she attended a nondenominational church.

I asked Karen if she knew what would happen to her when she died. She had no idea. Like most people, she believed she was a good person. She believed that people who do "bad things" will go to hell. So, I took Karen through the Ten Commandments. She admitted to being a liar who dishonored her parents by lying to them. She was concerned as she came to the realization that if she were to die today, she would spend eternity in hell as the just punishment for her sins against God.

Then Karen asked me a question that broke my heart. "My dad raped me. Do I still have to honor him?"

She told me that although the crime was reported to the police, her father was never arrested and never faced charges for the assault. She no longer lives with her father.

It was difficult, and I was as gentle as I could be, but I explained to her that honoring one's parents is something children are to do, regardless of whether or not the parents are honorable. I was quick to assure her that what her father did to her was despicable and he should be in prison for the rest of his life.

She asked me what honoring her father, considering the circumstances, would look like. I told her that she shouldn't seek vengeance or act out of hatred toward her father. But, I found words difficult. I told her how sorry I was that she had been victimized in such a horrible way. My blood was boiling toward a man I would never meet, who violated a girl the age of my youngest daughter, Amanda.

I used the courtroom analogy with Karen as a transition to the gospel. I asked her what she would think of someone who would pay her fine so she could be set free. She said, "I would be forever grateful and I would love him and follow him the rest of my life."

I shared the gospel with Karen, which she understood. She had been waiting to meet friends but seemed to be in no hurry to leave. As we continued to chat on the corner, I told her where I attend church. I learned Karen aspired to be a college hockey player. She graduated with a 5.0 GPA and was offered a scholastic scholarship to a prestigious university. If the hockey goal (no pun intended) didn't work out, her back-up plan was to be a photographer.

We talked until she received a call from her friends. I encouraged her to read the Gospel of John and explained to her where she could find it in the Bible. She said she would read it. Karen walked away to meet her friends, and I thanked God for the opportunity to talk to her.

Karen and I talked for almost an hour. Before the conversation was over, we were no longer strangers. I knew about Karen's spiritual beliefs, her aspirations, and her pain. There's nothing "cold" about this kind of evangelism (as some would errantly characterize it)—not if you care about the people with whom you are blessed to speak.

Evangelism Tip #2: Friendship Evangelism
It's neither Friendship nor Evangelism

I received the following message from a friend on Facebook. While it is a topic I have addressed many times in the past, I thought the way my friend honestly asked her questions accurately expressed how many Christians feel about sharing the gospel with their friends. Her words also helped to reaffirm what I have believed for a very long time: "Friendship Evangelism," as it is most commonly taught and practiced by Christians, is neither friendship nor evangelism.

With my friend's permission, I would like to share her note with you, and then I will answer her questions.

> I have made a lifetime of friends, and up until about 6 years ago, I was a partier and not walking with the Lord. Since become a Christian, I have made myself known to all but not gone out of my way to share the gospel. I know my friends "think" they know what the Bible says, and I also know that they don't want me to preach or share. I have hoped that Facebook would encourage them to ask me, but they don't.
>
> I watch, like a voyeur, their lives on Facebook, and I hate it. I see them post pictures of nights on the town, glazed eyes, draped over a different guy in each shot. Today I read as they talked about spending money frivolously and obnoxiously. I see so much "selfism" and today it really started to hurt.
>
> I keep thinking that, by example, they might want to know more or ask… Instead, I see them avoid my page and my comments. They never address anything I say regarding our Savior, God, or the written word, and only comment on the "regular" things I post.
>
> Most of my "friends" from the past, I still DO care about their salvation. I'm certain that my approach will mean the end of life-long friendships. Should I just keep exposing the Lord to them? Our Christmas cards and small other things are about all the contact we really have. Should I just go for broke

and risk turning them off completely? I know it would mean the end of friendships in most cases.

Part of me knows that losing these friendships shouldn't matter. I'm more concerned that if I can keep the door open, they might...might...someday come to repentance. I want the door to remain open.

I need some advice. I'm pretty sure you're going to tell me to go for it...but I thought you might have a perspective or a way that I should use as an approach...

[P.S.] I'm thinking of how to approach evangelizing them. I know the approach that Ray [Comfort] uses, letting them convict themselves through the 10 Commandments (which really works) and you, too, have mastered it. I have also been told to have them read the word themselves because the word has power. As a chicken, I was hoping to be "non-confrontational" and send it in a letter. A letter of love and a pouring out of my heart for them. But that leaves them with the ability to not answer or reply. I know that God would use me MUCH better if I had the nerve to deliver my (HIS) message in person. I want to engage their minds. I've never been a "chicken." I don't want to fail God. I want my (HIS) words to pierce. So...praying and waiting for His inspiration and His way to lead me, and maybe your words will help push me into the world. I'm NOT ashamed of Him, I'm afraid of them, so to speak. I know if He is with me, who can be against me? Why...do I struggle? Oh, the flesh.

Before I answer my friend's questions, it is important that I preface my commentary with a few clarifying remarks. First, my commentary is not a critique of my friend—neither of her love for Christ nor of her love for people. I do not question her salvation or the genuineness of her desire for her friends to be saved. My commentary will be, however, a pointed critique of "Friendship Evangelism" or "Relationship Evangelism," which I believe is a profoundly effective tool of Satan (1 Peter 5:8).

What Is Friendship Evangelism?

I believe many Christians practice "Friendship Evangelism" with sincerity. But sadly, it is a sincerity most often born out of an ignorance (1 Peter 1:13-16) of the Word of God in general and biblical evangelism in particular. At the same time, I feel no such obligation to extend charity toward authors, pastors, teachers, speakers, and movement leaders who propagate this spiritual fraud upon followers of Christ—both true and false converts. Theirs will be a stricter judgment (James 3:1).

Now, let me take a moment to answer a couple of baseless objections before I articulate my position. I do this in advance of making my case because I know some Christians treat "Friendship Evangelism" as if it is sacrosanct—an essential evangelism tradition. I use the word "tradition" since there is no biblical support for this methodology/philosophy for ministry. Traditions like "friendship evangelism" demonstrate the sad reality that modern-day evangelicalism, especially the American variety, has yet to completely break free of Rome. For Rome also holds traditions with more reverence and gives tradition more authority than Scripture (Matthew 15:1-6).

Let me make it very clear that Christians are called by the Word of God to be both friendly and relational. "And if I give all my possessions to feed the poor, and if I surrender my body to be burned, but do not have love, it profits me nothing" (1 Corinthians 13:3). To be opposed to "Friendship Evangelism" as it is most commonly practiced is not to be opposed to friendship or relationships. But a godly and biblical Christian will put God and friends before and above friendships (Luke 14:25-27).

A second common objection to any argument against "Friendship Evangelism" is this: "There are many ways to share the gospel and 'Friendship Evangelism' is one of them." Not so. There is only one way to communicate the gospel, the Bible's way, though it can take different forms. Any methodology that is extra-biblical (meaning the Bible neither commands nor condemns the activity) should be approached and applied with extra care and caution. The immeasurable harm done by "Friendship Evangelism" is evidence that the American Church has thrown caution to the wind and has operated carelessly when applying this extra-biblical, faux-evangelistic methodology.

Does Friendship Evangelism Cause Harm?

How do I know "Friendship Evangelism" has done great harm? I meet false converts who are byproducts of this unbiblical form of evangelism almost daily on the streets. They have been welcomed into the Christian community. They have been converted to the creature comforts of the church, but they have never been converted by and to the Lord Jesus Christ.

I once attended a baptism where several people were baptized. One teenage girl stood in the pool to share her "testimony" before being baptized by the pastor. Her testimony, albeit paraphrased, went something like this: "I grew up Roman Catholic. I started to attend this church. I'm more comfortable with Christianity, so I want to be baptized." And the pastor baptized her as a follower of Jesus Christ.

With the above in mind, I will now address my friend's questions and concerns.

Friendship Evangelism Doesn't Preach Christ

My friend wrote: "I have made myself known to all but not gone out of my way to share the gospel."

In a sentence my friend summed up one of the great deficiencies of "Friendship Evangelism." A shockingly low number of professing Christians share the gospel with a single person in a year's time (or in a lifetime), and it's obvious most Christians practicing "Friendship Evangelism" are part of that indefensible number. Why? By engaging in the practice of "Friendship Evangelism," the Christian spends far more time making themselves known to their friends than making Christ known (1 Corinthians 2:2) to their friends.

Many Christians who practice "Friendship Evangelism" have been led to believe that it is evangelistic to live a perceptible Christian life in front of unbelievers or to openly admit to unbelievers that they are Christians. There is nothing remarkable about such an admission, especially in America. The majority of the American population will indicate on surveys and censuses that they are Christians. Many Christians will answer the "What religion are you?" question with "I'm a Christian" for no other reason than they are not Jewish, Muslim, or Atheist. To check the Christian box is the default position of most Americans. But many are no more Christian than the Jew, Muslim, or Atheist.

Making yourself known as a Christian is not the same as evangelistically making Christ known.

My Friends Don't Want Me to Preach Christ to Them

My friend wrote: "They [her friends] don't want me to preach or share."

Modern evangelicalism has wrongly valued an unregenerate sinner's "felt needs" over their very real need of salvation. This is not to say that we shouldn't address a person's felt needs. In doing so, one can often discover that the root of a particular need is sin, which then presents the opportunity to share the law of God and the gospel with that person. However, evangelicalism has woefully dropped the ball by trying to meet felt needs and stopping there—as if addressing felt needs were the same as evangelism.

Dear reader, if you feed, clothe, and house people for the glory of God (Matthew 5:16) but you do not share the gospel with them, all you have ultimately accomplished is making those people warmed and filled on their way to hell. You have merely made their bodies more comfortable. You have done nothing for their souls.

More to the point regarding my friend's observation: of course the unregenerate person doesn't want their Christian friends to proclaim the gospel to them. Why? They hate Jesus (John 15:18). They love their sin (Job 15:16) and they hate God (Romans 1:30). Cockroaches don't run to the center of the floor and square dance when you turn on the kitchen light. They flee to the dark regions underneath the cabinets and appliances. They hate the light and so does the unregenerate sinner (John 3:20). Their love for the darkness of their sin is so great that any holy light brought to bear in their lives is not only uncomfortable and unpleasant but also detestable.

Sadly, modern evangelicalism has responded to this reality by doing everything it can to engage lost sinners in their culture and according to their felt needs without ever bothering to flip on the light switch of the gospel. Some modern evangelical churches have allowed a lost person's feelings about "the light" to determine whether or not they shine the light. Many Christians have become man-pleasers to the point of hiding the gospel from people (Matthew 5:15). In doing so, they cease to live as servants of God (Galatians 1:10). Frankly, it doesn't matter what lost people want. What matters is what they need, and what they need is salvation by the grace of God alone (Ephesians 2:8-9), through faith alone (Romans 1:17), in Jesus Christ alone (Acts 4:12). What they need, whether they feel it or not, is to repent and believe the gospel (Mark 1:15; Luke 13:1-5; Acts 17:29-31).

Friendship Evangelism is not Evangelistic

My friend wrote: "I keep thinking that, by example, they might want to know more or ask… Instead I see them avoid my page and my comments."

Part of the evidence that "Friendship Evangelism" is not evangelistic is the practice of "Assisi-ism."

Francis of Assisi is far too often quoted as saying, "Preach the gospel at all times and when necessary use words." There are two problems with this quote.

1. It is unbiblical.
2. Assisi never said it.

Catholic scholars have methodically and exhaustively searched the extant writings of Assisi and cannot attribute the quote to him. These days, this is common knowledge. Yet Christians continue to refer to the mythical quote, and worse, they errantly apply it in their lives. The quote also has a modern-day translation. It goes something like this: "Live your life in such a way that people ask you why."

While it is true that our good works, when performed for the glory of God alone, can cause lost people to glorify God (Matthew 5:16), living a Christian life in front of lost people does not mean they are going to see Jesus in you. Why? The reason is simple enough. Unregenerate sinners are spiritually blind. "But a natural man does not accept the things of the Spirit of God, for they are foolishness to him; and he cannot understand them, because they are spiritually appraised." (1 Corinthians 2:14).

It is also important to note what Matthew 5:16 doesn't say. The verse says nothing about people coming to genuine repentance and faith in the Lord Jesus Christ.

Not only are unbelievers spiritually blind, but they are also dead in their sins. Not asleep. Not sick. Not in need of a little help. They are dead.

> And you were dead in your trespasses and sins, in which you formerly walked according to the course of this world, according to the prince of the power of the air, of the spirit that is now working in the sons of disobedience. Among them we too all formerly lived in the lusts of our flesh, indulging the desires of the flesh and of the mind, and were by nature children of wrath, even as the rest. (Ephesians 2:1-3).

The Gospel is a Spoken Message

The gospel is a spoken message, meaning it is communicated in verbal and/or written formats. The gospel is not communicated through interpretive dance, random acts of kindness, or mimes.

> How then will they call on Him in whom they have not believed? How will they believe in Him whom they have not heard? And how will they hear without a preacher? How will they preach unless they are sent? Just as it is written, "How beautiful are the feet of those who bring good news of good things!" However, they did not all heed the good news; for Isaiah says, "Lord, who has believed our report?" So faith comes from hearing, and hearing by the word of Christ (Romans 10:14-17).

With 160,000 people dying every day and the vast majority of them facing God's judgment (Matthew 7:13-14), it amounts to depraved indifference to wait for the lost people around us to see something special in us and ask what's different about us. We are commanded by God's Word to go (Matthew 28:18-20) and preach (Mark 16:15) the gospel to as many people as we can, whenever we can, as often as we can (Acts 1:8). Time is far too short to wait for spiritually dead and blind people to see Jesus in Christians who are still clothed in sinful human flesh. It will never happen.

Christians also should not assume that they regularly look like Jesus. Jesus was and is God (John 8:58; John 10:30; Philippians 2:6-11; Hebrews 2:5-18). The Christian is not. Jesus was and is without sin (2 Corinthians 5:21). The Christian is not. Jesus was and is perfect (Hebrews 1:3). The Christian never will be perfect this side of Heaven. Since an unbelieving world hates Jesus, the spiritually dead and blind are going to see in you what is most appealing to them (Romans 1:28-32; 2 Timothy 3:1-5)—your sin. People are also going to look for you to sin in a failed attempt to justify their own unbelief (Luke 10:29; 16:15).

Friendship Evangelism Makes Friendship More Important than Evangelism

My friend wrote: "I'm certain that my approach will mean the end of life-long friendships."

The tragic result of "Friendship Evangelism," as Christians most often practice it, is that friendships often become more important than the souls of friends. Christians have been wrongly convinced that they must take time to cultivate relationships with people so that someday they may gain the lost person's permission ("earn the right") to share the gospel with them. So the Christian invests time, energy, and resources, sincerely trying to establish loving and caring relationships with people. Is it wrong to do that? No. But the all-too-often tragic result of the practice is that the Christian won't share the gospel with his lost friend even if he desires to do so. Why? The Christian doesn't want to do anything to jeopardize the relationship he has worked so hard to build.

This is a selfish perspective. Does the Christian believe he is so valuable that his lost friend can't live without him? Or does the Christian derive so much pleasure out of the relationship and what his lost friend does for him that he doesn't want to ruin a "good thing"?

Jesus said, "Greater love has no one than this, that one lay down his life for his friends." (John 15:13). If Christians truly loved their lost friends, they would be willing to give up their very lives and certainly their relationships so that those same lost friends might have eternal life. Or do Christians really want their friends to be with them in this life more than they want them to be with Jesus?

No One Goes to Hell Because You Weren't Their Friend

My friend wrote: "Part of me knows that losing these friendships shouldn't matter. I'm more concerned that if I can keep the door open, they might...might...someday come to repentance. I want the door to remain open."

No Christian can close a door that God wants open. No Christian can open a door that God wants shut (Revelation 3:8). God is sovereign (Acts 4:24), and He doesn't need our help. God needs nothing from people (Psalm 50:7-15). The gospel alone is the power of God for salvation (Romans 1:16). God, by His grace, chooses to use His children to communicate the life-saving gospel to a lost and dying world. No one goes to heaven because we've made friends with them, and no one goes to hell because we've failed to establish relationships with them.

Conclusion

In closing, let me reiterate that Christians should be loving (1 Peter 4:8), merciful (Zechariah 7:9), gentle (Galatians 5:23), and kind (Proverbs 21:21) to people. We should speak the truth in love (Ephesians 4:15). Evangelism is not a game. It is not a sport. It is what God has commanded every follower of Christ to do. Evangelism is a lifestyle, which is not to say that living the Christian life is evangelism. Rather, our verbal proclamation of the gospel should permeate every aspect of our lives and impact every relationship we have. My friend understands all of this. She knows what she must do. She acknowledged as much toward the end of her note. I hope I've answered her questions and maybe some of yours, too.

Spiritual Tug-of-War

You don't know what converts God has given to you. There are scattered up and down the world—perhaps some precious ones who owe their salvation instrumentally to you, and could they all stand before you, you would blush with shame at the thought of leaving a harvest field that has really been so prolific though not in your sight. Go back again to thy work, for the Lord has blessed thee. Play not the fool by deserting the post where he will give thee honour yet.
Charles Spurgeon

Over the years, I have had many encounters on the street in which I've tried to engage a small group of three or more people in conversation. Most often there is one person in the group who is invested in the conversation while the others either joke around or talk among themselves. It is common for the disinterested members in the group to try to convince the interested person to leave. I refer to times like these as "spiritual tug-of-wars." I feel like I'm literally hanging on to one of the person's arms, while the group is hanging on to the other. I'm trying to pull the person toward life. The others are trying to pull the person toward death.

One afternoon I spent an hour with my cross at the corner of Bouquet Canyon Road and Alamogordo Road in Saugus, a neighborhood of Santa Clarita.

Within minutes after arriving at the corner, I saw three young men on the opposite side of Bouquet Canyon Road walking toward the intersection. One of the three yelled, "I'm Jewish!"

"What's your point?!" I replied.

That got their attention.

When the light turned green, they started across the street in my direction. Chris was the first to speak. "I just want to ask you a question. Ready for what?"

"Are you ready for eternity? Are you ready to stand before God and give an account for your life?" I asked.

"I'm ready?"

"What makes you ready?"

"I have Jesus."

"What does that mean?"

"I'm a Christian."

"What does that mean? A lot of people claim to be Christian, but they don't know Jesus. They don't know the Jesus of the Bible."

"I'm a good person."

"You consider yourself to be a good person?"

"Yes."

"What's your definition of a good person?"

"I don't know. A good soul."

"Do you read the Bible?"

"No. But I used to go to a Bible study."

"The Bible says that every man will declare his own goodness."

One of Chris's friends interjected and asked, "Do you go to church on Sunday?"

"Yeah, but that doesn't make me a good person," I replied. "I'm not a good person."

"I feel like you don't have to go to church on Sunday. I haven't been to church in 15 years. I don't feel like I have to go to church to be a good person," Chris's friend asserted.

"In the end, it doesn't matter what we feel or believe. What matters is whether or not what we feel and believe is true. A lot of people have different feelings and beliefs out there. Some people feel and believe it's good to fly planes into buildings for their god. That's doesn't make it right," I answered before returning my attention to Chris. "Are you familiar with the Ten Commandments?"

"Yeah."

"Okay. That's actually God's moral standard. In fact, the definition of 'good' is moral perfection. I'm not that."

I took Chris through several of the commandments. He admitted to being a liar, thief, blasphemer, and adulterer-at-heart.

"Chris, does that sound like the definition of a good person?"

"I guess I'm going to hell." Chris's response seemed a bit sarcastic, but I could see in his eyes that there was more to his answer than that. He had a look of concern and conviction on his face.

It was at this moment that Chris's two friends became uncomfortable and wanted to leave. "Come on, man!" one of his friends said. "It's time to go drink some beer!"

"You can get beer in a little bit. You can stick around for a bit and have a reasonable conversation," I said.

"Okay," they replied.

I once again turned my attention back to Chris and shared the courtroom analogy with him. It was during the analogy that his friends made one last ditch effort to pull Chris out of the conversation. It didn't work. Chris wanted to stay and talk. Chris's friends made some mocking comments, but a couple minutes later they walked away.

When I finished the courtroom analogy (of which there are several variations), ending with a stranger coming into the courtroom to pay Chris's fine, I asked Chris, "Would that be good news?"

"Yep."

"What would you think of the person that did that for you?"

"I would love him."

"Okay. Let's see if that's true, because that's exactly what God did." I then proclaimed the gospel to Chris. Throughout the presentation of the gospel, Christ nodded in the affirmative.

"Chris, it seems you are agreeing with me, because you've heard this before," I said. "But you think you're going to heaven because you believe you're a good person. The Word of God says that there is no one who is good [Romans 3:10-18]. All of our good deeds are nothing but filthy rags before a holy God [Isaiah 64:6].

"God's standard is perfection, and we can't live up to that. That's why Jesus came to Earth. We need a savior. The Bible says that the demons believe and tremble. Satan and his demons know exactly who Jesus Christ is and what He came to do. Their knowledge is far superior to our own. But they're not going to heaven simply because they know the truth about Jesus.

"What God commands of us is that we repent, that we turn from our sin, turn to God, and put our faith in Jesus Christ alone to save us, not in our own goodness, not in a church, not in anything else but Jesus Christ. It's on the basis of what He did on the cross, and not on the basis of anything we have done, that we can be saved. So you need to consider where you really stand with God."

Chris's eyes were watery, as if he was fighting back tears.

"Now, you're standing here and your friends walked away for a reason. There's something going on inside you. I can't read your mind and I don't know your heart, but you're staying here for a reason. They walked away for a reason.

"As soon as you walk down that street, they're going to try to talk you out of everything you just heard. But there's nothing more important than your soul, Chris. When you die and stand before God, there are no second chances. There are no 'do-overs.' That's why God has given you the opportunity to hear the gospel today. He is giving you the opportunity to repent and put your trust in Christ today."

Chris and I talked for another minute or two. We shook hands and thanked each other for the conversation before he walked down the sidewalk in the same direction his friends went several minutes earlier. I knew what the conversation would be like when Chris reached his friends, so I prayed, asking the Lord to allow the seeds I tossed to land on good soil. I asked that He would save Chris.

While two mocked and walked, one stayed, and I thank God for that.

Wayne Was Compelled to Stop

If one should spend one's whole life for God, and win only one soul by the most earnest and devoted efforts, it would be a rich reward to see that one star shining forever in the firmament of heaven, to see that one gem glistening forever in the diadem of Christ, to see that one sheep feeding forever in the pastures of eternal life.
Charles Spurgeon

Liza was 29 years old, married, with two small children. She was athletic and beautiful with what I'm sure she thought was her whole life ahead of her. Sadly, she died suddenly after suffering a massive heart attack.

In Liza's obituary, which appeared in our local paper, her family wrote:

Liza was a devoted wife, a caring mother of two wonderful young children, and an awesome daughter. She loved being in the water, the outdoors, camping and exploring. She was fond of all God's creatures with cats, dogs, birds, fish, rabbits, and turtles, all being a part of her life. Her love of family and friends was endless. Liza was 29 and married for almost four years. She was loved by many and is sorely missed. While our grief is deep and at times unbearable, our comfort is knowing Liza is now with the Lord. We love you Liza.

The memorial service was scheduled for 4 p.m. at the Lutheran Church across the street from my condo community. Reading her tragic story, feeling for her young family, realizing that many people (saved and unsaved) would gather at the church across the street, and not knowing (because I know nothing about the church) if the gospel would be preached during the memorial service, I felt compelled to take out my cross.

Initially, I thought to stand across the street from the church. I decided that I would wait until the service was well underway so as not to be a distraction to anyone before the service. I wanted the conversation inside the church during the memorial to be about Liza and not the man standing across the street with a cross.

As the time of the service drew near, I grew increasingly uncomfortable with the idea of standing across the street from the church. Thoughts of the Westboro Baptist Church cult[1] came to mind. The last thing I wanted was to leave anyone with the impression that I was either protesting the church or the memorial service.

The cross is not a protest sign or political tool. It is a symbol of the sacrifice my sin required: my heavenly Father crushing His only Son on a rugged piece of wood. It is a symbol of my precious Lord and Savior's propitiation and love that defeated sin and death.

So, I decided to walk up the hill, about 3/10 of a mile away from the church, to a corner where I had previously stood with the cross several times. This way I would be out of sight of the church. But I was in a position where people leaving the memorial service could see the cross without necessarily seeing my presence there as directly related to the memorial service. I wanted the message I was displaying to draw their attention without anyone assuming I was there to be a distraction or an unnecessary offense.

"Hail Satan," "Get a life," "@#$%^&," and multiple one-finger salutes were the responses I received from some tolerant, forward-thinking Santa Clarita residents. It is interesting to note that none of the negativity came from people driving from the direction of church. Of course, there were also several positive waves (with all five fingers), thumbs up, car horn honks, and smiles.

---

[1] From the church's website ("About Us," *God Hates Fags*, accessed April 22, 2016, www.godhatesfags.com/wbcinfo/aboutwbc.html.): "WBC engages in daily peaceful sidewalk demonstrations opposing the homosexual lifestyle of soul-damning, nation-destroying filth. We display large, colorful signs containing Bible words and sentiments, including: GOD HATES FAGS, FAGS HATE GOD, AIDS CURES FAGS, THANK GOD FOR AIDS, FAGS BURN IN HELL, GOD IS NOT MOCKED, FAGS ARE NATURE FREAKS, GOD GAVE FAGS UP, NO SPECIAL LAWS FOR FAGS, FAGS DOOM NATIONS, THANK GOD FOR DEAD SOLDIERS, FAG TROOPS, GOD BLEW UP THE TROOPS, GOD HATES AMERICA, AMERICA IS DOOMED, THE WORLD IS DOOMED, etc." Westboro Baptist Church is *not* a Christian church. It is a small band of very hateful people who do not represent Christ or His gospel.

I had been on the corner for two hours when my daughter Marissa walked to the corner. It was starting to get dark. She said that she had walked by the church the parking lot and it was no longer very full. After chatting for a few minutes, I told Marissa that we would walk home after one more cycle of traffic lights. Marissa kindly reminded me that I had said that to her a few times already.

"Okay, honey. Let's go home."

But, we had only taken a few steps when I heard a voice coming from behind me.

"Excuse me, sir."

I turned around to see a young man, probably in his early twenties, with disheveled hair and the makings of a small Mohawk. Both of his shoulders, exposed through his sleeveless tank top, were marked with fresh tattoos. His eyes were glassy and he had a troubled expression on his face. I could tell this kid was hurting. His name was Wayne.

"Yes?" I said.

"Could you tell me what 'Are you ready' means?"

"Well, it asks if you are ready to stand before Jesus Christ and give an account for your life."

"I've seen you all over town with the cross. And every time I see you I think, 'I need to stop and talk to him about what "Are you ready" means.' You see, my life is kind of messed up right now. And when I see you standing with the cross it kind of scares me. I'm sure you're not trying to scare people."

"Wayne, it's not always a bad thing to be scared. What if you were walking toward a 500-foot cliff and you didn't know it? I know what's about to happen to you. What if I didn't say anything to you and just let you walk over the cliff? Would you think I was a caring person?"

"No."

"That's right. If I cared about you, I would grab you by the arm and tell you to turn around. Better for me to scare you so that you can live instead of saying nothing to you and watch you die."

"That makes sense."

"Wayne, what do you think is going to happen to you when you die?"

"I really don't know."

"Do you know when you're going to die?"

"No."

"Neither do I. But we're both going to die someday."

"That's true."

"There's a memorial service happening right now at the church down the street."

"Really?"

"A young woman, only 29 years old, died suddenly of a massive heart attack."

"Whoa."

"We're all going to die someday. And when that day comes, we are going to stand before God, and He is going to judge us according to His Law. Do you think heaven and hell exist?" I asked.

"Well, I think that if there is a heaven, there must be a hell. But, I don't think hell is like how most people describe it—you know, a fiery place."

"Do you think our version of hell that we've created in our mind to make us feel better or what Jesus said about hell is the truth?"

"Probably what Jesus said."

"Jesus described hell as a place where there is weeping and gnashing of teeth, where the worm never dies and the fire never goes out. The Bible says that all liars will have their part in the lake of fire (Revelation 21:8). We're certainly not in hell now, are we?"

"No."

"So, if heaven and hell are real places, Wayne, what do you think a person has to do to go to heaven?"

"Be as good a person as they possibly can be. I know I don't look like..." he said, dropping his head.

"Wayne, I don't care what you look like."

"Thanks," he said, lifting his head smiling slightly.

"Wayne, what if you and I committed a crime together and we got caught? We find ourselves standing before the judge, and the judge asks us what we have to say for ourselves. So, we tell the judge why he should let us go. He looks at us and says, 'Wayne, I like your haircut, so you're free to go. Tony, I don't like your haircut, so you're going to prison.' Would that be just?"

"Not at all."

"God is not going to judge us according to how we see ourselves. And He is not going to be arbitrary about His judgment. Because He is good, He will judge both of us equitably, according to the perfect moral standard of His Law. Have you ever told a lie?"

"Yes."

"So have I. So, God will see us as liars."

"Have you ever stolen anything?"

"Yes."

"And so have I. So, in God's eyes we are thieves."

"Have you ever looked at a woman and had a sexual thought?"

"Yes. That's lust."

"That's right. And because God is good, because He is a righteous and holy Judge, He must punish our sin. And the punishment He has determined for sin is eternity in hell."

"I know," Wayne said, nodding his head.

"Wayne, that's the bad news. But, here's the good news. Have you ever been in court?"

"Yes I have."

"So have I. What if you were standing before a judge, having been found guilty of breaking the law, and the judge tells you it will be either a $1,000,000 fine or the rest of your life in prison? You can't pay the fine, so the judge is going to send you away for the rest of your life. Just then, someone walks into the courtroom—someone you've never met. He walks up to the judge's bench and says, 'Your honor, I've sold everything. I've sacrificed everything. And because I love Wayne, I'm going to pay his fine. Please let him go.' The judge looks at you and says, 'You are free to go, not because you're a good person—you're a lawbreaker—not because you deserve to be set free, and not because you asked to be let go, but because this other person came in and paid your fine.' Wayne, would that be good news?" I asked.

"It would be good for me."

"And what would you think of the person who came in and paid your fine?"

"I would fall in love with him."

"That's a beautiful answer, because what I just described to you is a picture of what God did. Two thousand years ago, God the Father sent His Son to earth in the person of Jesus Christ—fully God and fully Man, yet without sin. Unlike you and me, He never once violated the Law of God in thought, word, or deed. He was perfect in every respect. About 30-33 years into that earthly existence, He voluntarily went to the cross. He suffered and died, shedding His innocent blood. The Bible says that Jesus was so badly mutilated that he could barely be recognized as human [Isaiah 52:14]. He took upon Himself the punishment you and I rightly deserve for our sins against God. Then, three days later, He rose from the dead, forever defeating sin and death. He is alive today and He will return at a time of the Father's choosing."

Wayne nodded his head almost nonstop as I shared the gospel with him.

"But Wayne, it's not enough for us to simply nod our head in agreement. Satan would nod his head, too. Satan and his demons know exactly who Jesus is and what He came to earth to do, but Satan won't spend a moment in heaven because he knows that."

Wayne continued to nod his head.

"What God requires of you, Wayne, is that you repent. God commands that you turn from your sin and by faith alone receive Jesus Christ as your Lord and Savior.

"Wayne, I don't know you."

"I know," Wayne agreed.

"Look, I don't know what's going on in your life right now. But Wayne, there is nothing in your life—no sin past or present—that Jesus Christ cannot forgive, because of His shed blood and sacrifice on the cross. You're never going to clean up your act enough to deserve heaven. You can't earn it. You can't deserve it. You can't go to church enough to work your way into heaven. It is a free gift of God's grace [Romans 6:23]. Does that make sense?"

"Those are some inspirational words."

"Do you have a Bible at home?"

"I have three. I have a Bible. I have a Mormon bible. And I have a Jehovah's Witness bible."

"Wayne, I don't mean to offend you, but..."

"Oh, that's okay," Wayne interrupted.

"Wayne, throw the Mormon and Jehovah's Witness bibles away. They're not bibles. They are religious books created by people who want to create gods to suite themselves. Their books cannot help you. The Bible is true."

"Okay. I will."

"Here, let me give you something else to read." I reached into my bag and gave Wayne a gospel tract. "And here's my business card. If you have any questions, or if you ever just want to talk, don't hesitate to give me a call."

"Thank you very much."

"And thank you for letting me talk to you."

"Okay. Well, goodnight."

"Good night, Wayne. And God bless you."

"Thanks."

"We'll be praying for you."

"Thanks."

We walked away in opposite directions.

"Dad, I'm pretty sure I saw him drive by a little while before he walked up to us," Marissa said.

"Well, you probably did, considering he said he has seen me with the cross around town," I answered.

"That was cool."

"Yes it was. And I'm glad you were here with me to see it. I think Wayne was the reason I came to this corner with the cross today."

"I think so, too."

Section II:
Fishing at the
Local Mall

Evangelism Tip #3: Mall Evangelism
A Great Fishing Pond while It Lasts

After reading Ray Comfort's book, *Militant Evangelism*, and being convicted by the Holy Spirit for my sins of evangelistic apathy and depraved indifference, I was determined to engage in biblical evangelism. Through the Living Waters website, I discovered there were other people (not many) in my area who had also come to the same realization.

It was about 2004 when I went to a mall for the first time to engage in evangelism. A man who would become a good friend, and remains one to this day, Dru Morgan, was my leader that evening. It was one of the first times I distributed gospel tracts, and I think it was the first time I ever engaged a stranger in evangelistic conversation. Wow. A lot of life and ministry has happened since. Thanks, Dru.

Fast forward a dozen years. I arrived at the Westfield Valencia Town Center, the only mall in my community, about half an hour before my appointed time. After I parked, I packed up my rolling cart with English and Spanish Bibles and gospel tracts and an assortment of other visual aids.

I made my way to the security office where I signed in. Liking to patronize the mall while I'm there, I stopped at Starbucks on my way to my assigned location on the second floor. My spot was at the top of the escalator and situated between the children's play area and the family lounge, a great location. Waiting for me was a table with a nice, black tablecloth and three chairs, provided and set up by mall staff.

It's a Different Kind of "Fishing"

Allow me to use some fishing analogies to describe the various kinds of evangelism in which I engage.

Open-air preaching is like commercial fishing with nets. The preacher casts a wide net, hoping to catch many fish at one time.

Engaging strangers in conversation is like fly fishing. The fly fisherman is hunting with rod and reel. He reads the flow of the stream. He looks for telltale signs of spots where fish might be hiding.

And then he tosses the fly in the general proximity of where he suspects fish to be, hoping they will bite. Engaging strangers in one-to-one conversation involves many of the same tactics. The Christian is constantly surveying the area in which he finds himself, looking for people who might be ready for a conversation.

Tract distribution is like chumming the water: throwing bait on the water to attract fish. The Christian distributes tracts hoping everyone who takes one from his hand will come to repentance and faith as they read the tract. He also hopes people will stop as they receive a gospel tract and engage in conversation.

Mall evangelism is like shoreline fishing, the kind you might see in a Norman Rockwell painting. Picture a fisherman sitting on a chair or his tackle box along the shore of a peaceful pond or lake. His pole is propped up on a Y-shaped stick. He eats a sandwich or reads a book while he waits for the pole to move, indicating that a fish is going after his bait.

All of the above scenarios have a common characteristic: fishing doesn't always equate to catching.

If you were to ask me to name my favorite kind of "fishing," my answer would be open-air preaching. If you were to ask me which form of evangelism is the most effective, I would tell you they are all tied for first place. Why? The effectiveness of evangelism, when the evangelism is biblical, is not found in a particular or preferred method. The effectiveness of evangelism is found in the power of the message (Romans 1:16). The gospel is the power of God for salvation.

While God has hard-wired me to be a herald on the streets and college campuses, I love all forms of biblical evangelism, including (but not limited to) conversations, tract distribution, and mall evangelism.

Helpful Resources

The very best mall evangelism team of which I am well aware is the NorCal Seedsowers.[1] This is the group, under the leadership of my good friend Daniel Beaudoin, that inspired me to starting "fishing"

---

[1] For more information about the NorCal Seedsowers, please visit www.norcalseedsowers.com.

at my local mall. Daniel is also a security supervisor for the Westfield Mall in San Jose, California, which gives him some obvious "street cred" (or should I say, "mall cred") when it comes to evangelizing in malls. The NorCal Seedsowers' website offers a wealth of free evangelism training videos and evangelist testimonies.

Legalities

Disclaimer: What I'm about to offer is NOT legal advice. I'm not an attorney, and I don't even play one on TV. The following is for informational purposes only.

A 1980 United States Supreme Court decision in a landmark case, *Pruneyard v. Robins*, set the standard for the exercise of free speech on private property that is accessible by the public.

Here is what happened.[2]

Soon after appellees had begun soliciting in appellant privately owned shopping center's central courtyard for signatures from passersby for petitions in opposition to a United Nations resolution, a security guard informed appellees that they would have to leave because their activity violated shopping center regulations prohibiting any visitor or tenant from engaging in any publicly expressive activity that is not directly related to the center's commercial purposes. Appellees immediately left the premises and later filed suit in a California state court to enjoin the shopping center and its owner (also an appellant) from denying appellees access to the center for the purpose of circulating their petitions. The trial court held that appellees were not entitled under either the Federal or California Constitution to exercise their asserted rights on the shopping center property, and the California Court of Appeal affirmed. The California Supreme Court reversed, holding that the California Constitution protects speech and petitioning, reasonably exercised, in shopping centers even when the center is privately owned, and that such result does not infringe

---

[2] "Pruneyard Shopping Center v. Robins," *Cornell University Law School Legal Information Institute*, accessed December 28, 2015, https://www.law.cornell.edu/supremecourt/text/447/74.

108 CROSS ENCOUNTERS: A Decade of Gospel Conversations

appellants' property rights protected by the Federal Constitution.

And, here is how the U.S. Supreme Court decided the case.[3]
Appellants first contend that Lloyd Corp. v. Tanner prevents the State from requiring a private shopping center owner to provide access to persons exercising their state constitutional rights of free speech and petition when adequate alternative avenues of communication are available...

Our reasoning in Lloyd, however, does not ex proprio vigore [by its own strength] limit the authority of the State to exercise its police power or its sovereign right to adopt in its own Constitution individual liberties more expansive than those conferred by the Federal Constitution...

Appellants next contend that a right to exclude others underlies the Fifth Amendment guarantee against the taking of property without just compensation and the Fourteenth Amendment guarantee against the deprivation of property without due process of law...

Here the requirement that appellants permit appellees to exercise state-protected rights of free expression and petition on shopping center property clearly does not amount to an unconstitutional infringement of appellants' property rights under the Taking Clause. There is nothing to suggest that preventing appellants from prohibiting this sort of activity will unreasonably impair the value or use of their property as a shopping center. The PruneYard is a large commercial complex that covers several city blocks, contains numerous separate business establishments, and is open to the public at large. The decision of the California Supreme Court makes it clear that the PruneYard may restrict expressive activity by adopting time, place, and manner regulations that will minimize any interference with its commercial functions.

---

[3] "Pruneyard Shopping Center v. Robins," *ACLU Pros & Cons*, last modified December 23, 2009, accessed December 28, 2015, http://aclu.procon.org/view.resource.php?resourceID=429.

Appellees were orderly, and they limited their activity to the common areas of the shopping center. In these circumstances, the fact that they may have "physically invaded" appellants' property cannot be viewed as determinative...

Appellants finally contend that a private property owner has a First Amendment right not to be forced by the State to use his property as a forum for the speech of others...

[T]he shopping center by choice of its owner is not limited to the personal use of appellants. It is instead a business establishment that is open to the public to come and go as they please. The views expressed by members of the public in passing out pamphlets or seeking signatures for a petition thus will not likely be identified with those of the owner. Second, no specific message is dictated by the State to be displayed on appellants' property. There consequently is no danger of governmental discrimination for or against a particular message. Finally, as far as appears here appellants can expressly disavow any connection with the message by simply posting signs in the area where the speakers or handbillers stand. Such signs, for example, could disclaim any sponsorship of the message and could explain that the persons are communicating their own messages by virtue of state law...

We conclude that neither appellants' federally recognized property rights nor their First Amendment rights have been infringed by the California Supreme Court's decision recognizing a right of appellees to exercise state-protected rights of expression and petition on appellants' property.

The U.S. Supreme Court affirmed the judgment of the Supreme Court of California.

While this court decision was good news for free speech advocates in California and 36 other states, as of this writing there remain 13 states that refuse to follow the precedent set in *Pruneyard v. Robins*. Those states are[4] Arizona, Connecticut, Georgia, Iowa,

---

[4] Richard J. Peltz, "Limited Powers in the Looking-Glass: Otiose Textualism, and an Empirical Analysis of Other Approaches, When Activists in Private Shopping

Michigan, New York, North Carolina, Ohio, Oregon, Pennsylvania, South Carolina, Wisconsin, and Washington. I know some of my friends who live in those 13 states just had their hearts broken. I'm so very sorry. I know what such news would do to my spirits.

But all is not lost.

Just because you live in a state that has not adopted the Supreme Court's decision as law doesn't mean the malls in your area will not allow you to engage in evangelism on mall property. It simply means they are not legally obligated to do so. That is an important distinction.

On the other hand, if you live in one of the 37 states that recognize the *Pruneyard v. Robins* decision, this does not mean you can simply walk into your local mall and do whatever you want. Don't expect to waltz into the mall, climb atop a table in the food court, and start open-air preaching without quickly being told to stop and escorted off mall property by mall security. In such a scenario (which has been tried by some zealous evangelists, by the way), mall management would have every legal right to send you and your gospel tracts packing.

If you look again at the Supreme Court's decision in *Pruneyard v. Robins,* you will see that business owners/management, while not allowed to prohibit free speech, do have the right to regulate it. The Supreme Court indicated that businesses can establish "time, place, and manner" regulations for free speech exercise on their property. This means malls can legally require you to fill out an application and determine where, when, and how you will engage in free speech while on their property. If you do not comply with their legitimate "time, place, and manner" policy, they can (and will) ask you to leave.

When it comes to mall evangelism, I want to strongly encourage you to play by the rules. Do not bring a reproach upon Christ by trying to be a law unto yourself and ignoring legitimate and legal policies of property owners.

Centers Claim State Constitutional Liberties," *Cleveland State Law Review* 53, (2005): 399-427, accessed December 28, 2015, http://engagedscholarship.csuohio.edu/cgi/viewcontent.cgi?article=1247&context=clevstlrev.

Getting Started
Step One: Talk to your pastors/elders about what you want to do.

Explain to them your plans to evangelize at the mall. If you attend a solid, Bible-believing church, it is unlikely your pastors/elders will balk. Get their blessing. Get their prayerful and maybe even their financial support (i.e. tracts, bibles, etc.). Do everything you can to make your mall evangelism a ministry of the church. Get your pastors'/elders' permission to hand out or share information about your church.

Step Two: Go to the management office of your local mall.

If your local mall is part of a larger corporation or groups of malls, as is the case with my local mall (Westfield), then you will likely discover your mall has a well-researched, legal "time, place, and manner" free speech policy. If the mall is an independent establishment but stays current on the issue, they will likewise have a solid free speech policy.

Go to the management office of your local mall and request a free speech application. Depending on your mall's policy, they might offer an application for the use of a common free speech area, the distribution of literature, or a free speech table. The application will likely ask for your name, address, phone number, and email address. It will also ask for information regarding the group, organization, ministry, or church you represent. Set your fears of "big brother" aside and give the information. Sharing the gospel with the lost is more important than the illusion of privacy. The mall has the legal right to know to whom they are granting permission to exercise free speech on their property.

When you go to the mall to complete and submit the application, have some samples of the material you plan to distribute. Mall management will probably request this, too. As part of the application process, you will likely be given choices regarding dates, times, and locations within the mall to exercise free speech. In my case, it has been a very pleasant experience working with mall management. My local mall provides me with the choice of seven different locations in the mall. Most of them are well-traveled areas, and a few of the options are high-traffic areas where I can go through hundreds of tracts in a matter of a few hours.

Step Three: Decide what materials you will display (if provided with a table).

Your mall may provide you with a table (6'-8') and a few chairs. My mall limits me to three people working my table at any given time. You can fill a table with Bibles, gospel tracts, DVDs, church information, and any other material you would like to give away. Try to include some eye-catching props that will draw attention. The mall may also allow you to use small, standing signs on the table. Get creative.

Step Four: Have the right demeanor.

So, you went to your pastor. He's enthusiastic about evangelism and loves that you have taken the initiative. You've gone to your local mall, completed and submitted the application, and picked your time and date. You've gathered all of your material and props together, and you're ready to go.

When the big day comes, you set everything up and let several brothers and sisters in Christ know to be praying for you. Then, you sit down behind the table or find a place to stand in the free speech area and begin to check your email on your phone or to dig into that new book you've been meaning to read.

STOP!!!!!!!!

How inviting do you think it is to a stranger walking toward you when all he or she can see is the top of your head? In my case, the reflection of mall lighting off my cranium could blind the person and potentially expose me to a civil suit.

Your demeanor need not (and should not) be over the top, but you should be at least as excited to be there as the kids working the different kiosks throughout the mall. Come to think of it, you should be more excited than the kids working the kiosks. Many of them look like they are waiting for a root canal.

Keep your head up. Keep your eyes open. And smile.

Yes, smile.

Look, I'm a retired deputy sheriff. I look like a cop. I sound like a cop. And when I make eye contact with a person, I can leave them thinking, "What? I haven't broken the law. Have I broken the law? Is he going to take me to jail? I think he wants to take me to jail." Sometimes their first impression would be accurate. But I digress.

The point is that I know enough about myself to know I have to be intentional to smile and to look and sound friendly. Remember, at the mall the majority of those who walk up to your table or through the free speech area will be people you have never met. You can have the best looking table on the planet, but if the look on your face, your body language, or your overall countenance is telling people to stay away, what do you think they are going to do?

When someone makes eye contact with you, say "Hello." Whether or not the person approaches, wish them a good day. If someone stops and his eyes seem to linger in the direction of your table or display, let them know that the material you are distributing is free. Ask them if they would like a free Bible. Engage them in conversation. Ask them about their day. Ask them what brings them to the mall. Ask them if they attend church locally or if they have any spiritual beliefs. One look at the table or display and the person will know why you're there (at least they should). So, you can skip all the uncomfortable formality of trying to engage a stranger in a conversation without the other person having any context for why you are talking to them.

Oh, one more thing.

Have fun! Let the joy of the Lord be your strength! Think nothing of how many or how few people are coming to the table. Remember, this is a different kind of "fishing." You're the fisherman sitting peacefully on the lake's shore, waiting for the big one to bite.

Conclusion

I've titled this chapter "The Mall: A Great Fishing Pond while It Lasts" because the availability of this kind of evangelism won't last forever. I think it's Pollyannaish for anyone to think laws are going to become more favorable toward Christian evangelism. Free speech rights for Christians are going to become more prohibitive rather than more accommodating. But for now, malls are still a wonderful place for reaching your community with the good news of the gospel of Jesus Christ.

The information in this chapter is not exhaustive; however, I hope you find it helpful. And I look forward to hearing testimonies of how readers have seen the Lord work through mall evangelism.

All He Wanted Was 60 Cents

Fish sometimes leap out of the water with great energy, but it would be foolish to conclude that they have left the liquid element forever, in a moment they are swimming again as if they had never forsaken the stream; indeed, it was but a fly that tempted them aloft, or a sudden freak, the water is still their home, sweet home. When we see long-accustomed sinners making a sudden leap at religion, we may not make too sure that they are converts; perhaps some gain allures them, or sudden excitement stirs them, and if so they will be back again at their old sins. Let us hope well, but let us not commend too soon.
Charles Spurgeon

One day, while manning an evangelism table at my local mall, I engaged in a public reading of 2 Timothy. As I read the Word of God, a young man stood a short distance from me. He would listen for a few moments, pace a short distance, stop and fix his attention on me, and then repeat the process. I could tell the young man wanted to talk to me. What he probably didn't realize was that I was even more eager to talk to him.

"Sir?" he said.

"Hey," I replied.

"Do you have 60 cents?" he asked.

"I'm sorry. I don't have any cash on me. Sorry."

"Alright. Yeah, I heard your reading earlier. Sounded good. Are you from Grace?"

"Grace Community Church? Yes."

"I used to go there," the young man said. "I started at Higher Vision and now I'm at a place called Haven House."

"Haven House? I'm familiar with it. What's your name?"

"James."

"James, I'm Tony. Good to meet you."

"Are you the worship leader or…"

"No, no, no. I'm just a member of the church," I interrupted with a smile.

"A member of the church?"

"Yep."

"So, how did you get involved in all this?" James asked, motioning to the table covered in Bibles and gospel tracts.

"Well, I've been doing street evangelism for about 10 years, and I spend Friday afternoons here at the mall."

"Do you know anyone named Kristin by any chance?"

"No."

"No? He goes to Haven House, but you actually remind me of him. He has the broad voice that you do when you speak. Your voice reminds me of him."

It's not uncommon, especially in America, for Christians to be part of several different churches in their lifetime. The fact that James mentioned three churches came as no surprise. One thing I have learned over the years, however, is that no one is a Christian simply because they say they attend Christian churches, even good churches. No one is a Christian simply because they profess to be one. When I'm engaged in evangelism and someone tells me they go to church or they go so far as to confess faith in Christ, it means only one thing to me: I'm going to proclaim the gospel to this person.

"So, James, where are you at today, spiritually? I asked.

"Um, in and out."

"What does that mean?" I asked.

"It's been a journey. Lately it has been kind of like I've been angry about a lot of things."

"What are you angry about?"

"Just the fact that I've made bad decisions in my past and so it's affecting my future, so…"

"So you're angry with you?" I asked.

"Yeah. I'm angry with me, but I'm not angry at God. I know He didn't do it. I did it. You know? So, I'm just angry at the fact that it's not all changing. I'm trying to do better. I have two jobs."

"That's good," I replied, trying to give James some affirmation.

"Yeah. I'm trying to get a car. I messed up financially and so everything is all over the place. How about you? Where you at?" James asked.

I tried to muffle a chuckle as I thought to myself, "Hang on, kid. I'm the one conducting this inquiry."

"Well, I'm here for one," I joked.

"I know you're here, but..."

"I know what you meant," I said, letting James off the hook. "Well, I came to faith in Christ about 27 years ago. I was raised in a Roman Catholic family. I was Catholic because my name ended in a vowel and I'm part of an Italian family, and so we were all Catholics, but..."

"But, you didn't choose to be?" James asked.

"Right. It didn't really mean much to us other than a couple of times a year," I said, referring to Christmas and Easter. "I grew up believing I was a relatively good guy, meaning I didn't get caught for the things I did. I believed in God, but that did not really have any real meaning to me at all. I served as a deputy sheriff for 20 years..."

"Oh, wow!" James exclaimed.

"Early in my career someone shared the gospel with me and brought me to the realization that I wasn't good. The Lord used that to bring me to repentance and faith in Him."

I did not communicate the entirety of my testimony to James. I knew from experience that a conversation like this one could end abruptly, with James saying he had to go or was running late for this or that. I wanted to stick to talking about James. People like to talk about their favorite subject—themselves. I stood a better chance of keeping James in the conversation if I talked to James about James.

"That's awesome. That's great. Oh yeah, I was raised in a Christian home my whole life," James said.

"Was that at Grace Community Church?" I asked.

"No. My granddad had his own church actually, and so he was the pastor of the church."

"Was that here in Southern California?"

"Yeah. Do you know where Canyon Country is?"

"Yes I do."

"It was called Little Brown Church."

"That's your grandfather's church?

"Yeah."

"Interesting."

"My grandfather passed away."

"Is the church still in existence?" I asked.

"No. The owner of the church passed away, too," James said. "When I came out of my mom, he said I was going to be a pastor, and I always thought until, you know…"

"So, you grew up with that pressure?"

"Yeah, I'd say so. I am not all over this like I should be, and that's actually causing a lot of problems. That's the main thing. I'm trying to work on it. I'm trying to get back into the Word and trying to focus more on my spiritual life, because it's affecting my outside life, like my job and everything and my girlfriend. You know what I mean?"

James quickly shifted gears and turned the conversation back to me. People will often do this when they either catch themselves giving what they think is too much personal information or when the conversation is making them feel self-conscious or convicted. "Are you married? Do you have kids?" he asked.

"I'm married. I have three adult daughters. I've been married for 30 years."

"Wow. How is your journey with that?"

"It's been wonderful," I said with a smile. "My wife has always been my best friend, and we get closer every day."

"You guys must have your arguments," James insisted.

"Well, yes. After all, we're sinners—sinners saved by grace. We have yet to have a perfect day together, but we do love each other and we both love the Lord. So, it's good. It's good."

This conversation was beginning to feel a bit like a tennis match. It was time for me to hit the ball back over the net.

"So now, when in your journey did you end up at Grace Community?" I asked.

"I met some friends of mine that I'm still friends with, and they got me kind of involved in the church."

"How long ago was that?"

"Oh, let's see. Probably three years ago. So I haven't been there in a little while, but I've been at Haven House on and off."

"So, how long you been there?"

"About a year or two. I'm doing two jobs, so I'm trying to go there. I'm not married and haven't made the commitment, to be perfectly honest."

James was trying to justify himself. I could tell it wasn't easy for him.

"What does that mean when you say, 'I haven't made the commitment'?" I asked.

"I don't go to church very often."

"Okay."

"I say I'm going to do things and then something will somehow get in the way to stop me, or I'll just let it stop me," James confessed. "I've got to be honest with myself and not say, 'Oh, you really tried.' I really haven't tried, to be honest."

"So, James, if you and I had not just met and we had been friends for some time, and you're a believer and you know that I'm not, and I came to you and said, 'James, I just got back from the doctor. It was just a regular checkup, no big deal. I feel great. But, my doctor told me I have cancer throughout my body. There's nothing they can do. I'm going to die soon, and I'm scared.' What would you tell me?"

"I'd tell you, 'Let's pray.' I'd tell you that God will, you know, make it change."

"Okay. And if He doesn't do that, what are you going to tell me?"

"If he *doesn't*? James asked.

"God doesn't promise to heal everybody," I said.

"Well, of course," James agreed.

"People die every day. Hospitals are filled with people."

"So, let's pray that you can live your life to the fullest. And, if it's in God's hands and He decides to heal you, let's make that happen. If not, then try to live to the best of your abilities."

It's painful to listen to professing Christians explain in such unbiblical ways how they would offer dying friends literally no hope at all. Yet, I have found that role playing with professing Christians like James is the best way to learn what they actually believe. Out of the abundance of the heart the mouth speaks (Mark 7:20-22).

"So, what would that look like in the short time I've got left? What would living my life to the fullest look like?" I asked.

"Spending every moment you have with your family, trying to be happy."

"And then when I die?"

"Then you die. Yeah. I actually should have said, 'Let's talk about your salvation. Where are you going when you die?' That's the question," James said.

"Well, I've been a pretty good guy, as you know. We're friends." I continued the role playing by staying in character. "So, I think God is going to weigh the good against the bad and I'm hoping it will work out in the end, but I'm not sure."

"Well, honestly, I'd say that you need Christ as your Savior."

"Why?" I asked.

"Because he's the only one that can change you."

"Why do I need to be changed?"

"Well…"

I let James ponder the question for several moments. When it seemed that James had no answer, I let him off the hook. I was confident that while James professed faith in Jesus Christ he did not actually know Jesus Christ as his Lord and Savior. One cannot be saved by a gospel one does not know.

"Okay. I put you on the spot, so now…"

"That's good, though," James interrupted.

"So now we'll switch," I said. "Now, you are *my* unsaved friend. I'm the believer. You came to me with the same news. Whether you're 51 or 24, anyone can get that diagnosis, right?"

"Exactly," James agreed.

"Or, you could be walking across the street when a driver who is texting nails you, right?"

"Yeah, exactly."

"So, here's what I would say to you, James. Of course, I would want to pray with you, too. I would want to do whatever I could to comfort you, because I'm your friend. The last thing I want is for my friend James to die."

"Right," James agreed. He was now fully invested in the conversation.

"I mean, your 24 years old. I'm having a hard time wrapping my head around the idea of someone so young dying of cancer." I wanted to make the situation as real as possible to James. I wanted him to only focus on our conversation for the next few minutes.

"But James, at some point I'm going to get to the point. I'm going to say, 'James, when you die you're going to stand before God and you're going to give an account for your life. He's going to judge you, not based on how James sees himself in the mirror or how James compares himself to other people. He's going to judge you based on the law that He's written on your heart.

"'You were created in the image of God. You know it's wrong to lie, because God is not a liar. You know it's wrong to steal, because God's not a thief. You know it's wrong to commit adultery or fornicate, because God's not an adulterer or a fornicator. You know it's wrong to take His name in vain, because God's not a blasphemer. God has written these realities on your heart. So, that's why we're all without excuse. We're not going to be able to stand before God and claim either innocence or ignorance of violating His law. And because all have sinned and fallen short of the glory of God, when you stand before Him, He's going to find you guilty of breaking His law. Because He's good, He *must* punish your sin.

"'The punishment God has determined for sin is eternity in hell. You're my friend, and that's absolutely the last thing I want for you. James, the same God who is angry with the wicked every day, the same God whose wrath abides upon the ungodly, is the same God who is loving and merciful and gracious and kind. He showed that great love 2,000 years ago when God the Father sent His Son to earth in the person of Jesus Christ—fully God, fully man, without sin. He lived a perfect life for some 33 years that you and I can't live for 33 seconds.

"'Then, Jesus voluntarily went to the cross. He suffered and died a horrific bloody death He did not deserve to take upon Himself the punishment you and I rightly deserve for our sins against God. Three days later, He forever defeated sin and death when He rose from the grave. James, what God commands of you is the same thing He commands of me and everybody in this mall, and that's that you repent and turn from your sin and by faith, and by faith alone, receive Jesus Christ as your Lord and your Savior.

"'Now, God is more than able to heal you of this cancer, but God makes no such promise to you. But, God is not a "get-away-from-cancer card," and God is not a "get-out-of-hell-free card." The promise to those who turn from their sin and put their trust in Christ isn't simply their best life now, health, wealth, and prosperity, but a future hope, an eternal hope, forgiveness of sin, a place in heaven for all eternity with Him.' Does that make sense?"

"Yes," James answered.

"Alright. So, James, what do you like to do? What makes James tick? What do you like to do?"

"I'm an entertainer."

"An entertainer?" I questioned.

"I'm a singer and a dancer. I do gymnastics. I do parkour—all these crazy tricks. That's what I love."

"Do you ever do any busking on the streets?" I asked.

"What's that?"

"Busking, street performing for tips," I explained.

"Yes, once in a while. I probably should do that more because it does make some good money. I've been trying to get into this, the whole singing career thing."

"So, what if I came to you one day and I said, 'Hey, James. I'm in the music industry and I know what you need to know to make it as an entertainer.' You're probably going to be a little skeptical because lots of guys say that."

"Yeah."

"But, curiosity gets the better of you and you say, 'Alright. What have you got, Tony? What do I need to know to make it in this business?' So, I tell you, 'Well, you've got to be able to carry a note and, if you dance, you've got to make sure your shoes are tied.'"

"Right," James agreed with a laugh.

"'That's all you need to know, James. Make sure you can carry a tune and make sure your shoes are tied.' If I said that to you, would you believe I knew anything about the music industry? Would you believe I knew anything about being an entertainer?"

"No."

"No," I said. "So, here's the tough question, James. If you wouldn't believe that I know anything about being an entertainer based on what I said to you, then why should I believe that you know Christ when you couldn't tell me how to know Him?" I asked.

"Yeah, that's true. Why would you believe me?"

"So then, what is your assurance? What is your assurance that you've truly turned from your sin and put your trust in Christ? You know yourself far better than I know you."

"Um, not much."

"I appreciate your honesty, because there is nothing more important than your soul. The Word of God says, 'What does it profit a man if he gains the whole world, but yet forfeits his soul? What will he give in exchange for his soul?'" (Matthew 16:26).

"Amen," said James.

"You came to me for 60 cents. If I had 60 cents, I probably wouldn't give it to you. If you're hungry, I'd give you something to eat. If you're thirsty, I'd get you something to drink. But, I don't give out cash."

"I understand," said James.

"If you're hungry, I'll feed you. If you're thirsty, I'll give you something to drink. But more important that the 60 cents you think you need is where you're going to spend eternity, James. Do you understand? You may have come up to me looking for something else with nothing but legitimate reasons. Only you know if that's the case. But everything is ordained by God. There are no coincidences. He's sovereign over everything. It's not by coincidence that you and I are at the mall today," I said.

"I agree."

"James, hopping from church to church is not going to make you right with God. Settling in one church is not going to make you right with God. Going to church on Sunday and living like hell Monday through Saturday is not going to make you right with God. Right? If I go to Starbucks every day, I am never going to become a caramel macchiato."

"Well, yeah," James agreed with a smile.

"Right? Going to Starbucks does not make me a coffee drink, right?" I asked. "Well, going to church doesn't make someone a Christian."

"Amen," James said. "That's true."

"So, James, is there any sin in your life that you love so much that you're willing to die and go to hell so that you can enjoy that sin in this life?"

James looked down and slowly shook his head.

"Then why wouldn't you turn from your sin and put your trust in Christ?" I pleaded.

"Yeah, I agree. That's a good question. I like that."

"James, doing that, coming to repentance and faith in Christ, is entirely a work of God. It's not a work of you. It's not a work of me. It's entirely a work of God. It doesn't mean He's going to give you that 60 cents. It does not mean He's going to give you that career in music. It doesn't mean He's going to allow you to settle down. You may get to do all that and more, but God is not a used car salesman with salvation being a cheap used car."

"Yeah, you've got to give yourself to Him," James asserted.

"Jesus said, 'Whoever is unwilling to deny themselves, take up their cross and follow Me, is unfit, unworthy to be My disciple' [Luke 14:26-33]. Now, that doesn't mean we do things to earn our salvation or to keep our salvation. It's a gift [Romans 6:23]. The Word of God says it is by grace we're saved through faith and not that of ourselves. It's a gift from God, not as a result of works so that no man may boast [Ephesians 2:8-9]. James, what if you and I were neighbors? You're 24. You're young enough to be my son. You knock on my door and you say, 'Hey, Tony. I'm going to mow your lawn so that I can be your son.'"

James and I both laughed at the idea.

"James, if you did that, I would smile and say two things to you. I would thank you for getting me out of yard work in 100° weather. I would appreciate that. It does an old man's soul good. I would also tell you that I think it is pretty cool that you want me to be your dad. But, I would also tell you that mowing my lawn, James, isn't going to make you my son.

"However, if you *were* my son and you said, 'Dad, I'm going to go mow the lawn, not for 60 cents, not for a raise in my allowance, not because I got a bomb to drop on you, not because I wrecked the car, not because I want the keys. I'm going to go mow the lawn because I love you, Dad. I'm grateful that you're my dad.' That would make this grown man cry."

"Oh, yeah," James said. He understood the point I was trying to make.

"James, no one is going to stand before God and say, 'Look, I mowed Your lawn. Welcome me into your kingdom. Look at all I've done.' But those who *do* know Him, who have been adopted by Him, who do know Him by the grace of God alone through faith alone in Christ alone, they will *want* to do those things to please God—not to earn or keep salvation, but because they are so grateful for the gift that they received. Does that make sense?"

"Yeah, absolutely. I've always known in my heart what's wrong and what s right. You know?"

"Right, because God has given you a conscience. Every human being knows the difference between right and wrong. It's not because of what mommy and daddy taught them; it's not because of what they learned at school; it's not because of what society has taught them. It's because they were created in the image of God and He's given them a conscience. He's given them a conscience, but the vast majority of people, even some of the most religious, even those attending Haven House or Grace Community Church or some other church, are in rebellion against Him. They live their lives the way they want to. They do the religious things because they know they should and they don't want to get too far off the religious beaten path. They're hoping that maybe God will weigh the good against the bad and it will all work out for them, and everything they do is blasphemy to God because of it. Everything.

"The Bible says that whatever a person does, if it is not done by faith in Christ, it is sin [Romans 14:23]. If you help a little old lady across the street and you do not do it for the love of Christ and in faith in Christ, that's sin. A young soldier jumps on a grenade to save his buddies. If he doesn't do it by faith in Christ and for the love of Christ, he's in sin. That heroic act will actually be counted against him in the Day of Judgment, not for him. That's how holy God is. But, He's so merciful and kind. He's so gracious that even though you and I deserve death, even though you and I deserve hell for all eternity, by His grace and His mercy He chooses to save some—not because they're worthy, but because of the worthiness of His Son and what He did on the cross. So, when are you going to get right with God? When are you going to stop playing the game?" I asked.

"Right now," James said with a tone of determination.

"James, if you do it for me, you're still lost. If you do it for what you want in the world, you're still lost. Only God can cause a person to be born again [1 Peter 1:3], to be born from above [John 3:3-7]."

"Amen."

"Turn from your sin and put your trust in Him," I said. "Do you have a Bible?"

"Yeah."

"When was the last time you read it?"

"Actually, four days ago."

"What did you read?"

"Ah, man. I read the chapter in Acts about how Paul was talking about... Shoot! I don't remember exactly what I read," James admitted. "I was reading Acts 17 where he was talking to a bunch of people and they were saying that they were grateful for him being there."

"And before that?" I asked. "What did you read in the Bible before that?"

"I think it was John."

"And how long ago was that?"

"About a month ago."

"James let me ask you this. Would you intentionally go a month without eating?"

"No. Definitely not." James thought for a few moments about the idea of going a month without food. "I like that question," he said.

"Did you say you have a girlfriend?" I asked.

"Yes. She works at a liquor store in town."

"So, let's say you went into the military and you get shipped out to Afghanistan or Iraq. Your girlfriend writes you like once a week, maybe twice a week, but she never hears back from you. She knows you're alive, because no one has knocked on her door to say, 'James was killed in action.' After your tour of duty, you finally return home. She meets you there on the tarmac or at shore or whatever it is.

The two of you run into each other's arms. You embrace. The first question she asks you is this: 'James, did you get those 66 letters I wrote to you?'

"You say, 'Yeah, honey, I got them. In fact, they're in my bag. I never opened them. I never bothered to read them. They weren't that important to me, but I love you.'"

"Wow. That would be messed up," James protested.

"So, James, who is the person that really loves the Lord but can't be bothered to open His Word? Who really loves the Lord and never reads the 66 letters He's written to mankind out of His love for them? It's time to get real. It's time to get serious. It's time to quit playing the Christian game."

"That's right," James agreed.

"There are so many people your age who have grown up in the church, some with similar expectations as were placed on you ('You're going to be pastor someday. You're going to be a missionary. You're going to do great things for the Lord.'), not knowing if they're ever going to come to faith in Christ. So, they grow up in the church, doing what they're told. They go to every service. They're at every youth meeting. They've prayed the prayer. They've asked Jesus into their hearts. They've walk the aisle. Maybe they've done it more than once…"

"But are you really walking the walk and talking the talk?" James interrupted.

"Right. Are you really saved, James? Have you really come to genuine repentance and faith in Christ? You know the answer to that. You've already admitted to it. Don't let another moment go by without turning to Christ. It's good news, James. Christ died to set sinners free. Quit being a slave to your sin. Quit being a slave to your own desires. Whatever you put before Jesus Christ at that moment is your god. Whether it's singing or dancing or your girlfriend or going to church, anything you put before Jesus Christ is your god. God is a jealous God—not just jealous *of* people, but jealous *for* His people. He doesn't settle. He doesn't negotiate with sinners. If He sees you worshipping something or someone else other than Him, He's going to do what's right. He's going to do what's just. So, turn from your sin and truly put your trust in Christ."

After sharing the gospel with James, it was my turn to change the subject just a bit. "Now, what did you need that 60 cents for? I asked. "What in the world would 60 cents get you?"

"I just...I just needed it for the bus."

"Where you going?"

"I'm going to work."

I asked James where he worked. He told me he worked at a small local fitness center.

"What time do you start work?" I asked.

"I start at 5:00."

"What time is it now?"

"It's 3:55. Sometimes I have to leave an hour early. So, I take the bus into work and get there at about 4:30. But I'm actually very glad I came and asked about that. I just wanted to talk to you because I heard you knew the Bible. I'm very, very insecure about myself right now, and I've been for a while. I've been insecure about myself and my faith and everything, and I figured it'd be nice to talk to someone."

"Well, the apostle John wrote in 1 John 5, 'these things I have written to you, so that you may know that you have eternal life' [1 John 5:13]. You can have assurance of salvation, but if you're putting any trust in James or in anything James can do, then you're never going to have that assurance—not until you truly put your trust in Christ," I explained.

"Amen."

"Jesus is always Lord. We don't make him Lord. We don't ask Him into our heart. We don't make Him the Lord of our life. He's always Lord. He always has been. Whether He sends us to hell for all eternity or grants us a place in His kingdom forever, He's always Lord. The question isn't whether or not He's Lord. The question is whether or not you're living in submission to Him as Lord."

"Amen."

"Don't go another day, James, without Christ."

I reached into my pocket and removed a public transit TAP (public transit) card from my wallet. "There's probably, I don't know, $30 or $40 dollars on that card." I said, as I handed the card to James.

"$30 or $40?" James said with a stunned look on his face.

"Yeah."

"Oh wow," James exclaimed.

"That will help you get around."

"Thank you so much. I really appreciate it. God bless you. Thank you. I honestly like, I just came to ask for 60 cents."

"I know," I said, assuring James I was taking him at his word. "Don't go down that escalator thinking, '*Wow, I just got $30-$40! Wow, I just got a card!*' Don't walk away from here still dead in your sin. Turn to Christ and live. Alright, man?"

"Amen."

I gave James a hug and watched him as he made his way down the escalator and out of the mall. I have neither seen nor heard of James since then. I hope that every time he used that TAP card he was reminded of our conversation.

During our conversation, James made more than one verbal indication that he wanted to repent and receive Jesus Christ as Lord and Savior. Only God knows if those verbal indications came out of a mouth of young man whose heart was changed by the power of God the Spirit for the glory of God the Son.

"I Want to Talk about God"

A caviller[1] in an omnibus said to a Christian man one day, "Why, you have nothing at all to rest upon. I can prove to you that your Scriptures are not authentic." The humble Christian man replied, "Sir, I am not a learned man, and I cannot answer your questions; but I believe in the Lord Jesus Christ, and I have experienced such a change of character, and I feel such joy and peace through believing, that I wish you knew my Saviour, too." The answer he received was a very unexpected one: the unbeliever said, "You have got me there; I cannot answer that."

Charles Spurgeon

It was my first time back at the Westfield Valencia Town Center, for the purpose of evangelism, in more than a year. A heavy travel schedule, changes to the focus and direction of my ministry, and the simple fact that I cannot be in multiple places at once, led me to step away from mall evangelism for a time. But, I had recently decided to focus more of my evangelism efforts in my own community, so the time was right to once again set up a table at my local mall.

Since I try to keep my evenings free to spend time with my family in the evenings, I opted for an afternoon slot at my mall's free speech table.

Afternoons at the mall, even during the holiday season, have an entirely different atmosphere than does a typical Friday and Saturday night. On most Friday and Saturday nights, the mall serves as a babysitter for parents who drop off their 10- to 15-year-old children. Packs of undisciplined young people fill the mall, doing what undisciplined young people do. The afternoon and early evening hours are much quieter, not as busy, and the average patron is often older than those who frequent the mall on weekend nights.

---

[1] A "caviller" is a quibbler, a person who raises annoying and/or petty objections. Hecklers are often cavillers.

So, from 1:30 to 5:30 p.m. I sat at a table covered with an assortment of gospel tracts, Bibles, and my laptop, which has a sign attached to the lid encouraging people to stop and chat.

This was a very slow day for shoreline fishing; the fish weren't biting well. I did have an opportunity to place a "Thank You" tract into the hands of a Marine, PFC, and a young man came to the table and took a Bible. Believing and trusting in the sovereignty of God, I found contentment in these two opportunities and continued to pray.

About midway through my time at the mall, I noticed a man who looked at me and the table out of the corner of his eye as he walked by. Many people do that. I'll watch folks like that and attempt to make eye contact with them so I can say hello and offer them a Bible.

The man moved on, but he stayed in the area, trying to remain inconspicuous as he circled the table like a curious, soaring bird. I'm sure he didn't think I noticed, but 20 years in the Los Angeles County Sheriff's Department has made me trained observer.

About 45 minutes before I was scheduled to leave the mall, the man finally approached the table.

"Let's talk," he said, pulling up a chair and gingerly sitting down. His left knee was in a brace. I would later learn he had received reconstructive knee surgery about eight weeks ago. We'll call him "Matt."

"What's on your mind? What do you want to talk about?" I asked.

"I want to talk about God."

"Where would you like to begin?"

Matt began to share his story. He was recently medically retired and had been placed on disability after 30 years of working in the movie industry's transportation services. He was a truck driver who, for decades, engaged in the literally back-breaking work that entails.

Matt was in his 22nd year of sobriety and, up until several months ago, was a regular participant in AA and NA. Matt had believed in God all his life and he finally tired of the "higher power/you can worship your doorknob" philosophy of AA/NA.

One day, he was in a Barnes & Noble browsing through the religious literature section. There, he found a Bible, which he purchased and started to read. He began in Genesis. When he reached Isaiah and started to read the prophet's account of seeing the Lord seated on His throne, with the train of His robe filling the temple with glory and the angels heralding the thrice-glorious truth ("Holy, Holy, Holy"), the veil was removed from Matt's eyes. Not long after that, he had occasion to stop at the Grand Canyon while trucking. There, surrounded by the majestic artistry of Almighty God and pondering what he read in Isaiah, as well as what he read in the Book of Acts, he was drawn by God to His Son Jesus Christ.

According to Matt, his transformation took place only six months ago. Yet, he was troubled. He was not content. He was not at peace as he sat in front of me, trying to rub the soreness out of his rebuilt knee.

"Why am I excited to read the Bible one minute but not the next? Why does my spiritual life seem to go well for a time, but then the fire fades?" Matt asked.

Did Matt have a nothing more than an emotional and spiritual experience at the Grand Canyon, or did he really come to repentance and faith in Jesus Christ? I couldn't provide biblical counsel to Matt until I had some assurance that a born-again follower of Christ was sitting in front of me. To apply biblical counsel to an unregenerate heart would be to set Matt up for a season of frustrating, harmful works-righteousness. The result would not be repentance and faith, but a deadly commitment to "moralistic, therapeutic deism."[2]

---

[2] In this online article, Albert Mohler wrote the following (Albert Mohler, "Moralistic Therapeutic Deism—The New American Religion," *Albert Mohler*, last modified April 11, 2005, accessed April 10, 2016, http://www.albertmohler.com/2005/04/11/moralistic-therapeutic-deism-the-new-american-religion-2/): "When Christian Smith and his fellow researchers with the National Study of Youth and Religion at the University of North Carolina at Chapel Hill took a close look at the religious beliefs held by American teenagers, they found that the faith held and described by most adolescents came down to something the researchers identified as 'Moralistic Therapeutic Deism.'

"As described by Smith and his team, Moralistic Therapeutic Deism consists of beliefs like these: 1. 'A god exists who created and ordered the world and

I opted to take Matt through a "Three Minutes to Live" scenario. He was unable to articulate the gospel. I've learned over the years that while a person cannot be saved by the gospel they do not know, they can be saved by the gospel they cannot articulate well.

As I switched roles with Matt (making him the unbeliever in the scenario), I preached the law and the gospel to him. With every biblical point I made came an affirming nod of the head from Matt. He not only affirmed that he believed everything I said, but added that he knew salvation was only through faith in Jesus Christ, not by works. I believed I had a brother in Christ sitting in front of me—a Christian man who was young in his faith and not well discipled.

Giving Matt the benefit of the doubt, I explained to him the doctrine of progressive sanctification.[3] I talked to him about how important it is for Christians to take every thought captive, to fight well the battle for the mind by not only meditating upon but also committing to practice the truths of Philippians 4:5-9.

---

watches over human life on earth.' 2. 'God wants people to be good, nice, and fair to each other, as taught in the Bible and by most world religions.' 3. 'The central goal of life is to be happy and to feel good about one's self.' 4. 'God does not need to be particularly involved in one's life except when God is needed to resolve a problem.' 5. 'Good people go to heaven when they die.'

"That, in sum, is the creed to which much adolescent faith can be reduced. After conducting more than 3,000 interviews with American adolescents, the researchers reported that, when it came to the most crucial questions of faith and beliefs, many adolescents responded with a shrug and 'whatever.'"

[3] Progressive Sanctification," *Association of Certified Biblical Counselors*, accessed April 10, 2016, http://www.biblicalcounseling.com/before-you-begin/theological-considerations/progressive-sanctification/: The Association of Certified Biblical Counselors website defines "progressive sanctification" as "that gracious work of God in a believer whereby He enables him to replace works of the flesh with the fruit of the Spirit, thereby causing him to become more and more like the Lord Jesus Christ.

"This process of spiritual growth continues over the course of a Christian's lifetime and is, therefore, neither instantaneous nor complete, but gradually occurs as he appropriates God's sanctifying truth which is found solely in the Scriptures of the Old and New Testaments."

I ended our conversation by putting my hand on Matt's shoulder and praying for him. I gave him my card, we shook hands, and he walked away with a smile on his face.

Did Timothy Become a "Timothy"?

No real faith was ever wrought in man by his own thoughts and imaginations; he must receive the gospel as a revelation from God, or he cannot receive it at all.
Charles Spurgeon

After checking in at the security office, I made my way to the second floor of the mall where my table was already set up near an escalator. I like this particular spot because people making their way up and down the escalator are funneled past the table. More foot traffic means more Bibles and tracts distributed, as well as better opportunities to engage people in conversation.

A young couple was relaxing at the table when I arrived. I greeted them and let them know I would be using the table to distribute Bibles. They were gracious and kind, and when I asked them if they would each like a Bible, both accepted the gift. It was a good start to my afternoon.

While I had other tracts on the table, two of my titles I focused on distributing were "Miranda" and "Thank You." As the Lord would have it, I was able to give "Thank You" tracts to five uniformed soldiers and a uniformed Marine Corps sergeant. I thanked each man for his service and, in turn, they thanked me for the support.

I also distributed about 150 of the "Miranda" tracts at the top of the escalator, greeting people by saying, "Happy Good Friday!"

Among the many people in the mall that afternoon, I noticed a young man looking at the table as he made his way to the escalator. "Would you like a free Bible?" I asked.

"No. I've got so many Bibles at home."

As he was about to step onto the escalator, I said, "Make sure to read at least one of them!"

That stopped the young man in his tracks. He quickly changed directions and came over to the table. I introduced myself and learned the young man's name was Timothy. He was 19 years old. "I'm trying to read the Bible. I wish I could read it every night, but, you know," Timothy said.

"Where do you worship?" I asked.

"I go to a Church of God in Christ in Pasadena. My uncle is the bishop."

"Can I ask you something?"

"Sure."

I took Timothy through a "Three Minutes to Live" scenario (of which there are several variations). The best Timothy could offer me, his hypothetical unsaved friend, was to invite me to church so his bishop-uncle could talk to me.

"Timothy, what if I don't want to go to your church and talk to your uncle? You're my friend. I have a relationship with you. I'm coming to you for help. What are you going to tell me?" I asked.

"I guess I would tell you to turn to God?"

"Why?"

"Why?" Timothy repeated.

"Yeah. Why would you tell me to turn to God? What will happen to me if I don't?"

Timothy stammered for a few moments, looked around to see if anyone was eavesdropping, and then lowered his voice and said, "I guess you would go to hell."

"Okay. I kind of put you on the spot."

"Uh-huh," Timothy replied with a half-smile.

"Let's switch. Now, I'm the Christian and you're my unbelieving, dying friend. Here's what I would say to you."

I communicated the law and the gospel to Timothy. He said he understood and believed everything I shared with him.

"What do you like to do, Timothy?" I asked.

"Play basketball." Timothy said that he was presently attending our local community college. His plan was to transfer to another Southern California community college where he hoped to make the basketball team.

"Timothy, what if I told you I could teach you everything you need to know about playing basketball?"

"Okay?" was his quizzical reply.

"Here's what you need to know about playing basketball. You need to make sure the ball you use is orange and round. There are two baskets at opposite ends of the court. You need to make sure you put the ball in the right one." I let the level of my "knowledge" of basketball sink into Timothy's mind. "Timothy, if I were to say that to you, would you think I knew anything about basketball?"

"Well, maybe. I don't like to judge people."

"Come on, Timothy! You judge all the time. If you're standing in front of two restaurants and one has a 'D' from the Health Department on the front door and the other restaurant has an 'A,' you're going to make a judgment and go into the restaurant with the letter 'A' on the door. Come on! Judge me!"

Timothy smiled. "Okay. I wouldn't think you knew anything about basketball."

"Now, I have a tough question for you. If you wouldn't think I knew anything about basketball, based on what I said to you, then why should I believe you know Christ when you can't tell me how to know Him?"

Timothy thought about that for a moment.

"Look, Timothy, I don't know your heart. But, there are millions of people your age who have grown up in church. They think they know Jesus because going to church is all they've ever known. They think they are Christians because they were raised in a Christian home. Yet, they have never repented of their sin and received Jesus Christ, by faith, as their Lord and Savior. They go to church on Sunday and they live like hell Monday through Saturday. They think because they prayed a prayer and asked Jesus into their hearts, raised their hands, and walked down an aisle that they're right with Jesus. And they live like they have some kind of 'get-out-of-hell-free' card. They say they know Jesus, but nothing has changed in their life. They are the same people they've always been.

"Timothy, can you point to a time in your life when your faith became your own—when you turned from your sin and received Jesus Christ as your Lord and Savior?" I asked.

Timothy thought about it.

"Timothy, something a friend taught me last weekend at a conference is this: a person doesn't have to hit rock bottom and be lying unconscious in an alley with a needle and syringe sticking out of his arm before they can come to faith in Christ. There are many people like you who grew up in church and can't point to an exact moment in time when they came to faith in Christ. That's okay. What matters is whether or not Christ has saved you and that you know you have turned from your sin and truly received Jesus Christ as your Lord and Savior."

I could tell Timothy wasn't sure how to respond.

"Timothy, what's going to happen to you when you die?"

"I'm going to heaven?" Timothy's response revealed a lack of assurance.

"Why?"

"Because of my faith?"

"And?" I prodded.

"Well, because God will see what I've done with my life...."

"Weigh the good against the bad you've done?" I interrupted.

"Yes."

Again, Timothy had affirmed everything I said when I communicated the law and the gospel to him. Yet, his faith was not in Christ alone. It was in Christ plus Timothy. I spent some time taking Timothy through a couple courtroom scenarios while explaining doctrines such as depravity, propitiation, and justification in terms he could understand. By the time we parted company, Timothy was asserting he was trusting in Christ alone for his salvation. Maybe he had been. Maybe he came to faith in Christ during our conversation. Or, maybe he remains a young man who, having grown up in church, is a false convert. God knows.

Maria's Theological Mess

Whatever a man depends upon, whatever rules his mind, whatever governs his affections, whatever is the chief object of his delight, is his god.
Charles Spurgeon

Just moments after I said goodbye to Timothy, a middle-aged woman dressed in summer hiking/walking clothes and carrying a backpack approached the table. Her skin was dark and leathery. She looked like she spent a lot of time outdoors.

"I'm a believer. I'm just wondering if you will pray for my friend," she said.

"Certainly," I replied.

"His name is Jerry. He is Jewish. I've been trying to get through to him for years, but he just won't believe."

I held out my hand to the woman. "My name's Tony."

The woman shook my hand. "I'm Maria."

"Well, I won't forget your name. My wife's name is Mahria. Where do you worship?"

The look on Maria's face told me she didn't like the question. "I worship everywhere, all the time." She went on to tell me that she was raised in the Roman Catholic Church and attends the largest Roman Catholic church in the community. She also attends a "seeker" mega-church and a charismatic church.

I happened to look to my right and saw my Mahria. She got off work early and was able to join me at the mall. What a blessing! I introduced the two ladies and brought Mahria up to speed on the conversation so far.

Maria talked for several more minutes about her spirituality. When it seemed like she was ready to pause, I asked, "May I tell you what I would say to Jerry?"

"Please."

"I would begin by reading Isaiah 53." I opened my Bible to Isaiah 53 and held the book so that both ladies could see the pages. As I read, something inside me said, "Maria is going to stop me."

"Yet it was the will of the Lord to crush him; he has put him to grief; when his soul makes an offering for guilt, he shall see his offspring; he shall prolong his days; the will of the Lord shall prosper in his hand. Out of the angui…"

Maria placed her hand over the page in order to stop me from continuing. Most unbelievers and false converts (they are one and the same) quickly tire of hearing the Word of God read aloud. Maria was no different.

"I read that to Jerry just today."

"You read all of Isaiah 53 to him today?"

"Well, not all of it. Look, I have to get going. I'm already late for an appointment. Please pray for Jerry."

"We will. But Maria, before you go there's something else I need to say to you. You need to find a Bible-believing, Bible-teaching church and settle there."

"I'm in church on Sunday. I go to all three churches every Sunday."

"I understand. But, the churches you are going to don't preach the real gospel."

"I don't believe that," she snapped back.

"Maria, you look like you are athletic. You probably run or hike?"

"I do it all," she said proudly.

"Maria, what if you were running a race and you came to a water station and I handed you a bottle of water. And just as you put the bottle to your mouth, I tell you there is a drop of poison in the water. Would you drink it?"

"I've heard this before. One church tells me there's poison in another church. Another church tells me there's poison in another church. They all have poison, but they also bear fruit."

"Maria, a bad tree cannot bear good fruit. It might look good. It may even taste good. But, the fruit is always bad from a bad tree. The churches you are going to are bad trees."

Maria then asserted that she believed she had been saved by the blood of Christ and faith in Him alone, apart from works. She acknowledged that the Roman Catholic Church teaches that works are necessary for salvation, but she didn't see it as a big deal. She said the

Bible is the only infallible authority and that there are no perfect human teachers.

We parted company with smiles and well wishes. While Maria made many biblical assertions I could affirm, our conversation left me with little confidence she was saved. She found comfort and peace in three of the worst churches in the community, where false gospels are taught and unbiblical traditions are practiced.

Ten Words in ASL

Have any of you known or heard of such a thing as conversion wrought by any other doctrine than that which is in the Word? I should like to have a catalogue of conversions wrought by modern theology.
Charles Spurgeon

Two ladies approached my table at the mall. One was a shorter lady of possible Latin American descent. The other appeared to be in her 30s. Their names were Julie and Cheri, respectively.

Cheri was immediately drawn to the Bibles on the table.

"Everything on the table is free," I said.

Julie touched Cheri to get her attention. Using American Sign Language (ASL) and her voice, Julie communicated to Cheri what I had just said.

Cheri quickly took a Bible from the table and joyfully put it into her bag.

"Would you like one, too?" I asked Julie.

"Oh, I can have one?" she asked.

"Of course. I would love for you to have one."

Julie, once again gaining Cheri's attention with a gentle touch, told her, "I will read this to you at bedtime."

Mahria and I looked at each other and smiled.

"She has the mind of a five-year-old," Julie said, indicating Cheri was also developmentally disabled.

Our hearts went out to both Julie and Cheri as Cheri continued to pick up tracts off the table and put them into her bag. Then something at the end of the table caught Cheri's eye: my marble Ten Commandment tablets (the Ten Words). Cheri pointed to the tablets and signed to Julie, indicating she wanted Julie to read what was written there.

I almost cried as I watched this absolutely beautiful, God-ordained scene. One by one, Julie signed the Ten Commandments, explaining to Cheri what each one meant. Julie thought Cheri would be satisfied to learn what was on the first of the two tablets, but when

Cheri realized Julie had stopped reading, she pointed to the second tablet. So, Julie continued signing the commandments.

She stopped before getting through all of them, and I asked, "Can I help? Does Cheri have a question?"

"Adultery. How do I explain that in terms she can understand?" Julie asked.

Together we explained to Cheri that adultery happens when a person in a marriage behaves toward their husband or wife in a way that is not loyal, trustworthy, or faithful. Julie asked Cheri if she wanted to get married. With the consternation of a child, Cheri made a pouty face, shook her head, and said, "No!" We all chuckled.

As the two ladies started to leave, I handed Julie one of my business cards. "My email address is on the card. If you find you or Cheri have any questions about what you are reading in the Bible, please email me. I would love to help the two of you in any way I can."

Both ladies made the sign to say, "Thank you." I did the same in return.

Before the two ladies reached the escalator, Cheri turned back, smiled, and made the sign for "I love you."

"I love you, too, Cheri," I said, repeating the hand gesture.

As the ladies made their way down the escalator, Mahria and I turned to each other and embraced, rejoicing in what the Lord had just done for His own glory. It was a moment I will never forget.

Section III:
The Power
of a Bible

400 Bibles Delivered and One Received

See what vitality the gospel has. Plunge her under the wave, and she rises, the purer for her washing; thrust her in the fire, and she comes out the more bright for her burning; cut her in sunder, and each piece shall make another church; behead her, and like the Hydra of old, she shall have a hundred heads for every one you cut away. She cannot die, she must live; for she has the power of God within her.
Charles Spurgeon

I was running low on giveaway Bibles. It had been less than a month since the donations of multiple supporters allowed me to purchase almost 1,000 Bibles in English and Spanish, but those had all since been given away to people across Southern California, largely through the multiple outreaches I had led during a recent conference. When I put out the word on social media that my Bible stock was almost gone, one family stepped up and made a donation that allowed me to purchase another 400 Bibles.

Shortly thereafter, I received a call from the truck driver making the delivery of one pallet loaded with ten cases of "books." He let me know he would arrive at 12:14 p.m. I thought he must have an excellent GPS system to be that exact with his arrival time, especially in the greater Los Angeles area. I was skeptical, of course. But sure enough, the truck drove down my street at 12:14 p.m. I'm easily impressed by such things.

The driver hopped down from the cab of the truck and introduced himself. His name was Javi. He was personable and looked about half his actual age of 42.

As Javi maneuvered the pallet jack in the truck's trailer, he asked, "Are these books?"

"Yes. They're Bibles."

"Really? Are you a minister?"

"I'm a street preacher. I give these Bibles away to people I meet on the streets."

"Oh. That's cool," Javi said.

Javi loaded the jacked pallet onto the lift gate and slowly lowered the gate to the ground. He offloaded the pallet and put it in the carport.

"I grew up Catholic," Javi said.

"So did I."

"Really?"

"Yep."

"I went to a big church with my girlfriend at the time, about three years ago. It was a big church off the 118. It was an experience. I liked it. The pastor was funny."

My heart sank a bit as Javi continued to describe the church and his experience. I knew with certainty that the church of which he spoke is not known for gospel. I have no doubt there are genuine followers of Jesus Christ who attend the church. I know this is true because I've met them. A few of my friends, whose salvation is not in question as far as I'm concerned, have attended and even served at the church in the past. But there have been times over the years when the church in question (or at least members of its staff) has been better known for its opposition to public evangelism than for reaching the lost with the gospel. But, I said nothing to Javi about all of this. I only acknowledged I was familiar with the church he attended.

"So, Javi," I began, "is it safe to assume that since you've attended church you believe in God?"

"Yes, I believe in God."

"What do you think is going to happen to you when you die?"

"I don't know."

"Nothing wrong with that. That's an honest answer," I assured him. "If you were to die today—and I don't want that to happen—and God were to ask you why He should allow you to enter heaven, what would you say?"

"I don't know. I've done some bad things in my life—a lot of bad things."

"Okay. How about this: would you consider yourself to be a good person?"

"Yeah. I guess so."

"What is your definition of a 'good person'? According to Javi, a 'good guy' is…?"

"Someone who helps other people. Someone who is considerate?"

"Did you just describe yourself?"

"Yeah," Javi acknowledged with a smile.

"And that's what most people do. When I ask people on the streets to describe a 'good person' for me, they look into the mirror and describe the first person they see."

Javi smiled again.

"But Javi, the problem is this. God's standard for goodness is moral perfection. Jesus said, 'You are to be perfect as your heavenly Father is perfect'" (Matthew 5:48).

"No one can live up to that," Javi said.

"That's right. No one can. The Bible says, 'All have sinned and fall short of the glory of God' [Romans 3:23]. You and I have both sinned against God. You've admitted you've done lots of bad things. If God gave you and me what we deserved for our sins against Him, we would both spend eternity in hell. Have you ever been inside a courtroom?" I asked.

"Yes I have."

I then shared the courtroom analogy with Javi, as I have done with thousands of people during conversations and while open-air preaching through the years.

"Javi, if the judge released you, would that be good news?"

"Yes," he said with a chuckle.

"What would you think of the man who paid your fine?"

"I would be indebted to him forever."

"Well, let's see if that's true." So, I proclaimed the gospel to Javi. I decided to go over the courtroom analogy again, this time changing the scenario.

"Let's go back to that courtroom. This time, let's say you broke into someone's home late at night. As you're going through the house, you notice pictures on the wall."

"Family pictures," Javi interjected.

"Right. Family pictures. Then, a teenager, hearing noise in the house, confronts you in the living room. You panic and you stab the kid. He dies. You are arrested and you confess to the crime. Now, instead of life in prison, the judge sentences you to death. Throughout the trial, you have this weird feeling that you had met the judge before."

Javi interrupted. "I know where this is going! The pictures on the wall!"

"Yep. You got it. Javi, you killed the judge's son. The man who just sentenced you to death is the victim's father."

Javi slowly dropped his head and looked at the ground.

"Javi, in this case, it's not like our court system today. In this case, you don't get 20 years of 'three hots and a cot' [meals and a bed], all the pornography you can look at, and all the weights you can lift. As soon as the judge sentences you to die, they start to take you into the room where they are going to strap you to a table, stick a needle in your arm, and put you to sleep like a stray dog. But, before you leave the courtroom, the judge stands up from his chair, takes off his robe of authority, and steps down from his bench. He looks at you and says, 'You deserve to die for murdering my son, but I'm going to take your place.'

"Javi, every time you sin it's like driving a knife through the heart of God's Son, Jesus Christ. It's as if you are murdering Christ over and over again. But, if you repent, if you turn from your sin and receive Jesus Christ as your Lord and Savior, God will forgive your crimes against Him. The Bible says, 'These things have been written so that *you may know* that you have eternal life' [a paraphrase of 1 John 5:13, emphasis mine]. Javi, you can know the forgiveness of God, the mercy of God, the love of God. You can know you will spend eternity with Him in heaven if you repent and receive Jesus Christ as your Lord and Savior."

Javi nodded his head. "I'm listening," he said.

"Javi, is there anything, any sin in your life that you love so much that you just won't give it up? Is there any sin you won't give up today, knowing if you don't repent and receive Christ you will spend eternity in hell?"

Javi looked skyward and thought for a moment. "That's a really good question. I'm going to have to think about that."

"Please do."

"I will."

"Do you have a Bible?" I asked, pointing to the pallet of 400 bibles Javi had just delivered.

"No, I don't."

"Can I give you one of these?"

"Sure!"

Together, Javi and I tore through the plastic shrink wrap holding the cases of Bibles. Once we exposed the top of one of the boxes, Javi pulled his keys out of his pocket and used it to break the seal of the box. I reached inside and removed a Bible. Before handing it to Javi, I took Javi's pen from his shirt pocket, signed the Bible "To Javi, from Tony," and wrote down my cell number and email address. Javi took the Bible and opened it up to look at the inscription I wrote. "Thank you," he said.

"A good place to start reading is the Gospel of John." I turned the pages in the Bible to the Gospel of John and dog-eared the first page so it would be easier for him to find.

"Javi, all I know about you is your first name. No salesman will come to your door."

Javi laughed.

"I wrote down my number and email address. If you have any questions about what we've talked about, or if you have any questions about what you read in the Bible, give me a holler."

"I will!"

As Javi opened the door and stepped up and into the cab, I called out, "Hey, Javi! I'm going to have more Bibles delivered here in the future. I hope you're the one to deliver them!"

"Me, too!" Javi said with a smile.

Javi drove away with only 399 fewer Bibles in his truck. Javi delivered 400 Bibles, and he received one.

Was It the Sound of Salvation?

We have not yet sufficiently learned the value of an immortal soul if we do not feel that we would be willing to live, say seventy years, to be the means of saving one soul, and be willing to compass the whole globe, and preach in every city, and town, and village, if we might only be rewarded at the last with just one convert.
Charles Spurgeon

It had been a very long week. A two-week re-piping of our home left me with the task of repainting almost every room in our condo, so I took a week's vacation to work on putting my home back in order. I used five vacation days, but it most certainly was not a vacation. As many of my close friends can attest, I am not a handyman. The one thing I can do with marginal competence is operate a paint brush, which I did for 10 hours a day six days that week.

During that time, my grandmother had not one, but two heart attacks—the second one in her doctor's office. She was rushed to the hospital where she underwent several hours of open-heart surgery. She was 85 and unsaved.

The surgery was successful, with the surgeon saying that my grandmother's heart was the most beautiful heart he ever held in his hands. Her recovery was going well enough for my grandmother to complain about the food at the hospital. Then something went tragically wrong.

One day, my grandmother began coughing uncontrollably. As a result, she began to bleed. Within minutes she was in full cardiac arrest. Hospital staff heroically performed CPR for 25 minutes until the surgeon arrived. She was rushed into surgery where the surgeon was able to repair the new damage to her heart. Unfortunately, the CPR that kept her alive did not provide enough oxygen to her brain. Although she was able to breathe a little on her own, my grandmother never came out of her vegetative state. She had made it clear to family members that she did not want to live in that condition. She died soon after life support was removed.

My relationship with my grandmother and my mother's side of the family has been estranged since I was about 10 years old, the result of my parents' divorce. But, I cared about her as a human being. Over the years, I had shared the law and the gospel with her on more than one occasion.

So, on top of the physical exhaustion from working on the house, there was the emotional stress of my grandmother's pending death and my desire to be an encouragement to my mom and my sister. Needless to say, there was very little time for evangelism that week.

This particular morning was my first opportunity in more than a week to hit the streets. Jimmy, one of my regular fishing buddies, was studying for an exam at The Master's College. David, another of my fishing buddies, was working and getting ready for the birth his daughter. All of my girls were busy with school. So, I headed to the North Hollywood Metro Station alone.

A strange feeling came over me as I placed my box in front of the palm tree on the sidewalk of Lankershim Boulevard (where we would set up to preach each week). I opened the box, removed my open-air preaching Bible, and turned to Luke 13—the passage I would read as part of my Project Ezra[1] effort and from which I would preach the law and the gospel. I could hear my heart pounding in my ears. Everything seemed loud: my breathing, turning the pages of the Bible, the traffic noise, people's footsteps. I felt like I was having a mild anxiety attack.

"I'm going home," I thought. "No one would know. The people here certainly won't care if I leave. I need a break. I'm tired. I don't feel like preaching today. The Lord will understand."

"No." Another set of thoughts came. "I've got to preach. What would so many of my friends say at this moment?" I asked myself with a smile. "'Don't quit!' Alright, Tony, get up on the box and preach!"

I read Luke 13 to myself as I waited for my courage to catch up to my conviction.

---

[1] "Project Ezra" was an effort I put together several years ago, in which I encouraged Christians to read the Bible aloud in a public square.

"Good morning, everyone. I would like to read to you this morning Luke 13..." As is so often the case, once I started reading the Word of God aloud, the anxiety quickly melted away. The stress and fatigue from the last week meant nothing in that moment. All I felt was the excitement of preaching God's Word. "Thank You, Lord," I silently prayed.

By the time I finished, I had been on the box for about 25 minutes. I offered those within the sound of my voice a free Bible. There were no immediate takers, so I started to pack up. My plan was to go home before heading to Cal State University Northridge. Little did I know what the Lord had in store for me.

As I put my PA equipment and Bible in the box, I looked up to see a woman standing in front of me. "I would like a Bible," she said quietly.

I gave her a paperback ESV New Testament, and for the next 15 minutes, the Lord blessed me as I got to reiterate the law and the gospel to a very nice lady. She confided that her boyfriend was a Christian and read the Bible to her from time to time. She also admitted that while she thought she was a Christian she wasn't sure where she would spend eternity. Toward the end of our conversation I asked, "Do you have a Bible at home?"

"No, I've never had a Bible."

"Here, let me have that one," I said.

She seemed to pout as she handed back the New Testament I had just given her.

"I would like you to have this one instead." I handed her a leather-bound compact ESV Bible. My pastor at the time would occasionally give me a few of these beautiful Bibles to use in my evangelism efforts. I reserved those special Bibles for people whom the Lord either appeared to save while I talked with them, or for those who seemed genuinely contrite and interested (more than curious) in reading the Bible.

"Oh!" she gasped. "Thank you so much!"

I gave her my business card and encouraged her to call me if she had any questions about either our conversation or what she read in the Bible. She then walked away, and I finished packing up and headed to my car. I praised God for His faithfulness and thanked Him for the opportunity to preach His Word and to talk to the lady who now had her first Bible.

Fast-forward to the following Wednesday afternoon.

I walked into my office at Living Waters to see the customary solid red light on my desk phone. I had at least one message waiting for me.

"Hello," the message began. "My name is Jane (not her real name to protect her anonymity). I'm here with my sister. You gave her a beautiful Bible the other day. It's beautiful. Thank you for talking to her. I think I would like to talk to you, too." She left her number with a request that I call her back. I dialed the number, got her voicemail, and left a message. I waited to hear from her again.

Some days later, I got into my car to run some ministry-related errands. As I pulled onto the street, my cell phone rang. I immediately recognized the number to be Jane's.

"Hi, this is Tony," I answered.

"Hi, Tony. It's Jane."

"I'm so glad you called."

"I'm sorry it's taken me so long to get back to you. It's been a busy week."

"No problem at all."

Jane told me that she was a Christian who was struggling with a failed relationship.

"Jane, since we don't know each other, I would like to ask you something. It will give me an idea as to where you're at spiritually."

"Okay."

"Let's say you're a Christian and I'm not. You learn that I only have three minutes to live. I believe there's a God out there, and I'm scared. What would you tell me?"

"Well...I would tell you to believe that there is a higher power. And I would tell you to repent and pray a prayer."

"Why do I need to repent?" I asked.

"Because we're all sinners."

"Yeah, but I think I'm a pretty good guy. I've never cheated on my wife. I love my kids. I pay my taxes. Won't God take all of that into account?" I answered, playing the role of an unbeliever.

"Um, that's a good question."

I let Jane stew on that for a moment or two.

"Okay. Let's switch roles now. I'm the Christian and you have three minutes to live. Here's what I would say to you: 'Jane, in just a few minutes you are going to stand before Almighty God, and He is going to judge you according to the perfect moral standard of His Law. If you've ever lied, He will see you as a liar. If you've ever stolen anything, He will see you as a thief. If you've ever taken His name in vain, He will see you as a blasphemer. If you've ever had a lustful thought about someone other than a spouse, then God will see you as an adulterer. If you've ever hated anyone, He will see you as a murderer. God is holy, righteous, just, and good. He must punish sin, and the punishment God has determined for sin is eternity in hell. And that's what you face in about two minutes, unless God does something.

"'This is what God did. Two thousand years ago, God the Father sent His Son to earth in the person of Jesus Christ—fully God and fully Man and without sin. Unlike you and me, He never once violated the Law of God in thought, word, or deed. He was perfect in every respect. About 30 to 33 years into that earthly existence, He voluntarily went to the cross. He suffered and died, shedding His innocent blood and taking upon Himself the punishment you rightly deserve for your sins against God. Then, three days later, He rose from the dead, forever defeating sin and death. He is alive today and He will return at a time of the Father's choosing.

"'What God requires of you, Jane, is that you repent. God commands that you turn from your sin and by faith, and by faith alone, receive Jesus Christ as your Lord and Savior. He is your only hope. In just a minute or so you are going to stand before God. Unless He saves you, you are going to spend eternity in hell. My hope is that instead of receiving what you deserve for your sins against God, you will receive what you and I don't deserve, which is grace, mercy, and the free gift of eternal life. So, please repent and receive Jesus Christ as your Lord and Savior while He has given you time.' Does that make sense?" I asked.

There was a moment of silence on the phone.

"Whoa!" she exclaimed. "How did you do that?"

Jane's response was almost humorous, but more importantly, I believe it served to reveal the condition of her heart. Jane thought she was a Christian but was likely not saved.

"Jane, I was able to do that because I know Jesus Christ as my Lord and Savior."

"Oh," she said with a somewhat downcast tone of voice.

"Jane, what I'm about to say to you may seem kind of hard, but even though we've never met, I care about you as a person. So, just know that as you listen to what I'm about to say."

"Okay."

"What do you do for a living?" I asked.

"Well, I'm going to school right now."

"What do you want to do when you finish school?"

"I would like to be an alcohol treatment counselor."

"Jane, what if I told you I know everything there is to know about alcohol treatment? You're curious, so you say, 'Okay, Tony. Tell me everything you know about alcohol treatment.' And I say, 'Well, people who drink a lot get drunk. And if they get drunk a lot it's hard to stop. So, I think people should stop drinking.'"

Jane chuckled.

"Would you believe I know anything about alcohol treatment," I asked.

"Well, you might know a little bit."

"But would you come to me for counseling?"

"No way!"

"Good. Neither would I."

We both laughed.

"Now Jane, I'm going to ask you a tough question. And again, I'm asking because I care about you."

"Okay."

"Jane, if you wouldn't believe I was an alcohol treatment counselor based on what I said to you, why should I believe you are a Christian when you can't tell me how to become a Christian?"

"You're right. I guess you shouldn't."

Jane and I talked for another half-hour about the difference between saving faith and religion and the difference between grace and works. We talked about the forgiveness of God, as seen in the story of

David and Bathsheba, and about the difference between real and false assurance. I explained the biblical understanding of adoption and the fact that not everyone born into the human race is a child of God. We also discussed what it meant to be "born again."

"Jane, is there any sin in your life (and you don't have to be specific with me) that you love so much that you are willing to spend eternity in hell so you can enjoy that sin in this life?" I asked.

Jane thought for a moment. "No. There is nothing in my life worth going to hell for."

"Then, again, I want to encourage you to cry out to God in repentance and faith. If He saves you, if He causes you to be born again, then He will take your heart of stone and give you a heart of flesh. You will begin to love the things that God loves and you will begin to hate the things that God hates. You will begin to love to read His Word. You will begin to love having fellowship with other followers of Christ. And there's another thing you will love to do."

"What's that?"

"Can you remember a time when you couldn't wait to share news with people?"

"When I found out I was pregnant with my daughter," Jane answered.

"How old is your daughter?"

"She's 12."

"I have three girls: 22, 20, and 15 [their ages at the time]."

"Nice."

"Remember how you couldn't wait to tell people that you were pregnant?"

"Yes."

"Remember how easy it was for you to talk about it and how often you talked about it?"

"Yes."

"Well, that's the way it is with people who know Jesus Christ as their Lord and Savior. They are so grateful for the free gift of eternal life God has given them that they can't wait to tell people what God has done for them. They can't wait to tell people how they can come to know Jesus as their Lord and Savior."

"Oh. I see what you mean." Jane's voice brightened.

"Jane, many people misunderstand what God did through His Son on the cross. Let's say you and your daughter were in court one day. You decided to take your daughter to court as a civics lesson. You wanted her to see a court trial. Well, as it turns out, the day you decide to go to court is the day of a murder trial. The judge finds a man guilty of murder and sentences him to death. Just as the judge is about to have the man taken away to be executed, he turns to you and says, 'Jane, I will let this convicted murderer go if you will allow me to execute your daughter in his place.' Would you do it?"

"No way!"

"Neither would I. There is no way I would sacrifice one of my daughters so that a convicted criminal could go free."

"That's right."

"But Jane, do you understand that's what God did. 'For God so loved the world, that He gave his only Son, that whoever believes in Him should not perish but have eternal life' (John 3:16). God the Father allowed God the Son to be executed in the place of convicted criminals like you and me. So great is God's love that He sent His Son to die for sinners."

"That's beautiful."

"Yes it is. It's beautiful, Jane. It's a miracle. And it's a miracle I hope God will allow to take place in your life. We may never meet in person, but I hope one day when I'm standing before God's throne and worshiping Him that I will turn to my right or my left and see you there, too."

"That's what I want."

"Well, I think you need to spend some time examining yourself and talking to God."

"You're right. That's what I'm going to do. Thank you so much for talking to me."

"I'm really glad we had a chance to talk."

"Can I come to your church?"

"Of course!" I gave Jane directions to the church and information about the time and format of the service.

"My wife and I will be praying for you and your sister today."

"Please do." Jane paused. "I might want to talk to you again. Would that be all right?"

"Absolutely. You have my number. If you have any questions or if you just need some encouragement, don't hesitate to call."

"Thank you."

"You have a blessed day."

"You have a blessed day, too."

I hung up the phone and immediately began to praise God, lifting my hands in thanksgiving for what He had just done. I thought to myself, "Did I just hear the sound of salvation? Did God save Jane during our conversation?"

Only He knows, but that is certainly my hope. Her voice was humble from the very start of the conversation. If anything, her voice became even more humble as our conversation progressed, and her response the gospel was, to use her word, "beautiful."

Amazing Grace! How sweet the sound
That saved a wretch like me.
I once was lost but now am found;
Was blind, but now I see.

Section IV:
Abortion Clinic
(Abortuary) Ministry

My First Abortuary Conversation

Conscience is a faculty of the mind, which, like every other, has suffered serious damage through our natural depravity, and it is by no means perfect.
Charles Spurgeon

While I was still served with Living Waters, the Lord allowed me to have a small part in the production and distribution of their exceptional short film called "180."[1] One of my post-production responsibilities was to read incoming emails regarding the film. While plenty of people emailed the ministry to voice their hatred for God and unborn children, many of the messages were encouraging and heartwarming. The emails from women who shared that they had watched the film and decided not to murder their unborn children were the best of all.

It didn't take long for me to realize that while I was helping the ministry to fight the good fight against abortion, I wasn't personally doing enough to oppose the premeditated killing of unborn children. A simple Google search revealed that there were two abortuaries[2] not far from the Living Waters headquarters.

As often as my duties at Living Waters permitted, I drove to one of the local abortuaries to spend time in prayer. I asked the Lord to stop the killing of innocents at the murder mill. I prayed that the Lord would convict the doctors, nurses, and staff of their part in the killings and that He would bring these blood-thirsty people to repentance and faith in the Lord Jesus Christ. I prayed for the salvation of the women who came to the abortuary to murder their children and for the boyfriends, husbands, or other family members who may have convinced or forced them to have an abortion.

---

[1] "180" is available for free viewing at www.180movie.com.

[2] A place where the murder of unborn children should not be referred to as a "clinic" any more than a Nazi death camp should be referred to as a resort.

One morning, as I sat praying in the parking lot of an abandoned restaurant adjacent to the abortuary, I saw a linen services truck pull up to the back door of that place of death. My heart began to race. I knew immediately what I should do and what I wanted to do. I knew I had to talk to the driver, to ask him if he knew what was happening inside the clinic. I wanted to proclaim the gospel to him.

It took several minutes for the driver to finish his duties, which included delivering clean linen and collecting soiled linen. My heart was grieved as I watched the man load bags of dirty linen, likely stained with the blood of now-deceased unborn children, into the back of his truck. It was hard to hold back the tears. There was a lump in my throat as I continued to pray.

I asked the Lord to allow me to have a conversation with the driver, and since he appeared to be of Hispanic descent, I prayed he spoke English.

As the man climbed back into the truck, I got out of my car and walked to the chain link fence that separated the restaurant parking lot from the abortion clinic property. I waved at the driver as he approached. He stopped the truck and opened the large sliding door on the passenger side.

"How are you today?" I asked.

"Good. How are you?" the driver replied.

"I'm doing well. My name's Tony. What's yours?"

"Ramon."

"Ramon, do you know what they do here at this place?" I didn't want to wrongly assume Ramon was aware of the abortuary's activities or begin the conversation with an unnecessary confrontation.

Ramon nodded his head and then lowered it with a look of shame on his face.

"You do," I said. "How do you feel about that?"

"I have to do my job."

"Do you have just a minute to talk?"

"About what?"

"About this." I pointed at the building.

"I know that they do it. But what can I do? What can I say?"

"The blood on some of the linen you just brought out of there is the blood of babies. How do you think God sees that, Ramon?"

"I know."

"Ramon, I care about you. I'm not angry with you. I'm not here to fight with you or call you names or anything like that, but they're killing children in there, Ramon."

There was a moment of silence before I continued.

"Do you have children? I have three daughters."

"I have three children," Ramon answered.

"How old are your kids?" I asked.

"24, 22, and 17."

"My daughters are 25, 22, and 17. So, they're about the same age. Are you a grandfather yet?"

"Yes."

"How old is your grandchild?"

"A year and a half. It's my son's child."

"What if your son came to you, Ramon, and said, 'We're going to kill your first grandchild.'?"

"My son is in the Air Force. And his wife is in the Air Force, too. When she got pregnant, that's what they told her to do."

"The military told her to get an abortion?" I asked with a repulsed tone of voice.

"Yes."

"But she didn't do it."

"Right."

"Praise God for that. But what if they had come to you Ramon and said, 'Dad, we're going to kill your grandchild.'? Wouldn't you try to stop them?"

"Yes."

"I know things are hard right now. I know everyone needs to keep their jobs. It's hard to find work. But, Ramon, when you stand before God He's not going to say, 'Ramon, it was okay for you to help this abortuary because you needed a job.'"

"I understand that, but there's no way I can... I mean..."

"How long have you been coming here?" I interrupted.

"Over a year."

"Have you been working for the company for a long time?"

"Thirteen years."

"Have you ever thought about talking to your supervisors about this part of the route?"

"I already talked to him. Before, I used to have a route in Pomona and it had another one of these places, so they switched me to this route. And then I get this place, another abortion clinic. So, I talked to them again, and I said, 'Hey, I don't want to have this one, just in case something happens while I'm there.' They said, 'It's a job. If you don't want to do the route, we'll get another driver to do it.' They don't care. They just care about the money."

I could tell that coming to the abortion clinic truly bothered Ramon.

"I know. I know." I sympathized with the tough position in which Ramon found himself.

"But, Ramon, do you think it's more important to please God or to please men?"

"Right now, it's hard. I have to support a family. If I don't work... It's not like I like to do it."

"Ramon, what do you think is going to happen to you when you die?"

"I don't know. I believe in God."

"Do you?"

"I pray. I go to church."

Ramon told me he attended a Christian church in the area.

"So, what do you think is going to happen after this life?" I asked.

Ramon shrugged his shoulders. "Well, right now, I think if I keep going to the church and I do whatever God says, I'm probably going to go to heaven. It's hard, because I'm doing this."

"Well, sometimes the most important things to do in our lives are the hardest things to do."

"Yeah, but sometimes you don't want to do the hard things because you want peace and quiet."

"But God doesn't accept our excuses."

"I know. I know."

I took Ramon through the law. "When you die and stand before God, He is going to see you as a liar and a thief and a blasphemer. What should God do with you, then? Heaven or hell?"

"Hell."

"Does that concern you?"

"Yes."

"Do you know what God did so that you might not have to go to hell?"

"Yes."

"What did He do?"

"God sent His Son, His only Son. And if we believe in His Son, we can go to heaven, right?"

I shared the gospel with Ramon, using the courtroom and parachute[3] analogies along the way to help him understand. I explained to him that, on the one hand, saving faith is more than mere intellectual assent to the truths of the gospel while, on the other hand, there is nothing a person can do to earn or deserve salvation from God. Salvation is not belief in Jesus plus good works. Salvation is a gift of God by the grace of God alone, through faith alone, in Jesus Christ alone. And then I called Ramon to repent and believe the gospel and to examine himself to make sure he is truly in the faith.

"Ramon, I know it's hard. But who are you going to trust for your life? Jesus or your company? Make sure you truly know God as your Lord and Savior. It's not enough to go to church. Lots of people go to church, but they don't know Jesus."

"I know."

"And I would encourage you to talk to your pastor about this route," I said.

"I already talked to him about it."

"What did he say?"

"We prayed. We prayed that my company would cancel the service. We prayed that they would close the clinic."

"And that's why I sit out here," I said. "I sit out here and pray that this place closes."

Ramon shared a little more about how he and his pastor had prayed for the situation in which he now found himself, engaged in work that clearly violated his conscience.

---

[3] See "Evangelism Tip #4: The 'Parachute' Analogy."

"Well, Ramon, I'm going to be praying for you. I would like to give you something." Through a hole in the chain link fence, I pushed a gospel tract and a 180 business card. Ramon walked over and accepted both.

"I'd shake your hand if I could reach through the fence, but I'm going to pray for you, Ramon."

"Thank you."

"God bless you, Ramon. Thank you for talking to me."

"God bless you."

"Have a good day."

With that, Ramon waved, returned to his truck, and drove away. I sat for several minutes afterward praying for Ramon and thanking God for the opportunity to talk to a nice man who seemed genuinely torn about servicing the abortuary.

I learned some important lessons as a result of my conversation with Ramon—lessons that would help me better serve Christ and love my neighbor while ministering outside abortuaries. I learned that I needed to pray with more love and compassion for those involved in every aspect of abortion, from the abortionist, to the mothers, to the fathers, to the linen servicemen. I had to pray more like a hurting father than an angry judge. There forever remains only one Lawgiver and Judge, only One who is able to save and destroy. That is God; it will never be me.

I also learned that while I must remain firm and resolute in my communication with people at abortuaries because lives are at stake, I am also mandated by God to speak the truth in love (Ephesians 4:15). I must remember: "A gentle answer turns away wrath, but a harsh word stirs up anger" (Proverbs 15:1).

Though it has been years since I had this conversation with Ramon, I am still a rookie compared to some of Christ's soldiers who daily do spiritual battle for the lives of unborn children and for the souls of those bent on murdering them. I so appreciate the wise counsel from brothers and sisters in Christ who have been working in these particularly gruesome trenches much longer than I have. However, I am thankful for what the Holy Spirit allowed me to learn during my first gospel encounter at an abortuary.

Evangelism Tip #4: The "Parachute" Analogy[1]

Introduction

Many of you are familiar with the Parachute Analogy developed by Ray Comfort. I love it and I use it often when articulating to a lost person the difference between intellectual assent to the truths about Jesus Christ and genuine trust and faith. For those of you who are unfamiliar with the analogy, it goes like this:

You and I are on a plane traveling to New York. We get about half-way there when we hear the pilot's voice over the loud speaker. We can hear fear in his voice. The pilot says, "We've lost the engines and we can't get them started again. The plane is going to crash. There is nothing we can do about it. There's a parachute under your seat."

We both look under our seats. We see that the parachute is there. We believe that the parachute is there.

The plane descends to about 10,000'. The pilot instructs the flight attendants to open the doors, and then he orders everyone to jump for their lives. I put my parachute on and jump out of the plane. You don't put your parachute on, and you jump out of the plane. Who survives the fall?

"You do?" is typically the answer I receive.

"Why?"

"Because you put on the parachute."

"But we both believed in it." I allow the person to stew on that for a moment, and then I explain the analogy.

It wasn't enough to simply believe in the parachute. You had to put it on and trust that it would open and save your life when you jump out of the plane. The same is true with Jesus Christ. It is not enough to simply have an intellectual belief in or agreement with Jesus. The demons believe and they tremble. You must put on the Lord Jesus Christ and, by faith,

---

[1] Tony Miano, "Another Look at the Parachute Analogy," *The Comfort Zone with Ray Comfort*, last modified September 14, 2011, accessed April 22, 2016, http://www.onthebox.us/2011/09/another-look-at-parachute-analogy.html.

trust Him to save you the same way you would trust a parachute.

Many people believe in Jesus (both inside and outside the walls of the church), but far fewer have placed their faith and trust in Jesus Christ alone for their salvation and so know Him as their Lord and Savior. This analogy drives that point home very nicely.

As I continue to study the Word of God and strive to apply sound doctrine to my open-air preaching and one-on-one witnessing, I have developed another parachute analogy that focuses on a different doctrinal truth—regeneration.

This new analogy does not replace the one I have described above, which has been used so effectively by many Christians. It merely places the emphasis on a different doctrine. The original analogy paints a wonderful picture of genuine, tangible faith and trust in the Lord Jesus Christ. My hope is that this new analogy will help Christians explain the essential doctrine of regeneration (new birth) to unbelievers.

The New Analogy

David Kingsley served as a Portland firefighter before entering the Army Air Corps in April 1942. He answered his nation's call to service when it needed him most.

Kingsley received his bombardier wings during the summer of 1943, after which he joined the 97th Bombardment Group. Kingsley's group was stationed in Italy. On June 23, 1944, Second Lieutenant Kingsley and the rest of his fellow bomber crewmen participated in an attack on oil targets around Ploesti, Romania. It was Kingsley's 20th mission over enemy territory. The flak and enemy fighter assaults had been particularly ferocious in the area of Ploesti and this day was no different.

Kingsley's bomber was badly damaged during the bomb run, but the pilot was able to maintain control of the aircraft, which allowed Kingsley to drop the bombs with devastating precision. Kingsley's bomber was so badly damaged that it fell behind the rest of the formation and began to lose altitude. Three German ME-109 fighter pilots saw an opportunity to exact vengeance and mercilessly fired upon the wounded bomber, severely wounding the tail gunner in the arm. Other crewmen yelled to Kingsley, asking him to render aid. They removed tail gunner's parachute and flak jacket and covered him in blankets in order to make him as comfortable as possible.

Moments later, eight ME-109s attacked the bomber. This time the ball turret gunner was severely wounded. The bomber was going down; there was no hope for the plane.

Kingsley immediately put the ball turret gunner's parachute on him. The tail gunner's parachute was lost in the chaos of flying blankets and equipment as the bomber continued to descend. Kingsley, with no regard for himself, took off his parachute and put it on the tail gunner. When the pilot ordered the crew to bail out, Kingsley helped his two wounded comrades to the open bomb bay and pushed them out of the plane, saving their lives.

As the bomber crewmembers jumped, they reported last seeing Kingsley standing on the bomb bay catwalk. The bomber remained in the air for just a few more moments until it crashed into the ground, exploded, and burned. Kingsley's body was later found in the wreckage.

For conspicuous gallantry and intrepidity in action at the risk of life above and beyond the call of duty, Second Lieutenant David Kingsley was posthumously awarded the Medal of Honor, our nation's highest military award.

Had Kingsley not put the parachutes on the wounded men, they would have died in the plane crash. This certainly was true for the wounded tail gunner to whom Kingsley gave his own parachute, sacrificing his life in the process. He literally took the tail gunner's place on the mortally wounded bomber.

What an extraordinary picture of Jesus Christ's substitutionary atonement on the cross and His regeneration of fallen, helpless people!

The Penal Substitutionary Atonement of Jesus Christ

"...just as the Son of Man did not come to be served, but to serve, and to give His life a ransom for many" (Matthew 20:28).

"Greater love has no one than this, that one lay down his life for his friends" (John 15:13).

I am the good shepherd; the good shepherd lays down His life for the sheep... I am the good shepherd, and I know My own and My own know Me, even as the Father knows Me and I know the Father; and I lay down My life for the sheep... For this reason the Father loves Me, because I lay down My life so that I may take it again. No one has taken it away from Me, but I lay it down on My own initiative. I have authority to lay it down, and I have authority to take it up again. This commandment I received from My Father (John 10:11, 14-15, 17-18).

...being justified as a gift by His grace through the redemption which is in Christ Jesus; whom God displayed publicly as a propitiation in His blood through faith. This was to demonstrate His righteousness, because in the forbearance of God He passed over the sins previously committed; for the demonstration, I say, of His righteousness at the present time, so that He would be just and the justifier of the one who has faith in Jesus (Romans 3:24-26).

"For while we were still helpless, at the right time Christ died for the ungodly. For one will hardly die for a righteous man; though perhaps for the good man someone would dare even to die. But God demonstrates His own love toward us, in that while we were yet sinners, Christ died for us" (Romans 5:6-8).

"He made Him who knew no sin to be sin on our behalf, so that we might become the righteousness of God in Him" (2 Corinthians 5:21).

"Christ redeemed us from the curse of the Law, having become a curse for us—for it is written, 'Cursed is everyone who hangs on a tree'—in order that in Christ Jesus the blessing of Abraham might come to the Gentiles, so that we would receive the promise of the Spirit through faith" (Galatians 3:13-14).

"But when the fullness of the time came, God sent forth His Son, born of a woman, born under the Law, so that He might redeem those who were under the Law, that we might receive the adoption as sons" (Galatians 4:4-5).

"For there is one God, and one mediator also between God and men, the man Christ Jesus, who gave Himself as a ransom for all, the testimony given at the proper time" (1 Timothy 2:5-6).

Without a propitiation to make payment for the sins of men, without a substitute to take the place of punishment for the penal debt men owe to God for their sins against Him, there would be no hope whatsoever for any member of the human race. When Jesus Christ, God in the flesh, voluntarily went to the cross and shed His perfect, innocent blood, He took upon Himself the punishment every person deserves. He acted in obedience to the Father's will and became a ransom for sinners who bear in their redeemed souls and who exhibit in their lives the fruit of the divine gifts: repentance and faith.

Without the substitutionary death of Jesus Christ, no one can be saved. But, praise and thanks be to Almighty God that instead of condemning all of mankind to that which they deserve—eternity in hell—He chose to save sinners through the sacrificial death and the glorious resurrection of His Son, Jesus Christ. God would be just to condemn everyone to hell. And God is also just if He chooses to pardon sinners in accordance with His loving, gracious, merciful, and kind nature, accepting as propitiation the death of His one and only Son.

The Beautiful Doctrine of Regeneration

"But as many as received Him, to them He gave the right to become children of God, even to those who believe in His name, who were born, not of blood nor of the will of the flesh nor of the will of man, but of God" (John 1:12-13).

"Jesus answered and said to him, 'Truly, truly, I say to you, unless one is born again he cannot see the kingdom of God... That which is born of the flesh is flesh, and that which is born of the Spirit is spirit. Do not be amazed that I said to you, "You must be born again."'" (John 3:3, 6-7).

"No one can come to Me unless the Father who sent Me draws him; and I will raise him up on the last day" (John 6:44).

"But God, being rich in mercy, because of His great love with which He loved us, even when we were dead in our transgressions, made us alive together with Christ (by grace you have been saved)...

For by grace you have been saved through faith; and that not of yourselves, it is the gift of God; not as a result of works, so that no one may boast" (Ephesians 2:4-5, 8-9).

> But when the kindness of God our Savior and His love for mankind appeared, He saved us, not on the basis of deeds which we have done in righteousness, but according to His mercy, by the washing of regeneration and renewing by the Holy Spirit, whom He poured out upon us richly through Jesus Christ our Savior, so that being justified by His grace we would be made heirs according to the hope of eternal life (Titus 3:4-7).

"In the exercise of His will He brought us forth by the word of truth, so that we would be a kind of first fruits among His creatures" (James 1:18).

> Blessed be the God and Father of our Lord Jesus Christ, who according to His great mercy has caused us to be born again to a living hope through the resurrection of Jesus Christ from the dead, to obtain an inheritance which is imperishable and undefiled and will not fade away, reserved in heaven for you, who are protected by the power of God through faith for a salvation ready to be revealed in the last time (1 Peter 1:3-5).

Only Jesus Christ could accomplish atonement acceptable to God for the remission of sins against God (Hebrews 9:15-28). Thus, salvation is a work of God for the glory of God, and by the grace of God alone, completely devoid of and separated from the works of sinful mankind. As I stated above, even repentance and faith are gifts from God (Acts 5:31; Ephesians 2:8; 2 Timothy 2:25), made manifest when God draws a person to Himself (John 6:44).

Application

Now that I have shared the analogy and the rich theology to which it points, I would like to explain how this analogy can be used in the context of biblical evangelism.

After sharing the law and the gospel, followed by the story of Lt. David Kingsley's heroism, I might say something like this to an unsaved person: "There was absolutely nothing the wounded bomber crewmen could do to save their own lives. They were helpless. Had Lt. Kingsley not sacrificially intervened on their behalf, they would have perished in a ball of flames when the bomber hit the ground. Likewise, there is nothing you can do to save yourself, spiritually. You are every bit as helpless as the wounded crewmen in the bomber. Unless God miraculously, graciously, and lovingly intervenes in your life, you will perish and spend eternity in the fires of Hell as the just punishment for your sins against God.

"Lt. Kingsley literally took the place of his fellow crewmembers and died a horrible death as he went down with the plane. 'Greater love has no one than this, that one lay down his life for his friends' (John 15:13). In addition to sacrificing his life, Lt. Kingsley actively saved the wounded crewmen by fitting them with parachutes and causing them to float to safety when he pushed them through the open bomb bay doors before the plane crashed.

"Likewise, Jesus Christ died a horrible, bloody death on the cross for the sins of those who repent and believe the gospel."

A Plea to the Unbelieving Reader

No expression of the love of God is more vivid and tangible than the cross of Jesus Christ. The evidence that God has extended to you the free gift of eternal life, literally causing you to be born again (1 Peter 1:3), will be this: you will repent. You will turn away from and forsake your sins against God. Instead, you will turn toward God and by faith alone receive Jesus Christ as your Lord and Savior. You will then continue to repent and continue to believe as you grow in your faith.

What do you think the attitude was of the wounded crewmen who were saved by Lt. Kingsley? Do you think they were grateful? Do you think they took any credit for their rescue? Do you think they forever had a fond affection for Lt. Kingsley? Do you think they spoke highly of him and spoke of him often? And how do you think those crewmen would respond to anyone who tried to drag Lt. Kingsley's name through the mud, deny his valor, or even deny his existence?

If God saves you, so too will it be with you. You will love the Lord Jesus Christ with thankfulness in your heart. You will gladly submit to him as the Lord of Your life and take no credit for your salvation. You will begin to love the things that God loves and to hate the things that God hates. You will think often about Jesus Christ. You will love to read His Word. You will want to spend time with Him in prayer. You will long to be with Him in Heaven. You will defend His name and His honor against anyone who would blaspheme His name or deny His existence and life-saving power. And you will tell others about what He has done for you, with the hope that God will extend to them the same salvation He has given you.

When you sin against Him, when you fall short of God's glory (and you will), instead of trying to justify your sin or exonerate yourself, you will cry out to God for mercy and forgiveness.

I wonder what the conversation was like in the bomber between Lt. Kingsley and the wounded crewmen. I can hear them crying out to Kingsley, begging him to help them. They realized that there was nothing they could do to save themselves. They knew that unless Kingsley intervened they would perish when the plane crashed.

Cry out to God right now. Repent. Confess your sins, all of which you've committed against Him. Beg for His forgiveness and ask Him to save you. Place your faith and trust in Jesus Christ alone for your salvation. Lt. Kingsley, a hero, was the only hope for the wounded crewmen. Jesus Christ, the Lord, is your only hope. Apart from Him, without His miraculous intervention in your life, you will perish in your sins. My hope is that He saves you.

Maggie's Informed Decision

Murders themselves arise from the evil passions of the human heart. If the fire was not there, temptation could not fan it to a flame. Is it not because men love themselves better than their neighbors that they commit murder?
Charles Spurgeon

Like so many young women before her and so many young women since, Maggie had come to the Family Planning Associates abortuary in Mission Hills, California to murder her unborn child. Unlike most of the young women who come to the abortuary, however, Maggie listened to our pleas to talk to us before she went inside.

Maggie was in her late teens or early twenties. She was a diminutive young woman who seemed scared, not of us, but of what she had come to the abortuary to do.

Like most mornings that I stand outside the abortuary, I was with my friend, Don McGinnis. Don and I have now served side by side for several years but we first met in a somewhat unusual manner.

One morning, during the early days of my abortuary ministry, when I would often stand outside the fence alone with my "Are You Ready" cross, a car approached my corner. The driver stopped, rolled down the passenger window, and asked in a gruff voice, "Are you Tony Miano?"

My first thought, as I lowered the cross to cover as much of my torso as possible, was, "I wonder what caliber round this wooden cross will stop?"

"Yes, I'm Tony Miano," I said, anticipating the worst.

"I've been watching some of your videos. I live not far from here and I go to Grace Community Church. When I saw that you were coming to this place, I was hoping to see you here. Would it be all right if I came out to stand with you?"

Don McGinnis has been a dear friend and a faithful warrior for lives and souls at the Mission Hills abortuary ever since. Rain or shine, Don is at his post outside the abortuary every Wednesday and

Saturday morning—mornings designated for the murder of unborn children by "surgical procedure."

Maggie was now standing in front of us. I can't help but to think of my own daughters when I talk to women Maggie's age.

"We're here to help you. We're not here to judge you or to harm you. We're here to help you, and there's a reason that God put us here today," Don began. "That child is just as precious in God's eyes as your life is. You know that inside; I know that because God puts a conscience inside us where He speaks to us and tells us what's right and wrong. I can see you're battling with that right now. Right?"

"Yeah?" Maggie replied.

"Please, do the right thing and don't take the child's life," Don begged.

"How, how far along are you; do you know?" I asked.

"Like two weeks."

"Two weeks? It's not long after that your baby's heart begins to beat. Is this your first pregnancy?"

"No, this is my second, and I'm scared."

"Did you have an abortion with your first child?

"No."

"Oh? How old is your child?"

"My child is four months old."

"Oh, man. So, you know how precious that life is?" Don interjected.

"Yes. I'm just scared to be alone again."

"Are you, are you being a mom alone? Do you have any help or support?" I asked.

"Yeah, I'm on my own."

"Do you have any help from your family?"

"Yeah, they help me, but it's just really hard, just like the other people struggle with their kids. I want to just go in there and ask questions and..."

"Do you know what they are going to tell you?" I asked.

"No."

"They're going to tell you to abort your child. They don't care about you in there; they care about the money you bring to abort your child. They are in business to make money. That's why they are here.

We can point you to adoption services. We have a family; we know of a family that is ready to adopt a baby right now. They are just a phone call away. We can also put you in touch with people who will help meet your needs, such as prenatal care. I'm sorry. Your name is?" I asked.

"Maggie."

"Maggie, I'm Tony."

"Maggie, I'm Don."

"Maggie, the most important thing is this: you know in your heart that God sees abortion as murder, because your baby was created in the image of God, just as you were. God has already numbered the hairs on your baby's head just as He did for you, and to have an abortion is to murder the image of God. Do you have any spiritual beliefs?" I asked.

"Yeah. Christian."

"Do you go to church regularly?"

"No, I don't go to church. I thought about adoption, but I can't let go of my child like that."

"But you're going to let go of your child like *this*?"

Sadly, I've heard this many times from women outside of abortuaries. When I suggest giving up their babies for adoption, it is not uncommon for women, even angrily, to say they would never allow someone else to raise their children. So sinfully twisted and wicked are the minds of abortive women that they would rather kill their children than allow others to raise them.

"I know, but...."

"Maggie, you're still going to be the mother of this baby. If you go through with this, you'll simply be the mother of a dead baby. You're always going to be this child's mother—always. And the Word of God says that no murderer can enter into the kingdom of God [Revelation 21:8].

"When you say you're a 'Christian,' what does that mean?" I asked.

"I don't know. I was just told we were Christian," Maggie replied.

"Your mom told you that you are a Christian?"

"Yeah."

"Okay. So what do you think happens to a person when they die?"

"They reincarnate?"

"No, that's not what the Bible says. That's not a Christian belief," I explained.

"No? I thought it was."

"The Bible says that it's appointed once for a person to die and after that the judgment [Hebrews 9:27]. When we die, we stand before God to give an account for our life, and He judges us according to His law. It's a law that He's written on our hearts. You know it's wrong to lie because God is not a liar. You know it's wrong to harbor bitterness or resentment, or..."

Maggie's cell phone rang. "Can I answer this?"

"Sure. Absolutely. Of course you can," I assured her.

Maggie spoke to someone on the phone for a few moments, hung up the phone, and put it back in her pocket.

"So, Maggie, when we stand before God and He judges us according to His law, if He finds that we've sinned against Him in any way—and we all have; we've all lied, we've all done things we know that are dishonoring and displeasing to God; we know that, because God has given us a conscience—He's going to do what's right because He's a good God. What God has determined as the punishment for sin is eternity in hell. In fact, to even have the thoughts of hatred in our heart, to even have the thought of murder in our heart, God sees these thoughts the same as actually committing the murder. But that same God—and again there is only one God—that same God who is angry with the wicked, that same God who will judge the world in righteousness, is also loving, merciful, gracious, and kind, and He showed His great love when He sent His Son to earth in the person of Jesus Christ, fully God..."

"That's scaring me," Maggie interrupted.

"What's scaring you? Am I scaring you?" I asked.

"No, just like the whole thought of it."

"The whole thought of what? Going through with this?" I asked.

"Yes."

"Maggie, that's your conscience at work because you know it's wrong. Killing your baby is not going to make your problems go away, because you know this is wrong. You know this is wrong in your heart and you know this is wrong in the eyes of God. The Bible says that it's the fear of the Lord that's the beginning of wisdom (Proverbs 1:7). Sometimes being afraid, Maggie, sometimes being scared is a good thing. You know, getting scared keeps us from driving 110 miles an hour down...."

"Do they show videos before you go for the abortion?" Maggie interrupted. It was difficult to keep her focused on what I was saying.

"Do you mean an ultrasound, to let you see your baby?" I asked.

"No. Do they show a video before you go inside to have the abortion, because I would really like to see a video? If I see a lot of things—because my cousin says if you hear anybody and you see people come out, just get out."

Apparently, Maggie's cousin tried to warn her about what she might hear and see inside the abortuary.

"Maggie, we're here every week and we see the people coming in and we see them coming out. Not only is there pain for you, but your baby feels pain. Your baby feels pain, because your baby is a human being just like you, but you can't hear your baby scream. You have a son right now?" I asked.

"I have a daughter."

"A daughter. And she's four months old? What's her name?"

"Isabella."

"Isabella? And I have no doubt, Maggie, that you love Isabella with all your heart, right? I mean, four months after having her, I'm sure you have no thought in your mind of killing Isabella."

"Oh, no!" Maggie exclaimed.

"No, of course not, because you're a mother and mothers love their children. You need to see yourself as a mother of this little child, too. *You are*. This baby *is* as Isabella *was,* as you carried her in the womb, as you carried her inside you."

"I just want to see for myself."

"What is it you want to see?" I asked.

"I want to see people come out of there. I want to see how they come. Once I'm there, and if I can't do it because I have a feeling that I won't be able to go through that whole place, so…"

"But Maggie, you're not going to see that. They're not going to let you see that."

"Yeah, I know. But my cousin says that people walk out after and they look like @#$%. I think I need to see that and be in that chair, and then I will say, 'I can't do it.'"

"Maggie, once you go inside, they are very convincing. They are very good at what they do. They murder for a living. As many as 50 babies a day will be murdered here, and they expect young ladies like you to come in scared and with doubts. They'll convince you that the baby in your womb is not really a baby but just a blob of tissues or a parasite and that you're going to be better off without this baby. They're going to tell you all of those things, Maggie, because they want your money. We're not out here because we want your money. We're out here because we care about you as a human being, and we care about your child. And, when God sent His Son to earth in the person of Jesus Christ, fully God and fully man and without sin, Jesus lived a perfect life that you and I can't live. He never once sinned in thought, word, or deed because He is God in the flesh. And then He voluntarily went to the cross, Maggie. He suffered and died a horrible death…"

"For us," Maggie interrupted.

"As horrible a death as these babies face in here," I continued. "And He did that, not because He had sinned, but to take upon Himself the punishment we deserved for our sins against Him. Then, He forever defeated sin and death when He rose from the grave. And Maggie, what God commands of you is the same thing He commands of me and my friend Don and all people everywhere, and that's that we repent, that we turn from these sinful thoughts, turn from these sinful actions, and turn to Jesus Christ by faith and receive Him as our Lord and our Savior. He will give us a new heart with new desires. Your life won't ever be perfect, but with Jesus Christ you'll have a future hope. You'll have the hope of one day being with Him for all eternity. And in those times when it seems very difficult to raise two children, you can lean on Him. The Bible says that for those who know Him that He never leaves them or forsakes them. All the people in the world could leave you, but He never will. He gives the kind of love to us that we can't give to each other. Maggie, you know God doesn't want you to murder this child," I said.

"I know He doesn't."

"How old are you, Maggie?"

"I'm 20," she answered. "I know God doesn't want me to do this, but I just feel I need to experience it, not experience it like going through it, but I'm still thinking about it. I just feel like I need to go inside there, and once I'm inside there, I think I'm going to seriously back out because I just, well, just feel like I need to experience it but not go through with it."

I took from my pocket a wonderful booklet published by Living Waters titled "In the Womb."[1] The booklet is a review of National Geographic's *In the Womb* video, which provides a unique look into the world of the developing child in the womb. Of course, the booklet also includes a gospel presentation written by Ray Comfort.

I opened the booklet. "Let me show you. There are no scary pictures in here. This is your child. This is your child growing inside you right now. They're not going to show you a picture like this inside."

"Can I take this inside and read it?" Maggie asked.

"Of course take it," I said. "But I urge you, Maggie, not to go. I can't stop you, obviously, and I'm doing the best I can to talk to you, but Maggie, going inside that place is one step closer to doing what you know is wrong, one step closer to doing what you already know in your heart is wrong. You already know this. God has given you a conscience, and you're scared because you know this is wrong. We're here to help. We care as much about you as we care about your baby. And if you need help with prenatal care, finding a good doctor, if you need help with baby supplies, we're here to help. We want to give to you. The people inside just want to take away."

---

[1] The "In the Womb" booklet is available for purchase on the Living Waters website: http://store.livingwaters.com/in-the-womb.html.

"Thank you. I'll go inside. I don't think I'll go through with it. I want to see. If anything, I think I will just come out again and go home."

"Well, Maggie, we'll be out here."

"I will think about that adoption thing. I'm really thinking that I won't go through with it and I will think of adoption."

"We can help with that, Maggie. We can help with that. There are a lot of resources here, Maggie," I said, pointing to the back cover of the booklet. "I put my name and my phone number on the bottom, and we're still going to be out here for a while. Maggie, I can't stress this enough. To go through with this is to murder your child and to sin against the God you know. With adoption as an option and with people who are willing to help you, Maggie, there's no reason to kill your child today. So please, let us help you."

"Okay. Thank you."

"Alright. We'll be right here. I'm praying for you right now, Maggie."

"Thank you."

Maggie entered the front door of the abortuary. Don and I immediately asked the Lord to intervene and to keep Maggie from murdering her child. But, we did not see Maggie again before we left the abortuary for the day. While we couldn't know for certain, she likely murdered her second child. Maggie, like everyone else, knew she carried in her womb a person who was as deserving of life as her four-month-old daughter Isabella. Like other women who murder their unborn children on the altar of convenience, Maggie was not a victim. She was a perpetrator of the most unthinkable violence: the murder of one's own child.

Yet there is forgiveness for Maggie's sin.

However, she must come to God on His terms, for He does not negotiate with sinners. Maggie's only hope for forgiveness is to repent, believe the gospel, and receive Jesus Christ as her Lord and Savior.

If you have had an abortion or have in any way participated in the abortion of a child, there is forgiveness for your sins through Jesus Christ. Turn to Christ. He will take your heart of stone that allowed you to agree to murder an unborn child, and He will replace it with a heart of flesh that will have the capacity to love the things God loves and hate the things God hates. You will love others more than you love yourself, because God first loved you.

Turn to Christ and live.

Section V:
Planes, Trains, and College Campuses – Evangelism Anywhere

Burt, a Broken Man

A man never lowers himself more than when he tries to lift himself up.
Charles Spurgeon

Many of the conversations I have had with strangers on the streets have been the direct result of open-air preaching. The preaching of the law of God and the cross of Christ is used by God to compel both the saved and the unsaved to engage in conversations that truly matter—conversations about eternity.

One evening, as I was preaching the gospel at the Jan Heidt Newhall Metrolink Station in Santa Clarita, I noticed a man listening. The conversation I had with this man, Burt, following my preaching is one I will always remember. So, to set the stage for the conversation, I thought it best to share the sermon I preached to those at the station before I sat down to talk to Burt.

"Good evening. My name is Tony. I'm a member of Grace Community Church in the San Fernando Valley, but I live up here in Santa Clarita. I have lived here for the last 26 years, and I'm here to bring to you this evening, before you hop on the train or go wherever you're going, the good news of the gospel of Jesus Christ. There is no better news, my friends, than salvation by the grace of God alone through faith alone in Jesus Christ alone.

"The Word of God says that there is no other name under heaven given among men by which we must be saved. That name is Jesus. My dear friends, each and every one of us will one day stand before God to give an account for our lives. And because God is good, because He is holy, righteous, and just, He will judge us according to the perfect moral standard of His Law. Now justice is an interesting thing…"

I was interrupted by Burt. He appeared disheveled and intoxicated.

"Thank the Lord!" he said. He was not flamboyant, he was not mocking the preaching, and he didn't seem to be trying to distract me from preaching or to draw attention to himself.

"God bless you, sir," I replied.

"I love you, man."

"Thank you. Thank you."

It was not the first time an intoxicated person has expressed his or her love for me. During my 20 years in law enforcement, the majority of that time working patrol, I came in contact with many people in various states of insobriety. Of those, there were several who began by expressing their love for me, only to become enraged moments later.

"I love Jesus Christ with all my heart," the man insisted.

"Good, good."

"I know God."

"Amen," I answered. It was time to get back to preaching. "Justice is an interesting thing, my friends. It seems that we all want justice so long as it applies to somebody else. It seems that none of us really want justice if it applies to us. Today I heard on the news that Adrian Peterson, one of the best running backs in football, accepted a plea agreement. He would pay a $4,000 fine. He will do 80 hours of community service. He admitted guilt to a misdemeanor when he was charged with felony cruelty to his own child."

Current events serve as compelling transitions into the preaching of the law and the gospel. Current events, especially those involving some sort of tragedy, often cause people to consider their own mortality. And what better time could there be for engaging a person in a gospel conversation than when they are thinking about life and death?

"If you follow the news, if you follow sports, you probably saw the pictures of this young boy. I believe he was only about four years old. The wounds on his legs and arms and other places on his body that, by the time the pictures were taken, were already old wounds, were still visible. The country was incensed. The sports world was incensed. The media pundits, the sports reporters on the news, they were incensed. They thought Adrian Peterson should have the book thrown at him. Many are saying he should never play football again.

"You should hear the people ranting and raving today about the plea bargain agreement that Adrian Peterson received. Everyone is saying it is a miscarriage of justice, that he should go to prison, that if it were someone other than Adrian Peterson (if it were you or me or

John Q Citizen on the streets), we would certainly find ourselves in prison. And that would be justice.

"The Word of God says in Proverbs 28:5, 'Evil men do not understand justice, but those who seek the Lord understand it completely.' When I talk to people and I ask them if when they stand before God, will they receive justice or mercy, many people say, 'Well, I'm going to receive mercy. God's going to forgive me. God is going to turn a blind eye to my sin. He is going to see the good things that I've done. He is going to look at my church attendance, and He's going to forget about my crimes against Him, and He's just going to let me into heaven.'

"Yet, when I ask them what God should do with the pedophile, well, they say, 'He should go to hell.'

"'What should God do with the child molester or the parent who abuses their child?' I ask.

"'Oh, well, that person should go to hell.'

"What should God do with the white collar criminal who has so much money he does not know what to do with it all, but he is still ripping off the average citizen, bilking them out of their money to line his own pockets? When I ask them what should God do with that man, they say, 'Oh, throw the book at him. He should go to hell.'

"Then I ask them what God should do with murderers. What should God do with men who kidnap children and murder them and bury their bodies, only to be found years later? 'Oh, well if God is just, he will get rid of them. He will send them to hell.'

"We all want justice for the other guy. We don't want justice for us. My friends, you need to understand that God's justice is perfect. It's perfect. Yes, He is going to judge the murderer who takes another life with malice aforethought, but God's standard of justice also sees murder as simply hating another human being. The Word of God says that whoever hates another person is a murderer [1 John 3:15]. In fact, the Word of God says if you so much as call another person a fool, using it as a term of derision, that you are deserving of hell [Matthew 5:21-22]. That's God's standard.

"We think that the man who cheats on his wife multiple times, well, God should throw the book at him. But, Jesus said if you even look at another person to lust after them, you've committed adultery in your heart [Matthew 5:27-30]. If you lust, you're no different than the person who has actually carried out the act.

"Again, the Word of God says, 'Evil men do not understand justice, but those who seek the Lord understand it completely' [Proverbs 28:5]. So, my friends, those who seek the Lord, those who know Jesus Christ as their Lord and their Savior, understand the justice of God because they are receiving His mercy and grace. They understand that, but for the mercy and grace of God, they would face the same punishment as the murderer, as the pedophile, as the white collar criminal. The reason: all of us have sinned, all of us have fallen short of the glory of God [Romans 3:23]. All of us have failed to live up to His perfect standard.

"Jesus said, 'You are to be perfect as your heavenly Father is perfect' [Matthew 5:48]. Now, I will be the first to admit that I cannot live up to that standard. And I think if you were honest with yourself, you would likewise say, 'I can't live up to that standard either.' Yet God, being holy, doesn't lower His standard simply because we're not able to live up to it. No sin can be in His presence. He is holy; He is righteous; He is just; He is good, and He must punish sin. He's not only going to punish the sin that we hate in other people, He's going to punish the sin that we love in ourselves, because He's holy—because he's Holy, my friends.

"This is the God before whom you will stand to give an account. And my dear friends, God has already written His Law on your heart. You already know it's wrong to lie, not because mommy and daddy taught you, but because you were created in the image of God and, as an image-bearer of God, you know the God who is true.

"You know it's wrong to hate, to murder in your heart. You know it's wrong to harbor bitterness or resentment towards another human being. You know that, not because you were taught that in school, but because you were created in the image of God and, as an image-bearer of God, you know the God who is love.

"You know it's wrong to engage in any form of sexual immorality, whether heterosexual or homosexual. You know it's wrong to surf porn sites on the computer. Ladies, you know it's wrong to read romance novels. You know it's wrong to not only commit adultery with your body, but to commit it with your mind as you are lusting after a man or woman walking down the street. You know that, not because you were taught that by your government, but because you were created in the image of God, and as His image-bearer, you know the God who is faithful.

"This is why, my friends, each and every one of us is without excuse. We will not be able to claim innocence or ignorance when we stand before God. We are without excuse, and He is going to do what is right. He is going to do what is just. He is not going to be a corrupt judge that will accept a bribe [Deuteronomy 10:17]. He's not going to accept the bribe of your religion. He's not going to accept the bribe of your good works. He's not going to accept the bribe of holding yourself up as better than the mass murderer when you hate people in your heart. No, He is going to judge righteously. He is going to judge with equity [Psalm 67:4; 75:2; 96:10; 98:9]. He's going to judge everyone the same way according to the same Law, a law to which we all fall short.

"Because He's good, He must punish that sin, and that punishment is eternity in hell. Now, many people yell and scream and say, 'That is not just!' Well, they do that because evil men do not understand justice. But, those who seek the Lord understand it completely. This God, this one God (there is only one God), who is angry with the wicked every day [Nahum 1:6], who will judge the world in righteousness [Psalm 9:8], whose wrath abides upon the ungodly [Proverbs 11:23], is also loving [John 3:16] and merciful [Titus 3:4-7] and gracious [Ephesians 2:8-9] and kind [Romans 2:4].

"God showed that great love, my friends, 2,000 years ago when God the Father sent His Son to earth in the person of Jesus Christ—fully God and fully man and without sin. Unlike you and me, my friends, He never once violated the Law of God in thought, word, or deed. He could not because He was and He is and He always will be the sinless Lamb of God who came in to take away the sins of the world. He lived a perfect life from cradle to that cross. He lived a perfect life for some 33 years that you and I cannot live for so much as 33 seconds, and then He voluntarily went to that cross. He suffered and died a horrific bloody death He did not deserve to take upon Himself the just punishment you and I rightly deserve for our sins against God, and then three days later, my friends, He forever defeated sin and death when He rose from the grave.

"Unlike Muhammad, unlike Buddha, unlike Joseph Smith, unlike Charles Taze Russell, unlike the false gods of Hinduism, Jesus Christ is alive today, and He will return at a time of the Father's choosing. What God commands of us, my friends—what He commands of me, what He commands of you, what He commands of all people everywhere—is that we repent, that we turn from our sin and by faith, and by faith alone, receive Jesus Christ as our Lord and our Savior.

"Because God is good, because He's loving and merciful and kind, He will not cast out those who humble themselves before Him, because God is opposed to the proud. Yet, He gives grace to the humble. God is opposed to the proud, but He gives grace to the humble. Those who humble themselves before the Lord, those who seek the Lord by faith, understand His justice perfectly, because they realize that that's exactly what they deserve. But God, by His love and His grace and His mercy and for His own glory, chose not to cover them in His wrath, not to sentence them to hell for all eternity. Rather, because of their faith in His Son Jesus Christ, God chose to save them, chose to justify them, to exonerate them, to put all of the punishment they deserve on His Son when He died on that cross.

"You see, my friends, that cross is where justice and mercy kissed, for only God could appease the just wrath of God, and only the perfect man, the God-Man, could take upon Himself the punishment we deserve for our sins against God. That happened at the cross. That's where justice and mercy kissed. For God the Father made Him, God the Son, who knew no sin, to become sin on our behalf so that, through Him, we might become, we might receive the righteousness of God [2 Corinthians 5:21]. That is the good news of the gospel.

"If you do not hear this message, dear friends, as a message of love—that Jesus Christ came to earth to save sinners like you and me—it is because evil men do not understand justice, and those who do not understand the justice of God cannot and will not appreciate the mercy of God. But if you humble yourself before Him, if you turn from your sin and by faith, and by faith alone, receive Jesus Christ as your Lord and Savior, you will understand His justice perfectly because you are a recipient of His grace and His mercy and His love. So turn to Christ and live, dear friends. Turn to Christ and live. And thank you for listening."

The man stood only a few feet away from me the entire time I preached. There were tears in his eyes. As soon as I finished preaching, I engaged him in conversation. He was a stocky Mexican man, and He spoke with the accent of his people.

"Thank you. My name is Burt," he said.

"I'm Tony. Nice to meet you, Burt. Do you live here in Santa Clarita?"

"Well, I'm homeless right now."

"Okay, okay."

"Now, you know what? When I pray to the Lord, it's like the devil is behind me. I be praying to the Lord and all of a sudden I get side-tracked. So, the devil is doing that to me. You know what I mean?"

"Yeah. When was the last time you ate, Burt?" I asked.

"This morning."

"Are you hungry?"

"Ah, no thanks."

"You sure?"

"Yeah."

"I'd be happy to spend some time with you and talk about it. We can walk over there to the Railroad Café and…"

"I'm good. Thank you," Burt interrupted.

"You sure?"

"I'm good. Thank you."

"Don't let pride get in the way, because I'd love to serve you. You want to sit down? You want to sit down and talk?" I asked.

"When I pray to the Lord, it seems that he's always gives me like bad vibes, and I hate that. You know what I mean? Like, so I be praying and I just like blank out and I go somewhere else. I don't understand."

"How long has this been going on, Burt?"

"For quite a while already."

"Yeah?"

"I hate that."

"So, Burt? Is Jesus Christ your Lord and your Savior?" I asked
"Yes, sir. I love Him."
"How did you come to know Him?"
"From birth."

This was the first obvious red flag in my conversation with Burt. No one is born a Christian. The apostle John wrote, "But as many as received Him, to them He gave the right to become children of God, even to those who believe in His name, who were born, not of blood nor of the will of the flesh nor of the will of man, but of God" (John 1:12-13).

"From birth?" I asked.

"Jesus is my one and only. You know what I mean? God is my one and only. You know, through him, through God, because God created him. But you know, as a user [drug addict], it seems like every time I pray to my Lord, I always like get side-tracked."

"Well, Burt, I think I can help with that a little bit, in just looking at what you just said."

"Why does that happen to me?" Burt pleaded.

"Well, part of it could be that you might have a misunderstanding of who Jesus is," I said. "God didn't create Him. Jesus is God. The Word of God says that Jesus, the Son of God, was with the Father in creation. It says that God is one God in three Persons—Father, Son, and Holy Spirit. The Triune God is eternal, one God in three Persons. Together they created everything. Jesus is not a created being. He is the Son of God who took on human flesh, came to earth, born of a virgin, lived a perfect life as God in the flesh, died a death He did not deserve, bodily rose from the grave. He is alive. He rules and reigns as He sits at the right hand of the Father, as He sits in the place of power," I explained.

"You know what?"
"Yeah?"
"I wish I could take his place."
"Yeah?"
"You know what I mean? He didn't deserve that, you know, what happened to him. I don't know if I could stand it, but I would try to, you know, do what he did."

"Well, Burt, I appreciate that thought, but that's not something you or I could ever do. The reason He took that punishment upon Himself, even though He didn't deserve it, is because sinful men like you and me couldn't do it. We can't pay the penalty for our own sin to set us free, let alone do that for the rest of mankind."

"Yeah, because he got whipped like 39 times."

"He did. Yes, He did."

"You know, I wish I could do that for him. You know, doing that in pain is a whole different thing. I would try. I would try to do it for him just to prove my love to him. I love him that much."

"Well, Burt, instead of focusing on what you *can't* do for Him, we should focus on living our lives to bring Him glory. We can only do that if we truly know Him as Lord and Savior."

"Yeah, but I'm still drinking and stuff like that. I'm homeless because the alcohol is getting between me and my family. I don't blame them for kicking me out."

"How long, how long you been out on the streets?"

"About a month."

"Just a month?" I was surprised Burt had only been on the streets for a month. Having met and talked to a lot of homeless people over the years, Burt's haggard look led me to believe he had been on the streets for much longer.

"Have you had any contact with your family?" I asked.

"No. I don't want them to know."

"Do they have any idea where you are?"

"Yeah, they know where I'm at, but that kid is following me, but I can't raise him." Burt rambled as if his mind was filled with thoughts he could not organize. His mental condition was no doubt negatively impacted by the alcoholic beverages he had consumed during the day.

"Why, why is that, Burt?"

"Because I messed up."

"Yeah? Well, we all do that. We sin in many different ways."

"Yeah," Burt agreed. "Plus, my niece, I know she cries for me. You know what I mean? Her husband had to do what he had to do, but I brought that on myself. I don't blame nobody for what happened to me."

"Burt, can you think back to a time when you truly turned from your sin and put your trust in Christ alone as your Savior?" I asked, trying to refocus our conversation. "No one is born with a relationship with Jesus. He has to call us to Himself and draw us to Himself."[1]

"Yeah. I would like for him to come into my life, but he hasn't answered my prayer. I don't know. Maybe he's mad at me, or maybe I'm not trying hard enough, because I'm still doing things I'm not supposed to do."

"Burt, this I *do* know. Salvation is the gift from God. It's not something we can work for [Ephesians 2:8-9]. It's not something we can earn by trying really hard. It's a free gift [Romans 6:23], and sometimes, because of our pride, we won't let go of that idea that we're going to show God that I can be good enough for Him. We can *never* be good enough for Him."

"I know it's hard," Burt said with resignation in his voice.

"It's not hard, Burt. It's impossible [Matthew 19:26; Mark 10:27; Luke 18:27]. It's impossible because if we want to make ourselves right with God, we have to perfect [Matthew 5:48]. We can't be perfect [Ecclesiastes 7:20]. That's why we need His Son. That's why we need a Savior, because we can't save ourselves. I don't know your heart, Burt. We just met. But, could be, Burt, that you're trying to get to Jesus on your terms—that you're trying to measure up to God. Maybe you have a lot of pride, and you're determined that you're going to clean yourself up and pull yourself together so that you can be acceptable to God. That's not how God gives salvation. He saves us and *then* He changes us. It's not that we change ourselves and then He sees us as good. He changes us.

"You see, Burt, I know I'm going to heaven, not because of who I am but *in spite* of who I am. I don't deserve it. I don't deserve His grace. I don't deserve His mercy. I don't deserve His love or His forgiveness. I don't deserve His help. It's when I came to the end of

---

[1] Since my conversation with Burt, I have preached differently about a "relationship with Jesus Christ." I no longer tell people they need to have a relationship with Jesus. I tell people that they have a relationship with Jesus, but it is broken because of their sin. What they need is to have their relationship with Jesus restored, reconciled, by the grace of God alone, through faith alone, in Jesus Christ alone.

myself and I realized that there was nothing in me that would make me pleasing to God—when I gave up that pride and I humbled myself before Him—that's when I realized salvation is a gift.

"You were probably a very hard-working man before you fell on hard times. What kind of work did you do?" I asked.

"Construction."

"That's back-breaking, hard work. When I shook your hand, it was the hand of a man who has worked for living. It was a strong hand, a manly hand, a rough hand. You have the same kind of hands (physically speaking) that Jesus probably had. He worked as a carpenter throughout his life, from His early years until towards the end of His life.

"Sometimes, Burt, we can become so proud of being hard workers that we refuse to accept the gift of salvation, just like when I tried to offer you a meal, you refused to accept the gift. Sometimes we do that with God and we say, 'I want to take your place, Jesus. I know I'm not good enough. I'm going to work really hard. I'm going to stop drinking. I'm going to do this, I'm going to do that, so that you'll accept me.' But that's not how God works, my friend. That's not how God works. God extends His love to those He draws to Himself [John 6:44]—not because we're good, but because He's good; not because we're worthy, but because His Son, Jesus Christ, is worthy to receive the reward for His suffering [Hebrews 2:9-10; Revelation 5:9-12], for His death on the cross.

"So again, I don't know your heart and I certainly don't sit as your judge, but it just sounds to me, Burt, like your pride is getting in your way. Your pride is getting in the way of you humbling yourself and going back to your family. Your pride is getting in the way of receiving the gift of a meal. Your pride is getting in the way of receiving the grace and the mercy and the love of God through faith in Jesus Christ alone. Does that make sense?"

"Yes."

"When did you have your last drink?"

"Oh, just earlier. And you know what? If I go back to my family, and I want to go back. You know what I mean? I want to get a car and get a place to stay. I want to comb my hair because my hair has never been this long…"

"Burt, I mean no disrespect, but that's pride, my friend. That's pride. I'm a proud man, too, Burt. I'm not pointing a finger at you. I struggle with pride, too. Yet, wanting to clean yourself up, cut your hair, get a car, do all that before you go to your family and say, 'Help me,' that's pride. How long have you struggled with alcohol?"

"Oh, about two years," Burt confessed.

"I have to believe your family would want you home so that they could help you. Did they kick you out or did you leave?"

"No," Burt hesitated. "Well, my niece's husband told me to get lost. Enough was enough, because I take methadone."[2]

"Okay. So, you've struggled with heroin, too?"

"Yeah, heroin. Sometimes I would be at the kitchen table and nodding off, you know? Or I would drink too much, I mean, in front of the kids. They seen all that for weeks and weeks and weeks. My niece had always told me, 'Uncle Burt, you're doing that around my kids. It doesn't look right. I don't want my kids to remember you like that.'"

"How long have you struggled with heroin?" I asked.

"All my life."

"All your life? How old are you now?"

"About 61."

"Are you married? Do you have kids?"

"Yeah, I got two grown."

"And a wife?"

"No, no."

"So my daughter wants me to come stay with her. But I can't stay with her."

---

[2] According to Addiction Center (Kayla Smith, "Methadone Addiction and Abuse," *Addiction Center: Guiding You from Rehab to Recovery*, last modified January 21, 2016, accessed on April 13, 2016, https://www.addictioncenter.com/painkillers/methadone/.): "Methadone is a synthetic opioid prescribed for moderate to severe pain. It is also commonly used to treat opiate addictions, especially addiction to heroin. Methadone acts on the same opioid receptors as morphine and heroin to stabilize patients and minimize withdrawal symptoms in the case of an addiction.

"Methadone is a federally designated Schedule II drug, meaning it has a legitimate legal use but also a high likelihood of its users developing a dependence. Other Schedule II drugs include hydrocodone and morphine."

"Why, Burt?"

"Because of…"

"Because of the pride," I interrupted.

"Yeah, but I can't."

"Do you think you stand a better chance fighting alone out here on the streets or being with your daughter who loves you?" I asked. "Burt, this is what is between you and God, my friend. Yes, using heroin is a sin. Yes, drunkenness is a sin. But Burt, the root of those sins is pride."

"Yeah, but I've been to every prison there is, except the Bay.[3] I've been to four yards.[4] I've been to the shoes.[5] You know what I mean?"

"I was a deputy sheriff for 20 years, so I know what you're talking about."

"I know what I mean. I know you know what I mean."

My conversation with Burt had reached another level. He didn't seem surprised or bothered to be talking to a retired deputy sheriff. I now knew the man in front of me was more than a homeless drunkard. If he was telling me the truth, Burt had done some serious time in prison, and he likely had connections to both street and prison gangs. Years ago, had Burt and I met on the streets, it is likely that our interaction would not have been so cordial.

---

[3] Pelican Bay State Prison is located in Crescent City, California. Built in 1989, "The Bay" houses the worst offenders in the State of California. At the time this prison was built, I was serving as a deputy sheriff/gang investigator in Los Angeles County's highest security jail, the North County Correctional Facility (NCCF). During my time at that facility, I talked to a number of inmates who were heading to "The Bay."

[4] "Four Yards" is slang for "Level IV Security" in the California Department of Corrections prison system. A Level IV facility has a secured perimeter and both internal and external armed guards, with cell block housing not directly connected to exterior facility walls. Level IV is the highest security level in the CDC prison system.

[5] "Shoe" is the slang term for a "Secured Housing Unit," which is a disciplinary unit in the California Department of Corrections prison system.

"I hear the homies[6] talking about, 'Why would you want to be with your daughter? You're still depending on her. That's not cool. You should be taking care of her.'"

"Burt, do you know what the Bible says? The Bible says that children are to honor their fathers [Exodus 20:12]."

"Really?"

"That's what the Bible says, Burt. It's fifth of the Ten Commandments. 'Honor your father and mother.' What your daughter is trying to do, at least what it sounds like to me, is that she is trying to honor her father, because she loves you. So let her, Burt. Let her love you. Let your daughter love you."

"Yeah, but that's kind of embarrassing."

"I understand that, Burt. But that's pride. That's pride, my friend. That's pride, and pride comes before destruction [Proverbs 16:18]. That's what the Bible says. It's your pride that's destroying you."

"But I don't want to hear the homies saying, 'Oh, look who you are staying with. You're staying with your daughter?'"

"It doesn't mean it always has to be that way, Burt."

"Yeah, but that's kind of embarrassing."

"So what, Burt!"

"I can't. I can't live like that."

"Isn't your love for your daughter stronger than that, Burt?" I asked. "Isn't your love for your daughter more important than your pride?"

"I would give my life for her," Burt firmly replied.

"Then do that by going to her and letting her help you, by letting her take care of you. If your love for your daughter goes beyond what you're saying with your lips, if you mean it in your heart, then give away your pride for her. You say you'd give your life for her. If that's true, then give your pride away for her and let her love you and help you, not because she pities you but because she loves you, because she's your daughter."

"You think so?"

"Yes."

---

[6] "Homies" is a slang term for fellow gang members.

"Yeah, but that's kind of embarrassing."

"More embarrassing than living on the streets?"

"Yeah, I think so. I don't know. Maybe I got my priorities all wrong."

"It sounds that way. Burt, do you think it's a coincidence that a guy who walked Level 4 yards and a retired deputy sheriff are sitting here at a train station talking about these things? Do you think this is a coincidence?"

"No," Burt replied.

"No. It was ordained by God that you and I would have this conversation. I don't know what He's going to do with all of it, but man, have a moment of sobriety and see what's going on around you right now! Jesus Christ will save you, Burt, if you turn to Him, if you set aside your pride. If you turn away from your pride and you turn to Christ, He will save you. That doesn't mean all your problems are going to go away but, Burt, He'll take your heart of stone and give you a heart of flesh, and He will love you like a son."

"That's what I want Him to do."

"Then turn to Him, Burt. You've got to let go of Burt before you can receive Christ. You've got to let go of you. Jesus said, unless a man is willing to deny himself, take up his cross and follow Me, he cannot be My disciple" (Luke 14:26-27).

"That's what he said?"

"That's what He said, my friend. That's what He said."

"Well, then I can't follow him."

"If you don't deny yourself, then no you can't follow Him. But if you deny yourself, Burt, and put all of your faith and trust in Him, then yes you can follow Him—not by your strength, not by your might, but by the power of the Holy Spirit [Zechariah 4:6] through faith in Jesus Christ. And it's not you doing it, Burt. It's Christ doing it for you. But you have to come to Him on His terms. Just like a judge doesn't negotiate with a con,[7] Jesus doesn't negotiate with sinners. A good judge, seeing you back in his courtroom for the third, fourth, fifth, or sixth time, isn't going to negotiate with you."

"No."

---

[7] "Con" is a slang term for a convict.

"That's right."

"You know what, I been to a lot of judges that know me now."

"God knows you better. He has seen everything you've ever done, but He is allowing you to walk His earth."

"Everything I've done—it's all been bad."

"Me too, Burt. The Bible says that even our good deeds are filthy rags to God [Isaiah 64:6]. God, the perfect judge, has seen everything you've done, but yet He says, 'Come to Me, Burt.' Jesus said, 'Come to Me all of you who are weary, tired, and I will give you rest' (Matthew 11:28-30). But you've got to come to Him on His terms, man!"

"I am tired," Burt mumbled with his head down.

"Then turn to Christ and live. Humble yourself before Him. And let your daughter love you the way she wants to. Does she live local?"

"No. She lives in Riverside. But first I got to go kick this methadone. I have to start Al-Anon,[8] because I can't go back to her with a habit."

"Burt, there are all kinds of people struggling with drugs down in Riverside, man. There are all kinds of places to get treatment and to get help."

"But methadone is something serious."

"I understand. Do you know what is right across the street?" I pointed across the street where a local Alcoholics/Narcotics Anonymous group regularly meets.

"Yeah."

"Have you been up there for some of the meetings?"

"Yeah."

"What you need more than meetings, my friend, is Christ."

"I know."

"You need Christ."

"So, I'm looking in the wrong direction, then?" Burt asked.

I pointed at Burt and said, "You're looking to Burt to fix everything. There is no reason for God *not* to let you keep falling until

---

[8] Al-Anon is a support organization for the family members of people struggling with alcohol and drug addiction.

you cry out to Him and say, 'I'm done. I'm done with me,' and give yourself completely to Him by faith in Christ. Turn to Christ and live, Burt—not just in this life, but forever.

"There is nothing you have done in your life, Burt, that Christ's shed blood on the cross can't forgive. There's nothing you have done that the power of the cross can't make new. The Bible says that when God forgives you through faith in His Son, He'll take your sin, all of it, and remove it as far as the east is from the west and He'll remember it no more, Burt. He'll remember it no more. That's the love of God. But to receive the love of God, you must be willing to set aside your pride.

"Sure you don't want some dinner?" I asked.

"No, thank you."

"Alright. Well, thank you for your time, Burt. I'm going to be praying for you."

"Thank you. Thank you."

"What church do you go to?" Burt asked.

"I go to Grace Community Church, down in the San Fernando Valley, but I live here in Santa Clarita. There are two really good churches that are walking distance from here." There's one down Newhall Avenue called Faith Community Church. I know the pastor. I know the people there. They are godly people. They are loving people. They love to help people.

"Another one is off of Placerita Canyon Road. The church is called Placerita Bible Church. Again, I know people who go there. They are loving people. They are kind people. They'll tell you the truth. They won't' blow smoke at you. They are not going to lie to you. They are not going to ask you for your money. But, the ball's in your court, Burt. I've told you the truth because I care about you as a human being. There was a day when I would have liked nothing better than to put you in the back seat of my patrol car."

"I know."

"But not today, Burt. I care about your soul. I don't care what you've done. I don't care who you are. I want you to receive the love and forgiveness of Christ."

"I've been trying so hard."

"Stop trying and receive Him."

"I can just do that?"

"Yes. Set aside your pride and cry out to Him. Ask for His mercy. Stop trying to clean yourself up to be right with Him, because you can't. You can't. You'll never be clean enough. But if you receive Christ, He will wash away those sins and God will no longer see you as a con walking in a Level 4 yard. He will see you as one walking with His Son in glory, through faith in Christ. Will you give that some thought?"

"Yes, I will."

Burt and I hugged each other and parted company. I don't know where Burt is today, but I hope I see him again. I hope I see him in heaven.

The Quittance of Quisha

"Christ never came to be the minister of sin. He came to save us, not in our sins, but from our sins."
Charles Spurgeon

As I did many times during more than four years serving with Living Waters, I spent part of a morning at Cerritos College in Norwalk, California. The campus of this community college was one of my favorite "fishing ponds" at the time.

Heather, a customer service representative for Living Waters, joined me on campus. She shared with me earlier in the week that she was relatively new to biblical evangelism and had been working up the courage to initiate her first spiritual conversation with a stranger. I offered to help.

As we turned into one of the college's several parking lots, I immediately noticed something different from my previous trips to the school: there weren't many cars in the lot. Then it dawned on me. Most community colleges have few classes on Fridays. We decided to give it a shot anyway. I thought the smaller campus population might be a little more comfortable for Heather on her first "fishing trip."

We made our way from the parking lot to the center of the campus. As we rounded the corner of a building, I noticed a young African American lady standing off in the distance. She didn't appear to be in a hurry to get anywhere. She looked lost in her thoughts.

"Heather, let's pray. And then we're going to talk to her," I said, pointing to the young lady.

After we prayed, we walked over to her, and I handed her a gospel tract, which she accepted with a wary look on her face.

"My name's Tony, and this is my friend, Heather. What's your name?"

"Quisha."

"Quisha, this may sound silly, but what if I told you the tract I just handed you was a billion-dollar bill and that I would give you a billion dollars for your right eye. Heather and I are medical researchers and we're looking for healthy eyes for research. Your eyes look very

212 CROSS ENCOUNTERS: A Decade of Gospel Conversations

healthy. We'll give you a billion dollars for one of your eyes. We'll also replace your eye with a glass eye that looks just like the one we removed. You just won't be able to see out of it. Would you do it?"

"No."

"Okay. What if I offered you five billion dollars for both of your eyes? You would be blind as a bat, but would be rich beyond your wildest dreams. Would you give me both of your eyes?"

"No."

"Why not?"

"Because without my eyes I wouldn't be able to see my one-year-old son."

"So, your eyes are precious to you?"

"Yes."

"Then let me ask you this. It's been said that the eyes are the window to the soul. If your eyes are precious to you, shouldn't your soul that looks out of the windows of your eyes be even more precious to you?"

"I guess so."

"Quisha, what do you think happens to someone when they die?"

"I hope they go to heaven."

"And what do you think a person must do to go to heaven?"

"Do good," she said with some uncertainty in her voice.

"Are you a good person, Quisha?"

"Yes. I think so. I try to be." Quisha answered the question with very little confidence.

"May I ask you a few questions to see if you are, in fact, a good person?"

"Okay." A curious smile appeared on her face.

I took Quisha through several of the Ten Commandments. She admitted to being a lying, thieving, blasphemous adulterer at heart.

"Quisha, does that sound like the definition of a good person?"

She shook her head.

"Think of it this way. Let's say that after meeting me and Heather, you invite us to your home for dinner. When we walk in the door, your family asks you who we are. And you introduce me this way, 'This is Tony. He's a lying, thieving, blasphemous adulterer at heart. But other than that, he's a pretty good guy.' Would your family think I'm a good person?"

"No."

"That's right. In fact, they would probably ask you why you brought someone like me to your house."

Quisha smiled and nodded her head.

"So, if you were to die and stand before God, based on what you admitted about yourself, do you think He would find you innocent or guilty of breaking His Law?"

"I guess I would be guilty."

"You guess?"

"I would be guilty."

"And if God were to find you guilty, would you go to heaven or hell?"

"Heaven?" she hesitantly replied.

"I'm sure that's where you would like to go. But what should God do with you?"

"Send me to hell. But I would ask for forgiveness."

"Quisha, let's say you were in Walmart one day with your little son. You're a good mom, very careful and attentive. But, for whatever reason, you turn away your attention for just a moment. And during that brief moment, someone kidnaps your child."

Quisha's eyes widened and her breathing became heavier; I could tell that her pulse was quickening.

"The man who kidnapped your son is caught before he could harm him. Your son is okay." I said that to try to help her calm down so she could focus on what I was saying.

"The case goes to trial. He is found guilty by the jury. It's the day of sentencing. You, your family, and your friends are in the courtroom. The man who kidnapped your precious son is standing before the judge awaiting his sentence. The man looks at the judge and says, 'Your honor, I am sorry that I kidnapped that little boy. I know it was wrong. So, since I said I was sorry, I think you should let me go.' The judge looks at the man for a moment and smiles. 'Well, since you're sorry, you're free to go.' Quisha, what would you and your family expect from the judge?"

"Justice."

"That's right. A good judge will not let a guilty criminal go just because the criminal apologizes and asks to be let go. A good judge will punish lawbreakers, right?"

"Yes."

"Well, God's standard is much higher than any human court. God's standard is perfection. Because God is good, He must punish sin. He cannot let us go simply on the basis of us asking to be let go. Does that make sense?"

"Yes it does."

"So, does it concern you that if God finds you guilty of breaking His Law He will send you to hell as the just punishment for your sins against Him?"

"Yes it does."

"Do you know what God did to make the way for you not to spend eternity in hell?"

"Jesus died on the cross."

"That's right. But you know what, Quisha? Many people believe what you just said. And like you, when I ask that question, most people give the same answer with about as much conviction and passion as when they order a hamburger from a fast food restaurant." So, I took Quisha back to the courtroom. This time, however, she was the person who broke the law, with a stranger entering the courtroom and paying her fine. "The judge turns to you and tells you that you are free to go, not on the basis of anything you did, not on the basis of your goodness, but on the basis of someone else paying your fine. Would that be good news?"

"Yes."

"What would you think of the stranger who came into the courtroom to pay your fine?"

"I would love that person and want to follow him the rest of my life."

"Interesting that you would answer that way, because that's exactly what God did." I don't know if Quisha blinked or moved a muscle as I shared the gospel of God's amazing grace with her. "God sent His Son to earth in the person of Jesus Christ. He was fully God and fully Man. He lived a sinless, perfect life. He died a horrible bloody death on the cross in order to take upon Himself the punishment you deserve for breaking God's Law. Three days later He rose from the dead and forever defeated death.

"But it's not enough to simply believe the truths about Jesus in your head. You must believe in your heart, to the point that you want to repent. That means to turn away from your sins. You must repent and put your trust in Jesus Christ alone for your salvation. There is nothing you can do to save yourself. None of us are good, according to God's standard. You cannot earn or deserve heaven. If you turn from your sin and receive Jesus Christ as your Lord and Savior, when you die and stand before Him, instead of receiving what you deserve for breaking His Law, which is eternity in hell, you will receive what you don't deserve, which is grace and mercy and the free gift of everlasting life with Him. Does that make sense?"

"Yes."

"Quisha, there's one statistic that no one can avoid. Ten out of ten people die."

"I know. Four people who were close to me have died recently."

"Then you know from experience what I'm telling you is true. The time to get right with God is not when you are standing before Him as a guilty criminal waiting to be judged. It will be too late, then. The Bible says today is the day of salvation [2 Corinthians 6:2]. Quisha, do you believe that what I am telling you is true?"

"Yes."

"Is there any reason why you wouldn't, right now, turn from your sin and receive Jesus Christ as your Lord and Savior?"

Tears immediately began to stream down Quisha's cheeks.

"Why the tears? Are you thinking about the people close to you who have died, or are you thinking about yourself?"

"Both, but more about me."

"Is there anything keeping you from repenting of your sin and receiving Jesus Christ as your Lord and Savior?"

"No."

"Would you like to receive forgiveness for your sins and the free gift of eternal life?"

"Yes."

I motioned toward a nearby bench and asked Quisha if the three of us could sit down. She agreed. I spent a little more time reiterating the gospel to make sure Quisha understood everything I shared with her. It was clear to me that she did. I also wanted to be sure, to the extent that I was able in my fallibility, that I was seeing not simply emotion, but the Holy Spirit working on the heart of this young woman. I believe it was the latter.

I encouraged Quisha to cry out to God, ask Him for His forgiveness, and ask Him to be her Lord and Savior. The three of us bowed our heads. Instantly, Quisha was undone. She wept so bitterly that her words were almost unintelligible, but Heather and I understood enough of what she was praying to soon be in tears ourselves. Quisha cried out to God in a way that I have not often seen. She asked Him for forgiveness of her sin. She begged Him to save her. She implored Him to help her be a good mother to her baby boy. She prayed and prayed—her sobs seeming to intensify with each sentence.

After what seemed like several minutes, Quisha grew quiet. Then I prayed for her. Heather and I spent another half-hour or so encouraging and counseling her. I explained to her that if she were born again (I never declare anyone saved), she would begin to bear fruit.

"Quisha, if God has truly saved you, then you will begin to love the things that God loves, and you will begin to hate the things that God hates. You won't become a perfect person, but when you do sin you will run to God for forgiveness, just as a loving little girl runs to her loving father. You will want to spend time with Him in prayer. You will want to read and understand His Word. You will want to fellowship with other genuine followers of Christ. You will want to grow in your faith and in your love for and obedience to Him. Some of the changes in your life will be instantaneous. And yet others will take time."

I spent a few minutes sharing parts of my own testimony with Quisha to explain the sometimes instant and sometimes gradual process of sanctification. Heather wrote her phone number on the back of the gospel tract we had given Quisha. We both encouraged her to call if she had any questions, needed encouragement, or wanted help finding a good, Bible-believing, Bible-teaching church.

Heather and I said goodbye to Quisha. We walked around the campus for several minutes. At first, few words were exchanged. We were both in awe of what we had just seen God do.

I am not the least bit hesitant to say that I believe Heather and I saw a miracle. We saw the quittance of Quisha. The dictionary defines "quittance" as the "release from a debt, obligation, or penalty." We saw a young woman who was a stranger to us just an hour before her outcry of repentance and faith. We believe that God, in His sovereign grace and mercy, allowed us to watch Him move upon the heart of Quisha and usher her from darkness into light, from death into life.

The quittance of Quisha was beautiful.

It Happened for Jocelyn's Sake

How vain, as well as wicked, are all attempts to kill the gospel. Those who attempt the crime, in any fashion, will be forever still beginning, and never coming near their end. They will be disappointed in all cases, whether they would slay it with persecution, smother it with worldliness, crush it with error, starve it with neglect, poison it with misrepresentation, or drown it with infidelity. While God liveth his Word shall live.
Charles Spurgeon

I could hear David's voice, assisted by a portable amplifier, from almost a block away. It was like sweet music to my ears. It had been several months since I preached at the North Hollywood Metro Station with David and the evangelism team from Calvary Bible Church.

I pulled my cross, my box, and my backpack out of my car and made my way toward David's voice. He soon finished preaching and stepped down from the box. Aaron Block, a missionary to Mexico who was back in the States for just a couple weeks, next stepped up to preach. I stood quietly beside to Aaron with my cross, blessed to be reunited with friends.

North Hollywood has a significant Mexican and Hispanic population. Aaron heralded the gospel in Spanish. While I only understood a few words here and there, I knew the content of his message. What a blessing to hear the gospel proclaimed in another language. Although there were not many people gathered there, many of those present seem to cling to every word that came out of Aaron's mouth. Once Aaron had finished preaching, David decided to move the team down to Hollywood Boulevard. The foot traffic in the area was very light for a Saturday night, likely due to the fact that it had been a cool and rainy day.

I had previously preached on Hollywood Boulevard several months earlier. That last occasion had ended as I stood in handcuffs at the back of an LAPD patrol car. My offense: opening the Bible and reading it aloud on a public sidewalk.

At the time, the Los Angeles Police Department was increasing its efforts to rid Hollywood Boulevard of street performers and street preachers. It mattered not to the officers that they were issuing many citations unnecessarily. The officer who issued my citation in May stated as much when he assured me the ticket would likely be dismissed by the judge.

But recently, I had read a newspaper article that led me and others who conduct evangelistic efforts on the boulevard to believe that things were changing for the better. Just a week prior, a federal judge issued an injunction against LAPD, which prohibited the selective arrest of costumed performers on Hollywood Boulevard for offenses such as loitering and blocking a sidewalk, until the case could be settled in court.

We thought this temporary injunction was significant and helpful to evangelists who once frequented Hollywood Boulevard. LAPD had lumped street preachers into the same category as street performers, having erroneously cited many street preachers for loitering and blocking a sidewalk. But now, we decided to give Hollywood Boulevard a try.

We hopped on the subway and made the short trip to Hollywood Boulevard. As we exited the subway station, my senses were immediately struck by the sights, sounds, and smells unique to one of L.A.'s most famous locations. They served as welcome reminders of the many days spent on the boulevard preaching the gospel of Jesus Christ.

The paint bucket drummers and hip-hop dancers were back, showcasing their various talents to passersby. The costumed street performers were back, all vying for the attention of tourists and hoping to make a living by soliciting tips for photographs. The Hare Krishnas were back, worshiping their false god and chanting and dancing in white robes with tambourines. Everything seemed "normal" again.

We were excited. We missed our time preaching the gospel on the boulevard.

The team quickly picked a spot near the Kodak Theater. I jumped onto the box and read from Isaiah 6. I used Isaiah's cry that he was a man of unclean lips as a springboard into the law and the gospel. After calling people to repentance and faith in the Lord Jesus Christ, I stepped down. Brother Aaron had been holding my cross while I preached. I relieved him of the duty.

It was now David's turn to preach. As David flipped through his Bible, preparing to herald the gospel, I noticed two LAPD officers a short distance east of us. They were talking to a woman who was pointing in our direction. I told David that there were officers down the street. We were both confident that we would not have any problems with the officers. After all, things seemed back to "normal."

That confidence soon diminished when we were contacted by the officers. One of them quickly told me that I could not carry my cross on a public street. He said there was a city ordinance that limited wood signs, such as picket signs, to a certain size.

I respectfully asked the officer to show me the section in the code that pertained to my cross. He asked me if I wanted to speak to his sergeant. I thanked him for the offer and said that I would. Within minutes, I found myself surrounded by several officers. At one point we counted as many as 13 uniformed officers in the immediate area. About 20 minutes into our initial contact, the sergeant arrived and showed me the municipal code in question. Section 55.07 of the Los Angeles Municipal Code, entitled "Demonstration Equipment Prohibited," reads as follows:

> No Person shall carry or possess, while participating in any demonstration, rally, picket line, or public assembly, any length of lumber, wood, or wood lath, unless that object is one-fourth inch or less in thickness and two inches or less in width, or if not generally rectangular in shape, such object shall not exceed three-quarters inch in its thickest dimension. Note: Heavy staffs for carrying placards during street demonstrations have been used as weapons, and have injured officers dutifully enforcing laws relating to public assemblies. The above ordinance is directed toward preserving the safety of officers, the general public, and persons taking part in demonstrations.

I assured the sergeant of the obvious. Standing with a wooden cross and preaching the gospel was not the same as participating in a strike or a large-scale protest or rally. The sergeant admitted that the usual application of this particular law was for those types of incidents. Nevertheless, he told me that if I did not leave the boulevard with my cross I would be issued a citation under the section for prohibited demonstration equipment.

So, instead of things getting better on Hollywood Boulevard, they had gotten worse. Now, it was not only impermissible to verbally exercise one's freedom of speech, but it was also apparently prohibited to silently do the same.

David and I decided that the best course of action was to comply and move the team back to the North Hollywood Metro Station. As we made our way toward the subway station, even the costumed characters (some of whom had never appreciated our presence on the boulevard) shook their heads in disbelief.

While on the subway train, David and I talked about whether or not the Lord might have us stop trying to preach on Hollywood Boulevard. Passages of Scripture like the following came to both our minds.

> And whatever city or village you enter, inquire who is worthy in it, and stay at his house until you leave that city. As you enter the house, give it your greeting. If the house is worthy, give it your blessing of peace. But if it is not worthy, take back your blessing of peace. Whoever does not receive you, nor heed your words, as you go out of that house or that city, shake the dust off your feet. Truly I say to you, it will be more tolerable for the land of Sodom and Gomorrah in the day of judgment than for that city (Matthew 10:11-15).

> And the word of the Lord was being spread through the whole region. But the Jews incited the devout women of prominence and the leading men of the city, and instigated a persecution against Paul and Barnabas, and drove them out of their district. But they shook off the dust of their feet in protest against them and went to Iconium. And the disciples were continually filled with joy and with the Holy Spirit (Acts 13:49-52).

But when Silas and Timothy came down from Macedonia, Paul began devoting himself completely to the word, solemnly testifying to the Jews that Jesus was the Christ. But when they resisted and blasphemed, he shook out his garments and said to them, "Your blood be on your own heads! I am clean. From now on I will go to the Gentiles" (Acts 18:5-6).

When we arrived in North Hollywood, there were fewer people at the metro station than when we left for Hollywood Boulevard. David decided to preach one last time (since his preaching had been interrupted in Hollywood) before calling it a night. I stood next to David holding my cross.

I scanned the small crowd, watching their reactions to David's preaching. Some were indifferent. Others listened. One homeless man began to rant about what he thought was an improper use of the name of God. A woman sat with her face in her hands. But there was one young lady who seemed to stand out to me. She wore a necklace with a large, stone-studded, heart-shaped pendant and a black t-shirt that read "Haters Love Me."

As David continued to preach, I glanced at her from time to time. She was standing near the bus stop, but each time I looked her way she was a few inches closer than the time before. She stood facing the street, but leaning in our direction. Eventually she settled against a light pole, which seemed to provide her with some false sense of concealment. She leaned ever-so-slightly around the pole, making sure not to give up her position of concealment, yet affording her the ability to both see and hear David. Her eyes were dark and expressed something I had seen before during my days as a deputy sheriff—hurt, pain, and sorrow. She had the eyes of a victim. Whether it was neglect or some other form of abuse, I do not know. But I had seen that look before.

When David finished preaching, as is his custom, he offered those within earshot free Bibles. He stood next to his box with his arm raised high in the air, Bible in hand.

After a few moments, I turned to the young lady standing next to the pole and gently asked, "Would you like a Bible?"

She silently nodded her head. Her name was Jocelyn and she was 18 years old.

I retrieved a Gideon pocket New Testament from David, and as I handed it to her I asked her what she thought about what she heard from David.

"It was good," she said.

"Do you believe it's true?"

"Yes."

"Is there any reason why you wouldn't repent of your sin and receive Jesus Christ as your Lord and Savior?"

"No."

"Is that something you would like to do tonight?"

"Yes."

I asked David and Si (the wife of Dean, one of our team members) to join me. I explained to them that Jocelyn had heard the gospel and her desire was to repent and receive Jesus Christ as her Lord and Savior.

David and I shared the gospel with her again, calling upon her to cry out to the Lord and ask for Him to forgive her sin and grant her everlasting life. She testified that she believed the gospel, that she was worthy of God's wrath and judgment because of her sin, and that salvation was only available by and through faith in the Lord Jesus Christ. She wanted to be saved.

She said she was scared because she didn't know how to pray. We told her that prayer was simply talking to God and that God already knew what was on her heart. We assured her that if God caused her to be born again and she repented of her sin and received Jesus Christ as her Lord and Savior, He would give her a new heart, with new desires. She would love the things that God loves and hate the things that God hates. David opened his Bible and asked Jocelyn to read Isaiah 61:10 aloud.

> I will rejoice greatly in the Lord,
> My soul will exult in my God;
> For He has clothed me with garments of salvation,
> He has wrapped me with a robe of righteousness,

As a bridegroom decks himself with a garland,
And as a bride adorns herself with her jewels.

David then beautifully explained the doctrine of imputed righteousness to Jocelyn in a way she could understand. Through the sacrificial death of the Lord Jesus Christ the Christian is seen by God as if they had lived Christ's perfect life, while He saw Christ on the cross as if He had lived our sinful life. God laid upon Christ the penalty for Jocelyn's sin.

Not knowing Jocelyn's background but sensing there was some deep hurt in this young lady, I talked with her for a moment about the Father's deep and perfect love for His children. David asked Jocelyn if we could pray for her. She welcomed it, so we gathered around her and asked the Lord to extend to her the gift of eternal life only He can give.

David invited Jocelyn to join him and his family at church, offering her to pick her up if she needed a ride.

I told Jocelyn it was not by coincidence that she heard the gospel at the bus stop. I explained what happened on Hollywood Boulevard, which led us to come back to preach at the metro station.

Thirteen police officers worked to shut down the preaching of the gospel on Hollywood Boulevard, going *beneath* the call of duty to do so. However, they could not thwart the plan of God. God used what those officers intended for evil to fulfill His good purposes. It happened for Jocelyn's' sake.

Oh, the depth of the riches both of the wisdom and knowledge of God! How unsearchable are His judgments and unfathomable His ways! For who has known the mind of the Lord, or who became His counselor? Or who has first given to Him that it might be paid back to him again? For from Him and through Him and to Him are all things. To Him be the glory forever. Amen (Romans 11:33-36).

Epilogue

As explained above, I complied with the officers' order to leave the boulevard with my cross. The following Monday I contacted my friends at Alliance Defending Freedom.[1] They investigated the matter and agreed that the officers wrongly applied an ordinance written to protect protesters and officers at work actions, strikes, and large scale protests. Then ADF drafted and sent a demand letter to the Los Angeles City Attorney's Office.

Three months after that evening on Hollywood Boulevard, I received the city's response, signed by then Los Angeles City Attorney Carmen Trutanich:

> The Los Angeles City Attorney's Office is in receipt of your letter, dated March 14, 2011, written on behalf of Mr. Anthony Miano, wherein you described Mr. Miano's desire to express his religious beliefs on the public sidewalks by utilizing a large wooden cross. Specifically, your letter explains that in November 2010, officers from the Los Angeles Police Department advised Mr. Miano that he could not carry the cross, as built, upon the public sidewalk as it constituted a violation of Los Angeles Municipal Code Section 55.07.
>
> We have reviewed Section 55.07 and do not believe that a single individual displaying such an item in the manner and location you have described would trigger a violation of this Municipal Code Section.

---

[1] From the Alliance Defending Freedom website ("Who We Are," *Alliance Defending Freedom*, accessed April 22, 2016, http://www.adflegal.org/about-us.): "The morning Alliance Defending Freedom was launched, Dr. Bill Bright told a story about a little boy who was lost in a wheat field. The townspeople frantically searched for the boy, but they couldn't find him. Finally, one of the searchers suggested that they all hold hands and walk together across the field. They found the boy, but sadly, not in time to save his life. One of the searchers lamented, 'If we had only linked arms sooner...' Dr. Bright compared the town's story to the Christian community. The gathered Christian leaders—more than 30 founders of ADF— recognized that Christians, like the town, needed to unite in order to defend religious freedom before it was too late. And so, Alliance Defending Freedom was launched on January 31, 1994 to ensure that religious freedom did not share the same fate as the boy in the field."

We appreciate you bringing this matter to our attention, and have taken steps to ensure that this Municipal Code section is being enforced in a manner consistent with its purpose.

Sincerely,

Carmen A. Trutanich, City Attorney

Evangelism Tip #5:
"Hello, Officer!"
Interacting with Law Enforcement and Security

I wrote this chapter several years ago as an article to provide some practical counsel (not legal advice) to Christians and help them avoid negative contact with law enforcement during their street evangelism efforts. It's much easier for a person to talk his way into the back seat of a patrol car than it is to talk his way out of the back seat of a patrol car. The goal is to honor governing authorities (Romans 13:1-5), such as law enforcement, without compromising the proclamation of the gospel (Acts 3-5). While it is unlikely one will win an argument with a police officer on the streets, he can win the officer to his side or at least explain his position through reasonable and respectful discourse.

It is important for Christians to keep in mind that while the Declaration of Independence promises citizens "life, liberty, and the pursuit of happiness," God makes no such promises to His people in His Word. Sadly, some Christians take to the streets convinced that they must fight *with* people for "their rights" instead of fighting *for* the souls of people through the proclamation of the gospel.

What follows is merely a guide with suggestions for handling contact with law enforcement and private security. No two situations are identical. No two officers or security guards are identical. In every situation you must use the wisdom and discernment God has given you through His Holy Spirit. And use this guide only to the extent that it helps you to conduct yourself in a Christ-glorifying way.

Police v. Security – Understanding the Difference

Police (law enforcement) officers represent the government (local, county, state, or federal). Security officers represent private businesses or individuals.

Police officers enforce laws. Security officers enforce policies.

Police officers are included in the "governing authorities" mentioned in Romans 13:1-5. Civilian security officers are not.

In most jurisdictions, security officers have no more and no less authority to detain a person than a private citizen. (Check the laws of your state.)

Police powers are limited only by law and jurisdiction. Security officer powers are limited to specific private property, which may or may not be open to the public. Security officers have no more authority than a private citizen on public property, even if that public property is immediately adjacent to the private property to which the security officer is assigned.

Do Your Homework

Contact local government agencies such as parks & recreation, public works, and traffic to find out if the area in which you are going to conduct evangelism is public or private property. When open-air preaching, pick an area on public property where a crowd can gather without impeding the free flow of pedestrian and/or vehicle traffic.

Once you have found an appropriate location, familiarize yourself with local ordinances that may lawfully regulate aspects of free speech (i.e. amplification, displays, etc). Check with secular organizations that may have also used the location you are considering. Did their activities require any permits? Were their activities ever impeded by law enforcement?

Demeanor with Private Security

Know and understand any written "time, place, and manner" policy of a mall, shopping center, or other private business where you plan to evangelize.

Security officers are often young and zealous and can misunderstand the definition of "soliciting" or the application of the First Amendment to free speech on private property accessible to the public. So, be kind and respectful when you speak to them.

If you are contacted by private security and you are asked to stop distributing material or engaging people in conversation, ask if your activities are a violation of law. If a favorable resolution cannot be reached with the security officer, ask to speak to his or her supervisor. If a favorable resolution cannot be reached with the security supervisor, ask to speak to a manager of the business. If the supervisor and manager both agree with the security guard's initial assessment, ask the manager to contact the police.

Be polite, but persevere!

In most jurisdictions, private security can lawfully detain an individual if they have probable cause to believe that the detainee has committed a crime (i.e. shoplifting, burglary, etc.). On the other hand, private security cannot lawfully detain an individual for a simple violation of mall or shopping center policy.

If you elect to submit to the security officer's or manager's request to cease evangelism activities, do not return to the mall for at least 24 hours.

Demeanor, Posture, and Speech with Police Officers

A favorable outcome to contact with a police officer is less about being right and more about being wise and diplomatic. Unfortunately, many people talk their way into jail, not out of jail. Attitude is everything. Police officers, by and large, want to resolve public disturbances peacefully. In situations involving simple disturbances, an officer would prefer to resolve the situation without using force or making an arrest. To help you understand the red flags that officers look for, I've provided a simple list of do's and don'ts.

- *Do* keep your hands out of your pockets and in plain view.
- *Don't* talk with your hands, make any sudden movements, or make movements the officer may perceive as furtive.
- *Don't* ever reach into a box, pouch, or backpack without the officer's knowledge and/or permission.
- *Don't* turn your back on an officer.
- *Do* refer to police officers as "officer," and refer to deputy sheriffs as "deputy." Avoid using the term "cop" when talking to law enforcement professionals. To many officers, the word "cop" is a derogatory or disrespectful term, particularly when used by those outside the law enforcement family.
- *Don't* debate an officer in a group setting. Don't put the officer in a position where he or she has to assert his or her authority

to control a crowd or to save face in front of a crowd.

Be respectful, even if you feel that the officer is not being respectful to you. You will not win a sinful, prideful war of words with an officer, nor should you want to. Instead, submit to the officer's reasonable orders. Anyone can get arrested. It's not difficult. The smart evangelist (at least in present day America) is the one who remains out of jail evangelizing the lost.

If an officer orders you to stop preaching or distributing tracts, respectfully ask what law(s) you have violated. Use an inquisitive tone of voice, not an argumentative tone. If the officer cannot or will not cite a specific penal code or municipal code section, respectfully ask why you must stop your activities and explain to the officer that you are exercising your freedom/right to express your strongly held religious beliefs in a public place.

If the officer persists in ordering you to stop, respectfully ask to speak to the officer's supervisor for clarification, not accusation or complaint. If the officer refuses to summon his or her supervisor, then you may have to cease your activities for the time being, or you can allow the officer to arrest you without incident (1 Peter 4:14-16).

Be respectful, but persevere!

If you are unable to reach a favorable resolution at the scene, respectfully ask for the officer's name and badge number before you leave the area. These days, most officers carry business cards, so ask for one.

After the Contact

When you return home, collect your thoughts and write a detailed account of the incident. Gather the names, addresses, and phone numbers of those who were with you at the time of the incident. The following day, go to the police/sheriff station at the same time of day that the incident occurred, when the same Watch Commander or Watch Sergeant is likely to be on duty. A Watch Commander or Watch Sergeant is typically the person who has overall command of a particular shift. Ask to speak with him.

Try to obtain a positive resolution without filing a formal complaint. (Remember, your goal is to preach the gospel unmolested, not to vengefully exact a pound of flesh from the officer who tried to stop you.) If you do not reach a positive resolution with the Watch Sergeant or Watch Commander, request a meeting with either the station commander, Chief of Police, or Sheriff. If you are still unable to reach a positive resolution with the law enforcement agency, contact a reputable Christian defense organization for further assistance.

Establishing Rapport with Law Enforcement

It is better for everyone if your local law enforcement is with you rather than against you. Take time to talk to police officers or sheriff's deputies in your community. Get to know those who frequently patrol the area where you conduct your evangelism activities. If officers happen to walk by when you are open-air preaching, respectfully acknowledge them, thank them for their service, and encourage the crowd to do the same. If you are in a coffee shop or fast food restaurant, offer to pay for the officer's coffee or meal. But, do not be offended if the officer does not accept your offer, and don't press the issue. In some jurisdictions, an officer can be reprimanded for accepting a gratuity of any kind.

Tactical Considerations

Carry a digital audio recorder or video camera (or both) with you whenever you are engaged in evangelism. Most states have what is commonly referred to as a "one-party consent" law. This means that in environments where there is no expectation of privacy (i.e. most public places), the law allows for only one person in a conversation to be aware that a recording is being made, and that person can be the one making the recording. (Important: Check the laws in your state.)

Partners/Witnesses: There is a reason why Jesus sent His disciples out in pairs and in small groups. For personal safety, accountability, and support, it is good to have at least one partner with you (whenever possible) during evangelism activities.

When All Else Fails

Scripture shows that the apostles submitted to the governing authorities without compromising the proclamation of the gospel. There may come a time when you will have to choose between proclaiming the gospel and your freedom. Will you deny yourself in that instance, take up your cross, and follow Christ?

Persevere no matter what the consequences!

Isaac's Search for Forgiveness

This body loves not death, nor is it right that it should, for the law of self-preservation is stamped upon us, and a natural fear of the mortal stroke hangs over us, lest in some evil hour we should be tempted to suicide.
Charles Spurgeon

One afternoon outside the Shasta County Library in Redding, California, I was distributing gospel tracts with members of a local church. Although Redding has a population of over 90,000 people, there are few places where people publicly gather en masse. One such place is the public library.

Even in 100-degree weather, we distributed quite a few tracts and engaged a number of people in conversation. As I distributed tracts, a young man caught my attention. I would learn his name was Isaac. Isaac, with disheveled hair and black clothing, looked troubled, as if he had at some point emotionally and spiritually lost his way.

"Young man, can I ask you a question?" I asked him. "Do you know if your sins are forgiven? And that's not a judgment; it's just a question."

"Well, I ask God for forgiveness every night...if I remember to."

"My name is Tony by the way."

"Isaac."

"Good to meet you. What do you think happens to somebody when they die?"

"Well, I want to go to heaven?"

"Yeah? Okay, I do, too. But how do you think God determines that? Do you think you have to be a good person to go to heaven?"

"I was raised a Christian. From what I know, I don't really know anything, so I don't know."

"Do you think that information is important enough that you would want to know?"

"I just ask him all the time if he can let me go to heaven."

"Do you have any assurance of that? Do you believe that is going to happen? That is certainly what I want for you."

"I know if you commit suicide you go to hell, but, so, yeah, I try not to do that."

"I'm glad you don't do that."

"The commandments, I guess," Isaac blurted out.

"Keeping the commandments? You need to keep the commandments?"

"I guess. I don't know."

"Do you think you've been able to do that—not lie, not steal, not take His name in vain, not look at a woman with lust, not..."

"Well, I do little things like maybe not tell the whole, complete truth or leave something out. I try to pray about it and ask forgiveness. I don't know."

"Well, Isaac, the reality is this. I appreciate you letting me talk to you, and I appreciate the fact that you want to go to heaven. Wonderful. The reality is this: each and everyone one of us, one day, is going to stand before God. We are a part of the ultimate statistic: ten out of ten people die. It is not a scare tactic; it's simply a reality. We're all going to die someday. I am 51. I could fall out today, or I might live to 90. You might live to 110. We might both get hit by a car today walking across the street, by someone who is texting and not paying attention. When we die we are going to stand before God, and we will give an account for our life. He is going to judge us, but it's not based on how people see us. It's not even based on how we see ourselves. It's based on those commandments that He has written on our heart.

"God is holy. He created us in His image. You and I look different, and we look different than my friend Tyler there in the white T-shirt, but we are all created in the image of God. Because we are created in the image of God, we know that it is wrong to lie, because God's not a liar. We know it's wrong to steal, because God's not a thief. We know it's wrong to look with lust at a man or a woman, because God's not an adulterer. God's not a fornicator. And so when we stand before Him, if He finds us guilty of breaking those commandments—and we all have, all of us have sinned, fallen short of that standard—He's going to do what is right. He has to because He's holy.

"The punishment that God has determined for sins and all of it, whether it's a little white lie or a school shooting, is eternity in hell. Now, I certainly don't want that for you, and you apparently don't want that for yourself. So, here's what God did. Here is what God did to make it not only possible but assured that those who believe will have eternal life. He sent his Son to earth in the person of Jesus Christ, fully God, fully man, and without sin. He lived a perfect life from cradle to grave that you and I can't live. None of us are perfect, but He was because He was God in the flesh. He lived a perfect life that we can't live, and then He voluntarily went to the cross. He suffered and died a horrific, bloody death He did not deserve to take upon Himself the punishment sinner's like you and me rightly deserve for our sins against God. Then three days later, He forever defeated sin and death when He rose from the grave.

"What He requires of us, Isaac, is not simply to believe that in our head, nod our head in agreement. What He requires of us is not good works, not being religious. He doesn't want us to go to church on Sunday and live like hell Monday through Saturday. That's hypocrisy. What He commands of us is that we repent, that we not only change our mind about the truth of who God is, but we turn from our sins and by faith, and by faith alone, we receive Jesus Chris as our Lord and our Savior. We put our trust in what He did on the cross for the forgiveness of our sin. We don't put our trust in our confession.

"If you got popped[1] for something and you're standing before the judge and you confess to the crime, is the judge obligated to release you because you confessed or is that simply more evidence against you?"

"I've never really done anything bad," Isaac said somewhat defensively. "Last time I was in court it was a technicality."

"Okay. But if all they needed to convict you was a confession and you provided that confession, is the judge going to let you go? You did the crime and you confess that crime. Is that going to be evidence against you?"

"Well, he's not God. He's not going to forgive you; he's going to give you a punishment or something," Isaac said.

---

[1] "Popped" is a slang term for being placed under arrest.

"God is forgiving and God is loving, but God is also the perfect Judge."

"Oh. Yeah."

"God will not turn a blind eye to sin. God will judge everybody in righteousness according to the standard of His law, and because He's good, He has to punish sin.

"If someone hurt someone close to you—and maybe you have experienced this, I don't know—but if someone hurt someone close to you and that person got caught and he confessed to hurting your friend and the evidence was there and he was found guilty. Let's say you and your friend's family and other people who loved your friend are in the courtroom. You're expecting the judge to do what is right. You are expecting justice. So, the judge asks the man who's already confessed to hurting your friend, 'What do you have to say for yourself?'

"The guy says, 'Your honor, I'm really sorry. I think you ought to let me go.'

"The judge rubs his chin and says, 'Yeah, okay, that sounds good. You're free to go.' Would you think that's a good judge?"

"No," Isaac answered quickly.

"No. And God's standard is perfection. God is not going to let anyone go simply because he says he's sorry, because he has to follow the law. And that's what's amazing about what Jesus did on behalf of sinners!"

"Then how come all those people kill everybody else and 'oh well, he's insane,' or 'oh, let's give him three years?'" Isaac objected.

"Well, that is man doing what man does. That's not man exercising perfect justice. That's man exercising his form of justice in a fallen world. But see, we have to see God for who He is. He's perfect. He's not going to make a mistake. He's not going to err. He's not going to sin. He can't be bribed. He can't be bought."

"Yeah, I know God is… But, but half of the time higher up humans can't do anything to help good humans."

Isaac, like virtually every person whom I've engaged in gospel conversation, whether professed unbeliever or professed believer, clings to one of the greatest lies ever told, the lie that people are, by nature, good. But the contrary is true: man is evil by nature. God's Word is explicit on the subject.[2]

"Well, there is no human who is perfect," I explained to Isaac. "There was only one, and He was the God-man, Jesus Christ. He was the only one who could take upon Himself the punishment you deserve, Isaac, for your sin against God, because He knew no sin, and He sacrificed Himself. Look, think of it this way…"

"I burned a Bible once," Isaac interrupted. "I asked God to forgive me, but I mean, I don't know. I probably got punished for it by all the bad things that happened to me."

"Well, I can't answer that because I don't know the mind of God. I don't know what God does from moment to moment. I'm not God, but doing something like that God sees as blasphemy. You're basically telling God to F-off. When the time comes and you stand before God, He will find you guilty of that sin. But, if you turn from your sin and you put your trust in Christ alone, He'll see the sacrifice of Jesus' as being on your behalf, and He will accept His sacrifice instead of your punishment.

"Think of it this way. Let's say you had a particularly bad day—and I'm not saying you would ever do this—but let's say you had a particularly bad day and you needed to score some cash and you decide to break into some family's home."

Isaac gave me a look as if to say, "No way! I would never do that!"

"Okay, like I said, this is just a story," I assured Isaac. "I'm not accusing you of anything. You're not good at it. You're not a career criminal. As you are going through the house you're making all kinds of noise. You're looking for stuff and you notice pictures on the family wall, family pictures. Well, you're making so much noise, you wake up one of the kids, a little boy. He comes out to see what's going on. He sees you in the living room in the dark; he screams. When he screams,

---

[2] For an extensive list of Scripture verses regarding the Total Depravity of Man, ordered in subcategories, visit http://www.traviscarden.com/total-depravity-verse-list. This resource recommendation is not an endorsement of Travis Carden or his ministry.

you scream, and you do the first thing that comes to mind, and you pull out a gun and you shoot him."

"No, don't," Isaac objected. "I would never kill anyone."

"Isaac, I'm not saying you ever would. But just hear me out."

"I've almost killed myself over and over. If I killed myself right now, would God be really mad that I forced him to talk to me immediately? Would he forgive me for giving me the life he gave me back? I always ask him to forgive me, but would I be forgiven?" Isaac pleaded.

"I have an answer for that, if you'll just give me a couple more minutes."

Isaac was becoming upset. I tried to calm him down so he could process what I was telling him. "I have an answer for that question," I told Isaac. "I'm not going to dodge it because that's a great question. Alright, so you kill the kid in the house; you get caught; you confess to the crime. As the trial is going on, you look at the judge and you say to yourself, 'I've seen him.'"

"I've never killed anybody," Isaac again insisted.

"I know, Isaac. I know. Again, I'm not accusing you of killing anybody. This is a 'what if.' This is just a 'what if'—just a hypothetical. During the trial, you look at the judge and something in you says, 'I know him. I've seen him before,' but you can't place him.

"You're found guilty. It's a capital offense because you committed a murder while committing a burglary. As the judge is sentencing you to death, it dawns on you where you've seen him. His picture was on the wall in the house. You killed his son.

"The judge is going to do what is right. He sentences you to death for that crime. However, before they take you into the chamber to stick a needle in your arm and put you to sleep like a stray dog, the judge gets up from behind his bench. He takes off his robe of authority. He steps down and he says, 'Isaac, it would be just, it would be right for me to send you to your death for the murder of my son, but I'm going to take your place.' The judge allows himself to be led off, to be put to sleep like a stray dog, and he sets you free.

"Now, I know that's hard to get your head around, but that is a picture, Isaac, of the forgiveness you seek. That is a picture of what God did. God sent His Son to earth in the person of Jesus Christ, fully

God and fully man and without sin. When He shed His innocent blood on that cross, He was taking upon Himself the punishment that the Father would be just to hand out to you and me.

"Then why did he get his innocent son to die instead of himself?" Isaac asked.

"Because God so loved the world that He gave His only Son, that whoever believes in Him will not perish but have everlasting life."

"But that's not fair at all; God appeared as a baby."

"What's that?"

"God could have transformed himself into a baby and then…"

"You see, because we are creatures and not the Creator, it's not majority rule. He is the Creator. He has the right to do whatever He wants with His creation, and this is how He decided to reconcile sinners to Himself, by allowing His Son to take upon Himself the full weight and fury of God's wrath against sin, so that those who put their faith and their trust in Him can receive the forgiveness that they need to be reconciled to God.

"Isaac, every time you've harmed yourself, you've sinned against God. When you burned that Bible, you sinned against God. And Jesus died for sinners, Isaac. He didn't die for the religious people. He didn't die for people who thought they were righteous. He died for sinners, so that sinners could be forgiven."

"So, every time I've tried really hard to be perfect and pray and read the Bible every day, bad stuff just starts happening."

"That's because you're doing it in your strength, Isaac. You're not doing it by faith in Christ. That's what's missing. You're trying to be religious. You're trying to work your way into heaven, hoping that God will forgive you if you clean up your act. But, the Bible says it's by grace, unmerited favor, that we're saved, by grace through faith and that not of ourselves. It's a gift from God, not as a result of works, so that no man may boast.

"Look, if I give you my cheap Wal-Mart watch, what…"

"I wouldn't accept it," Isaac insisted.

"And that's pride."

"No, because I have a phone that has a watch."

"Oh, oh. Okay. This is another story. I'm not going to give you my watch." Isaac and I shared a chuckle. "But, if I *were* to give you my watch," I continued. "If I were to give you my watch, and I said, 'Isaac, I want you to have this as a gift,' and as you put my watch on, I say, 'That will be $300,' is it still a gift?"

"No."

"That's right. The Bible says the wages of sin (what we earn for our sin) is death, but the free gift of God is eternal life in Christ Jesus. Forgiveness for your sins, salvation, heaven are free gifts from God. But Isaac, you have to come to God on His terms. God doesn't negotiate with sinners.

"God has commanded you to turn from your sin and put your trust in Christ alone for the forgiveness you seek. The Bible says, 'These things have been written so that you may know that you have eternal life.' You *can* have assurance of forgiveness. You *can* have the confident hope of heaven—not because Isaac is good, not because of anything you did to earn it, but because of the goodness of God that allowed His Son to sacrifice His life on behalf of sinners. That's good news."

"So, if I had sat down and prayed the other day for forgiveness, because I almost died, or maybe I almost fainted, but would I've gone to heaven?"

"If you do not know Jesus Christ as your Lord and your Savior, it doesn't matter how much you've prayed for forgiveness, you will not be forgiven. But, if you know Jesus Christ as your Lord and your Savior, it doesn't matter how much you've done, Isaac, you will be forgiven.

"Now, that doesn't mean Isaac can just go about living his life with reckless abandon and live like hell. If God changes you from the inside, if He takes your heart of stone and He gives you a heart of flesh, if He causes you literally to be born again—born from above—you're going to begin to love the things that God loves, and you're going to begin to hate the things that God hates. When you do mess up, when you do sin (and you will, we all do) you'll no longer presume upon God's forgiveness as if it's something He should give you because you asked for forgiveness. You'll have assurance of the forgiveness because of what Jesus did on the cross for sinners like you and me.

"So again, the answer is, if the last time you hurt yourself and you asked for forgiveness but you did not know Jesus Christ as your Lord and your Savior, your prayers bounced off the heavens, because God says He does not hear the prayers of the wicked. But the prayers of His children, of those who He has adopted by faith in His son in Jesus Christ, He hears and He answers perfectly according to His will. So, Isaac, is there anything that would keep you from turning from your sin and putting your trust in Christ alone for your salvation?"

"No."

"Then do that, my friend. Do that. Do that. Trust Him. Put your trust and your faith in Christ alone for your forgiveness. He will hear your prayer. He will forgive your sin and you will spend eternity with Him in heaven, not because you're good, but because of the goodness of the God that has saved you. That's good news. Alright?"

"Okay. Thank you."

"I don't know if you ever go down to the mission, but I'm going to be speaking there tonight. So if you're there, I'd love to shake your hand again."

"Okay."

"Do you have a Bible?"

"Yeah."

"Okay. God bless you, Isaac. Have a good day."

I didn't see Isaac that night at the mission. He was not among the 100 or more people to whom I had the privilege of preaching the gospel. But, I hope I will one day see Isaac in heaven.

Discipleship at 30,000'

Did the apostles preach the sacrifice of Christ?—the devil's apostles preached the sacrifice of the mass. Did the saints uplift the cross?—the devil's servants upheld the crucifix. Did God's ministers speak of Jesus as the one infallible Head of the Church?—the devil's servants proclaimed the false priest of Rome as standing in the self-same place. Romanism is a most ingenious imitation of the gospel: it is the magicians "doing so with their enchantments."
Charles Spurgeon

The five of us climbed out of the car—five grown men exiting a compact car like coiled snakes leaping from a trick can. The rest of our team drove up in a second car, and then it was time to say our goodbyes. The JeremiahCry Ministries "No Hope in the Pope" outreach[1] was finished. Brian Ingalls said he hoped the Lord would provide us with additional ministry opportunities as Pastor Chuck O'Neal and I traveled to our respective homes. After hugs and well wishes all around, Pastor Chuck and I made our way up the steps and into the Egloff family's home.

James, Christine, and their three lovely daughters were our hosts during our time in Philadelphia. Each night after an extremely long day of ministry, we walked into the Egloffs' home to see their beaming faces. Each night they eagerly waited, with genuine excitement and anticipation, to hear our stories from the streets. This wonderful Christian family firmly, hospitably, and lovingly held the rope for us as we climbed deep into the well of Roman Catholic idolatry with the message of freedom in Christ.

---

[1] The "No Hope in the Pope" outreach took place in Philadelphia, Pennsylvania in October 2015. Pope Francis was in Philadelphia, wrapping up his tour of the East Coast. More than one million Roman Catholics descended upon the city to pay homage to the pontiff. I joined more than a dozen fellow evangelists in bringing the gospel to the throngs of people gathered in the city. We accomplished this through several days of open-air preaching, gospel tract distribution, and one-on-one gospel conversations.

The next morning, James Egloff drove Pastor Chuck and me to Philadelphia International Airport. As providence would have it, our flights were scheduled to leave at about the same time from the same terminal, only a few gates apart. The airport was surprisingly quiet considering the fact that a million people had traveled to Philadelphia to catch a glimpse of Pope Francis. We quickly made it through check-in and security, which afforded us some extra time for fellowship.

Pastor Chuck and I enjoyed a truly edifying time of mutual counsel and exhortation over authentic Philly Cheese Steak sandwiches. Few brothers in Christ are as close and dear to me as Pastor Chuck O'Neal. Years of shoulder-to-shoulder defense and communication of the gospel, in addition to our mutual love for Christ and shared indwelling of the Holy Spirit, have knit us together by a cord of three strands (Ecclesiastes 4:12). By God's continued grace, it will never be broken.

I boarded my crowded flight and made my way to my seat. Finding myself in the middle of Row 8, I sat down and started to settle in for my six-hour flight home. To my right sat a businessman named Jim. He was traveling to Los Angeles from his home outside Philadelphia.

Jim soon took notice of the shirt I was wearing, from Johan Henao's Wrath and Grace Clothing line. It was black with four words in large white letters across the front: "EVERY KNEE SHALL BOW."

"I like your shirt," Jim said.

"Thanks."

"Did you get that in Philly, or did you bring it from home?"

"I brought it from home."

"Were you in Philly for the festivities?"

"Yes. I came with a group of men to preach the gospel on the streets."

"Oh."

As I expected, after I answered Jim's last question there was a time of silence between us. I thought, with a level of certainty, that our conversation had ended and would not likely restart during the remainder of our flight. Surely, Jim was now thinking, "Oh, great. I'm stuck sitting next to a Christian, and not only a Christian, but a fanatical Christian—a crazy street preacher."

"So, how was your message received?" Jim asked.

Surprised that Jim wanted to continue the conversation, I answered, "I guess I would describe the response as similar to what the Apostle Paul experienced in Athens. 'Now when they heard of the resurrection of the dead, some mocked. But others said, "We will hear you again about this." So Paul went out from their midst. But some men joined him and believed'" (Acts 17:32-34).

"Oh, were there some there who didn't agree with the pope's message?" Jim asked. He thought I had traveled to Philadelphia to celebrate the pope's visit to America and that my preaching would be something Roman Catholics would affirm.

"Yes. I am one of those who disagree with the pope's message. You see, I don't believe the pope's message agrees with the Bible, with the true gospel."

"That's interesting," Jim said. "I thought his message is a positive one. Isn't his message about feeding the poor and looking out for people who are hurting?"

"Yes, it is."

"I thought his mission is to bring people back to the church? Isn't he saying that for a long time people have been pushed away from Jesus because the church is seen as a list of 'don'ts'—what people aren't supposed to do, instead of what people are supposed to do?"

"I understand," I said. "But there is a fundamental problem with all of that."

"Really? What's that?" Jim's tone was inquisitive, not argumentative.

"The Roman Catholic Church and the pope, the leader of the religion, believe and teach a gospel that is different from the one in the Bible. Roman Catholicism teaches that salvation comes by the grace of God through faith in Jesus. But it does not teach, as the Bible teaches, that salvation is by the grace of God alone, through faith alone, in Jesus Christ alone. Rather, Roman Catholicism teaches that the believer must do good works, in addition to having faith in Jesus, or be at risk of losing the grace of God in his life. Sadly, the Roman Catholic has no assurance of salvation. The Apostle Paul wrote to the Galatians that if anyone, whether a man or an angel from heaven, brings a different gospel than the gospel the Bible teaches, then they are anathema—accursed [Galatians 1:6-10]. The gospel of the Roman Catholic Church is an accursed gospel."

"Hmm," Jim pondered. "My wife and I recently became Christians. We joined a Pentecostal church. We're still learning what 'Pentecostal' means. I'm not trying to argue," he continued, "but doesn't the Bible say it's wrong to judge?"

Sadly, one of the first things Jim had learned as a new Christian was the commonly held, albeit wrong interpretation of Matthew 7:1-5.

"Matthew 7:1, the verse to which you are referring, doesn't teach that Christians should never judge," I explained. "Rather, it teaches that Christians should not be hypocritical in their judgments. I should not harshly judge you for a sin you are committing when I am committing the same sin."

"Ah. I understand."

"The Bible actually teaches that Christians should judge, but with right judgment. John 7:24 says, 'Do not judge by appearances, but judge with right judgment.' Let me explain it this way," I continued. "You said you have small children?"

"Yes, three," Jim confirmed.

"What would you do if you saw one of your children reaching for a hot stove top? Would you judge the behavior as wrong?"

"Yes, I would," Jim answered.

"Would you correct your child, even firmly if necessary?"

"Yes."

"Would it be unloving and inappropriately judgmental of you to correct your child?"

"No."

"That's right. In fact, it would be unloving if you didn't tell your child not to touch the stove top and, if necessary, physically pull your child away from the stove."

"I see now what you mean. That's a good analogy. That helped a lot," Jim said.

"Sometimes the most loving thing we can do for another human being is point out their error and plead with them to turn from it."

"That's true." Jim paused to think for a moment. "So, does the pope not believe in Jesus?"

"I don't believe he does. In order to be pope, he has to believe what the Roman Catholic Church teaches. He has to believe he is the Vicar of Christ, the Holy See, Christ's representative on earth. Did you happen to see the pope's speech before Congress?" I asked.

"No."

"He mentioned Gandhi, Martin Luther King, Abraham Lincoln, and a Catholic mystic named Thomas Merton multiple times. He talked about global warming, strife in the Middle East, and Syrian refugees. But, he did not once mention Jesus. If he was really Jesus' representative on earth, you would think he would mention the One he is supposed to represent at least once."

"You would think."

"Can I show you what the Roman Catholic Church teaches about the papacy?" I asked.

"Sure."

Across the aisle and one row in front of us sat two Roman Catholic priests. The one who sat in the aisle seat was the older of the two. I had glanced at him several times as I talked to Jim, looking for body language that might indicate he was eavesdropping on our conversation. I wanted him to eavesdrop. I made sure to speak loud enough so that Jim could clearly hear me over the engine noise, which meant others in close proximity could hear me as well.

When I asked Jim if he wanted to see what the Roman Catholic Church believes about the papacy, the Roman Catholic priest lowered the newspaper he had been reading to his lap. He tilted his chin slightly upward and stared straight ahead. He was listening; I was sure of it.

As I turned to the front of my Bible where I have several pages set aside for note-taking, I once again thanked God for His grace and sovereignty. The notes I was about to share with Jim were taken from a powerful sermon that Pastor Don Green[2] had preached about the papacy.

First, with Jim looking on, I read several excerpts from the Catechism of the Roman Catholic Church (CCC) and the First Vatican Council (FVC) regarding the papacy. The excerpts included:

1. The belief that there is no salvation outside the Roman Catholic Church (CCC, 846).
2. The belief that the pope has "full, supreme, and universal power of the whole church" (CCC, 882).
3. The belief that the apostle Peter is the "rock" upon whom Christ built the Church (CCC, 881).
4. The belief that the papacy traces back to the Apostle Peter (CCC, 936).
5. The belief that the pope has "world-wide primacy" over all Christians (FVC, Chap. 3, Par. 1).
6. The belief that a person is forever accursed who denies the supreme authority of the pope (FVC, Chap. 3, Par. 9).
7. The belief that the pope is infallible when he speaks ex cathedra about all things regarding faith and morals, and anyone who denies papal infallibility is forever accursed (FVC, Chap. 4, Par. 9).

Jim was surprised, even a bit stunned by the information he had just received. Even as a relatively new believer, the error of the Roman Catholic Church regarding the papacy was obvious to him.

"Would you like to see what the Bible actually says about Peter and this idea of a papacy?" I asked Jim.

"Sure."

I turned in my Bible to the passage of Scripture the Roman Catholic Church considers the cornerstone of the doctrine of the papacy: Matthew 16:13-20. With Jim following along, I read the passage aloud.

---

[2] Don Green is the pastor of Truth Community Church (Cincinnati, Ohio). "Why Are We 'Protestants'?, #1 (We Reject the Papacy)," *Truth Community Church*, last modified March 14, 2013, accessed April 22, 2016, http://www.truthcommunitychurch.org/sermons/sermon/why-are-we-protestants-1-we-reject-the-papacy.

"Now when Jesus came into the district of Caesarea Philippi, He asked his disciples, 'Who do people say that the Son of Man is?' And they said, 'Some say John the Baptist, others say Elijah, and others Jeremiah or one of the prophets.' He said to them, 'But who do you say that I am?' Simon Peter replied, 'You are the Christ, the Son of the living God.' And Jesus answered him, 'Blessed are you, Simon Bar-Jonah! For flesh and blood has not revealed this to you, but my Father who is in heaven. And I tell you, you are Peter, and on this rock I will build my church, and the gates of hell shall not prevail against it. I will give you the keys of the kingdom of heaven, and whatever you bind on earth shall be bound in heaven, and whatever you loose on earth shall be loosed in heaven.' Then He strictly charged the disciples to tell no one that he was the Christ."

Then, I turned back to my pages of notes from Pastor Don's sermon to explain what the Bible actually teaches about the apostle Peter. The New Testament leaves no doubt that Peter was not the first "Bishop of Rome," was therefore not the first pope, and would reject the papacy if he were alive today.

I walked Jim through my notes, showing him that the context of Matthew 16:13-20 does not allow for the Roman Catholic notion that Peter was "the rock" upon whom Christ would build His Church. Jesus Christ is the Rock. In the passage, Jesus declares that He is the Rock, not Peter. He tells Peter that his confession, "You are the Christ, the Son of the Living God," was the confession upon which He would build His Church.

I took Jim to several passages of Scripture that leave no doubt about Jesus Christ's position as the Lord God Almighty and the only Rock (1 Samuel 2:2; Psalm 18:31; Isaiah 44:8b; 1 Corinthians 10:4). I showed Jim what Peter said about himself and how he acknowledged Jesus as the Rock (1 Peter 2:8), never exerting any authority over the Bride of Christ that resembled the unholy authority exerted by the papacy (Acts 15:1-29; 1 Peter 5:1-3).

I then took Jim to several of passages of Scripture that demonstrate Peter's sinful nature. Just like us and just like every pope, Peter's character, including his actions and speech regarding matters of faith (apart from the two Holy Spirit-inspired letters we have from

Peter in the New Testament), was fallible (Matthew 16:23; 26:36-46, 69-75; Galatians 2:11).

Lastly, I showed Jim an important piece of biblical, historical data that destroys the notion that Peter was the first Bishop of Rome. Peter, whose primary mission was to the Jews and not to the Gentiles (Galatians 2:7), was not the leader of the church in Rome. Paul writes his extraordinary letter to the church in Rome, the letter many Christians today refer to as the "Constitution of the Christian Faith." At the end of the letter (Romans 16), Paul mentions 25 people in the church by name. One person Paul does not mention is Peter. Had Peter been the leader of the church in Rome, it would have been the height of impropriety and disrespect for Paul to not personally greet Peter, an apostle, in his letter to the church.

Jim told me that while he wanted to continue talking and, as he put it, was "appreciative of what I was teaching him," he had an online meeting for which he needed to prepare. I asked Jim for just another minute or two of his time. He agreed with a smile. So, I turned in my Bible to Colossians 1 and again read aloud while moving my index finger across the page:

"He is the image of the invisible God, the firstborn of all creation. For by him all things were created, in heaven and on earth, visible and invisible, whether thrones or dominions or rulers or authorities—all things were created through him and for him. And he is before all things, and in him all things hold together. And he is the head of the body, the church. He is the beginning, the firstborn from the dead, that in everything he might be preeminent. For in him all the fullness of God was pleased to dwell, and through him to reconcile to himself all things, whether on earth or in heaven, making peace by the blood of his cross" (Colossians 1:15-20).

For the benefit of the eavesdropping priest, I think I may have read the passage with a little extra volume, and I'm sure I read it with more passion (I usually do when I read this passage in the open air). I wanted to leave no doubt whatsoever that Jesus Christ, not Peter or any member of the false Roman Catholic priesthood, is the head of His Body, the Church. Jesus Christ is the Perfect Prophet, Great High Priest, and Sovereign King!

Just as Jesus never descends from His throne to assume a cracker or a cup of wine in Roman Catholicism's blasphemous mass, so too no man (whether priest or parishioner) ever ascends from his pitiful human existence to assume the place and authority of Christ on earth. I wanted Jim to know exactly where he should stand as a Christian. I wanted the priest to know exactly where he stood as an idolater and to understand that I knew his papal house of cards (all Jokers) was built upon a weak, crumbling, sandy foundation of human tradition and sin.

"Thank you for sharing all this with me. You've taught me a lot," Jim said.

"My pleasure."

Jim pulled down his food tray, opened his laptop, and went to work.

I, on the other hand, closed my eyes and worshiped. I thanked God for His amazing providence. The Holy Spirit, I believe, pointed me to Pastor Don Green's sermon. He compelled me to take good notes and then motivated me to take that same message to the streets of Philadelphia. He allowed me to preach the message to an untold number of lost Roman Catholics and lost people of other stripes. Yet, as God often does, He surprised me. I was confident that taking Pastor Green's sermon to Broad Street, Philadelphia was God's will. I was content with that. But God's plan was better than mine. His ways and His thoughts are all higher than my own.

I worshiped in seat 8B, thanking my great God and King for allowing me to take what I had learned from Pastor Green and use it to disciple Jim. I thanked God that members of an unholy priesthood were sitting nearby, close enough to hear what was said.

What a testimony of God's sovereign grace! He allowed me to communicate the truths about Jesus, Peter, the Church, and salvation to a new believer and an eavesdropping Roman Catholic priest. Others likely heard as well. Wouldn't it be amazing if the Lord saved one or more of the other people who heard the proclamation of the gospel through a time of discipleship at 30,000 feet? I pray the Lord would do so for His glory.

Lost Between Catholicism and Christianity

One of my favorite places to engage people in conversation is on college and university campuses. College-age young adults find themselves in an extraordinarily exciting, challenging, and stressful time of life. They have their whole lives ahead of them, and they know it. But sometimes it's difficult for them to see the forest for the trees. Many find themselves working harder than anything close to what they've experienced in the past. Academic standards make high school seem like kindergarten. Many students who were considered "kids" just a few months ago are now away from home and maybe holding down a job for the first time.

Add to all of this the constant pressures to conform to new social and philosophical structures and perform in the classroom in order to keep up with an increasingly competitive academic environment. It's not unusual to find a student sitting under a tree staring off into space. These are the students with whom I like to speak. In most cases, they are already deep in thought. So, I approach them, introduce myself and invite them to think even more deeply—maybe in ways they have never thought before.

Take for example a conversation I had with a young man on the campus of California State University Northridge (CSUN).

"Hi. I'm Tony." I introduced myself with an extended hand.

"Keith."

Like many students, Keith was a bit wary. He had a look on his face that said, *"Who is this old guy and what does he want?"*

"Nice to meet you, Keith. Is this your first year here?

"Yeah."

"What are you studying?" I asked.

"Social work."

"What do you hope to do?"

"I hope to be a social worker?"

"That's good work to be in. What drew you to that?"

"Well, I just have this idea of helping people."

"What high school did you go to? Did you attend locally?"

"Van Nuys High."

"This is my friend, Steven." Steven, who also attended CSUN, was a friend who would join me from time to time to evangelize his fellow students.

"Hi, Keith," Steven said.

"So, do you have any spiritual beliefs, Keith?" I asked.

"I do. I'm Christian," Keith answered.

"Where do you go to church?" I asked.

"I go to a place called St. Elizabeth's."

"Where is that?"

"It's in Van Nuys."

"Is St. Elizabeth's a Roman Catholic church?"

"Yeah."

"How long, have you been going there? Have you attended all your life?"

"Not all my life but quite a while."

"So, did you basically grow up in the church? I asked.

"Yeah."

"So, in your mind, Keith, what is a Christian? I ask because a lot of people say they are Christians, but the word 'Christian' means different things to different people."

"I'm mostly a Christian Catholic, if you will. I've actually kind of stepped away from Catholicism."

"Why is that?" I asked.

"Um."

"I grew up Roman Catholic, too," I offered.

"I don't know. I just I felt like, um, well…" Keith struggled to find the words. "I actually went to a Protestant conference and I enjoyed it a lot more," Keith explained.

"What kind of conference was it?"

"It was a church conference."

"Was it about anything in particular?"

"Well, it was mostly for pastors."

"Oh really?"

"Yeah. They mostly spoke to pastors but there was one particular message that got to me and it was, wow, beautiful."

"So, Keith, based on what you believe today, what do you think happens to somebody when they die?" I asked.

"Well, there are only two places in my view: heaven and hell," Keith answered.

"I would agree with that. What do you think a person has to do to go hell?"

"Well, basically not following Jesus, the Word of God, and not really believing in God—just lack of faith and not worshipping the Lord. Things like that."

"Do you think good people go to heaven?"

"That's a good question. Define a good person."

"What would be your definition of a good person?" I asked.

"I think someone who loves and worships the Lord, someone who tries to walk that straighter path. You know what I mean? A good person is someone who tries to live a life that represents a person of God."

"Does a person have to be a good person to go to heaven?" I asked.

"I think that's a really good question. I guess I would lean toward saying yes."

"Would you say that because God is a righteous judge?"

"Yeah. And He's the only one."

"Right, of course. We can't judge, certainly."

"And, at the same time, even in our unrighteousness He still loves us. He still has love for us all. So, that's my belief. He's got love for us."

"So how do you think He reconciles that love with justice? Because God is good, He must punish sin. But He's also loving. He loves sinners. How is that reconciled?" I asked.

"I think when a person says, 'I'm tired of this life,' and they get touched by the Lord, and the Lord reveals Himself in a way that they can understand, then that's when a person can give his life over to the Lord. At times even the Lord will say, 'You're mine. You're not going to live that life anymore. You're mine.'"

"And when you say 'the Lord,' who are you referring to?"

"Jesus."

"Keith, have you ever been in a courtroom before?" I asked.

"Yes, I have. I had to do jury duty. It was for a civil case."

"Let's say you had a particularly bad day. You got caught breaking the law and you're standing before the judge, and the judge says, 'Keith, you will pay a $1,000,000 fine or spend the rest of your life in prison.' Now, as a freshman in college, I'm guessing you probably don't have a million lying around to pay your fine."

"No."

"So, the judge is going to do what's right. He's got to follow the law. He's found you guilty. You can't pay the fine, and so he's going to send you to prison for the rest of your life. But before he does that, somebody walks into the courtroom, someone you've never met. He walks up to the judge's bench, puts $1,000,000 on the judge's bench and says, 'Your Honor, I've sold everything. I've sacrificed everything. And because I love Keith, I'm going to pay his fine.'

"So, the judge looks at you and says, 'Keith, you're free to go, not because you're good and not because you're sorry (you should be sorry; you broke the law) and not because you could pay the fine. I'm going to let you go because this other person paid the fine for you. You're free to go.' Wouldn't that be good news?"

"It would be awesome," Keith answered with excitement in his voice.

"What would you think of the person who did that for you?"

"I think that person is not only good, but I'm thinking the man is a man of God, a man who believes in the Lord."

"Well, that's a picture of what God actually did," I explained. "Two thousand years ago, God the Father sent His Son to earth in the person of Jesus Christ—fully God and fully man and without sin. He lived the perfect life that you and I can't live and, about 33 years into that earthly existence, He voluntarily went to the cross. He suffered and died a horrific, bloody death He did not deserve to take upon Himself the punishment you and I rightly deserve. He literally went to the cross and shed His blood to pay a fine neither you nor I could pay.

"Three days later He forever defeated sin and death when He rose from the grave. What the Lord commands of us in response to that is to not simply believe that in our head. It's an issue of the heart. He commands us to repent (to turn from our sin) and to put our trust and our faith in Jesus Christ alone for our salvation. See, it's not on the basis of anything we do that we're forgiven. It's based entirely on

God's mercy through what His Son accomplished on the cross. It's on the basis of what Jesus did on the cross that we can be forgiven.

"The promise is this. If God causes you to be born again, He changes your heart, changes you from the inside out. As a result, you will turn from your sin and put your trust in Him alone. You will freely receive that gift and that grace and that love and that mercy—eternal life with Jesus Christ. You will receive it, not through religion, not through being a good person, but entirely through what Jesus did on the cross. Does that make sense?"

"Yes."

"Now Keith, it sounds like you're still working your way through some of these things. It sounds like you're in an intellectual transition from Catholicism to Christianity. Do you think there has yet been a time when you've truly turned from your sin and put your trust in Jesus Christ alone for your salvation—not Jesus plus Keith's ability to please God, not Jesus plus being a religious man, but in Jesus Christ alone for your salvation?

"You know, I don't think I've ever come full circle to that," Keith replied. "You know what I mean? In my mind, obviously, I've come to discover that the Lord has love for me. You know what I mean? He can see me through anything. And whenever it is that I'm not able to do something, He can, because He's capable of anything."

"But you must first belong to Him," I explained.

"Right," Keith agreed.

"God is good. God is love. There's no doubt about that. The Bible makes that so clear. 'God so loved the world that He gave His only begotten Son that whoever believes in Him will not perish but have everlasting life' [John 3:16]. In fact, Jesus said shortly before He went to the cross, 'Greater love has no one than this, that someone lay down his life for his friends' [John 15:13]. But God is also just and we must come to God on His terms, because God does not negotiate with sinners."

"Right," Keith agreed again.

"God commands us to turn from our sin and put our trust in Him alone in order to receive that grace and that mercy and love."

"Right, right."

"Is there is any reason, Keith, why you wouldn't turn from your sin and put your trust in Christ alone for your salvation?"

"I don't think there is. I want to have trust in the Lord, because I think, like I said, He's capable of anything and He can do anything. So, I mean, that's what I want in my life. You know, the Lord, I mean, to have His presence with me. I want to have that confidence, you know, that faith in Him. He's faithful."

"Even when we are faithless, He is faithful, for He cannot deny Himself [2 Timothy 2:13]," I interjected.

"Yeah, even when we lack faith, even when we're kind of like in that state of 'I don't know what am I going to do; I'm so worried and everything,' but He's there. He's going to take care of it."

"He will be there for those who love Him, for those who have been called according to His purpose. The Word of God says that He causes all things to work together for good to those who love Him, to those who are called according to His purposes, and the good that He does is seen in the very next verse. It is conforming us to the image of his Son [Romans 8:28-29]. It's doing what we can't do on our own, and that is to be more like Christ. But again, all of that is reserved for those who have turned from their sin and put their trust in Him alone—not just those who are thinking about the love of God, but those who have appropriated it by faith in Jesus Christ alone.

"So, if you don't think you've come to that point yet, and you're saying there is no reason why you wouldn't repent and receive Jesus Christ as your Lord and Savior, then I would encourage you in your own way with your own words to cry out to Him and ask Him to forgive your sin. Ask Him to be your Lord and Savior. He'll take your heart of stone and He'll give you a heart of flesh. You'll begin to love the things that God loves. You'll begin to hate the things that God hates. You'll no longer presume upon His forgiveness as if you've earned it, but you'll have the confident assurance that you will receive His forgiveness because of His grace and His mercy—not because of anything that you've done, but because of everything that Jesus did on your behalf."

"Right," Keith agreed.

"Can I give you my card? Would that be alright?" I asked.

"Sure. Yeah. I'd love it."

"Are you living down here in the Van Nuys area? I asked.

"Yep, sure do."

"If you ever have any questions about what we've been talking about, give me a call. And if you're looking for a church, a solid church, a Bible teaching church, I would like to help. I live in Santa Clarita. You're certainly welcome to come to my church. But again, I would be glad to help you find one in this area. The most important thing, Keith, is to get right with God today. Don't stand on the fence anymore. You know the truth. He's written that on your heart. I think you believe what I'm telling you is true."

"I do."

"So, turn from your sin and put your trust in Him. Alright?"

"Okay."

"God bless you, Keith."

"God bless you."

"And remember, Steven is a student here. I've had a couple daughters graduate from here, and I try to make a point to be on the campus at least once or twice a week during the semester. So, if you see me around, come say 'hi,' and if you have any questions just let me know."

"That's wonderful, man. That's really great. I think my biggest concern is just being able to get through the whole semester this semester. I haven't done full-time in a while and it gets me worried, man."

"How long you been out of high school?" I asked.

"It's been years. I actually went to a community college and just transferred here."

"Excellent. Would it be alright if we prayed for you right now?" I asked.

"Sure. Fine. Yeah, I'd love it. That's good."

I put my hand on Keith's shoulder and prayed.

"Father, there are no coincides. Lord, You are sovereign over everything. It is not a coincidence that we have met Keith today or that he has met us. Father, I thank You for his openness—the openness of his heart—and for his willingness to hear the truth. I pray, Lord, that for Keith this would go from a mere head knowledge to a changed heart. For Your own glory I ask that You would cause him to be born again, that you would bring him to repentance and faith, that he would have the assurance of salvation and never again have to worry if You are in his life.

"More important than school and career and everything else is the condition of our souls. You said, Lord Jesus, 'What does it profit a man to gain the whole world, yet he forfeits his soul, or what will a man give up in exchange for his soul.' So, Father, first and foremost, I pray before this day is out, I pray that you would save Keith and that you would adopt him as one of Your beloved children, for Your own glory.

"Lord, having been out of school for a while, I know what that's like. I know how difficult it can be to go from being a working man and living the adult life to coming back to being a student and learning how to study and organize time and cram again. Father, the older we get, the more difficult it is. But Father, we can do all things through You who gives us strength. Lord, Your Word tells us that You will never leave us or forsake us—that with whatever trial that You place in our path, You will give us the ability to endure it [1 Corinthians 10:13] by Your grace and through the power of Your Holy Spirit. So Lord, I lift up Keith's soul to You. I ask that You would redeem him for Your glory. I ask that you would bless his studies and that he would do all things for Your glory, whether it's studying or taking a test or serving as a social worker or whatever it may be, Father. May you use Keith for the rest of his life to bring Yourself glory. In Jesus' name, I pray. Amen."

"Amen. That was beautiful," Keith said. "God bless you, sir."

"God bless you. I just want to say how glad I am to meet you. I'm going to keep you in my prayers. Don't ever hesitate to contact me if I could ever be of any encouragement to you. You can't be a bother to me. You can't put me out. That's why I'm down here. I'm down here to love students and, whether saved or unsaved, share the good news with them. So, anything I can do to be an encouragement to you, whether it's here on campus or email or on the phone, you just let me know."

"Wow. Thank you so much. I really appreciate you."

"You're welcome, buddy. God bless you, Keith."

"God bless you, too."

Steven and I parted company with Keith. As we walked away, we quietly rejoiced over what we believe the Lord had just done for His glory.

Section VI:
Loving Our
Muslim Neighbors

Nargis Knows the Way

He took the payment and bore it to God—took his wounds, his rent body, his flowing blood, up to his Father's very eyes, and there he spread his wounded hands and pleaded for his people. Now here is a proof that the Christian cannot be condemned, because the blood is on the mercy-seat. It is not poured out on the ground; it is on the mercy-seat, it is on the throne; it speaks in the very ears of God, and it must of a surety prevail.
Charles Spurgeon

Fellow evangelists John, Tom, and I arrived on the campus of Cal State Northridge shortly before noon. We picked a spot well away from the "free speech" zone. The "free speech" zone on this campus is in an area where there is very little student activity. We positioned ourselves on a sloping hill in front of a shaded patio area where students gather throughout the day. The hill provided enough elevation, so standing on a box was not necessary.

John got things started with a solid open-air sermon. I immediately followed John and preached from the slope for about 45 minutes. The Lord provided plenty of hecklers, both reasonable and profane, who kept the crowd interested and engaged. When I later watched the video footage, I discovered that my presentation of the gospel was not succinct, but rather elements of the gospel were interspersed throughout the preaching. I was hit with so many questions and objections that it was a challenge to focus on the main point of my sermon. But by the time I stepped down from the hill, all of the essential elements of the gospel had been presented.

After 45 minutes in the sun (it was in the 80s, a warm day for mid-November), I walked to a shady area near the patio. I was immediately approached by a young lady who appeared to be of Middle Eastern descent. Her name was Nargis. I had seen Nargis and a friend stop to listen toward the end of my preaching.

She extended her hand to shake mine. "I am Muslim. But I want to thank you."

"Well, that's very nice of you. Thank you for the encouragement."

"I know we don't believe the same way about Jesus. I believe he is a prophet."

"I understand. I believe He is the Son of God. I believe He is God in the flesh."

"Yes. I know."

"Nargis, may I ask you a question?"

"Yes."

"Can a good prophet lie?"

"No."

"Then what do you do with what Jesus said? He said, 'I am the way, and the truth, and the life; no one comes to the Father but through Me'" (John 14:6).

I could tell that the question gave Nargis a moment of pause.

"Nargis, according to your beliefs, how does a person go to heaven?"

"Well, we believe that a person must obey the Ten Commandments and be seen by God as a good person."

"Have you been able to keep the commandments? Have you ever told a lie?"

"Of course."

"So have I. So, we've both broken that commandment. Have you ever stolen something, even if it's small or when you were younger?"

"Well, yes I have."

"So have I. So, we've both broken that commandment, too. Have you ever hated anyone?"

"Yes."

"God sees our hatred of people as murder [1 John 3:15]. Have you ever wanted something that doesn't belong to you?"

"Yes I have."

"Nargis, if going to heaven is based on your ability to keep the commandments, where does that leave you since you've already broken the commandments?"

"Well, we believe that God will see our goodness."

"But Nargis, you're not good according to God's standards. Neither am I. We've broken God's law. And only God is good. So, again I ask, where does that leave you?"

Nargis thought about it for a few moments. And then she asked the most wonderful question.

"Then what does a person have to do to go to heaven?"

"Nargis, that is a wonderful question, and I'm very glad you asked. The Bible teaches that there can be *no* forgiveness of sin without the shedding of blood. And the sacrifice God requires for sin is a perfect sacrifice. The sacrifice could not be stained by sin. That's why the sacrifice had to be fully human and fully God to satisfy God's wrath and righteous judgment against sin. Two thousand years ago, God the Father sent His Son to earth in the person of Jesus Christ— fully God and fully Man and without sin. He was so much more than a prophet. He was God in the flesh. And unlike you and me, He never once violated the Law of God in thought, word, or deed. He was perfect in every respect.

"About 30 to 33 years into that earthly existence, He voluntarily went to the cross. He suffered and died, shedding His innocent blood, taking upon Himself the punishment you and I rightly deserve for our sins against God. Then, three days later, He rose from the dead, forever defeating sin and death. He is alive today and He will return at a time of the Father's choosing. What God requires of you, Nargis, is that you repent and by faith receive Jesus Christ as your Lord and Savior."

Nargis looked into my eyes for several moments.

"Nargis, does that make sense?"

"Yes it does."

"Do you see the difference between what you believe and what I just shared with you?"

"I do."

There was another quiet moment before Nargis told me she had to get to class. I took Nargis' hand and thanked her for talking to me. I also took her friend's hand and thanked her for listening.

"It was a pleasure talking to you, Nargis."

"Thank you."

And with that, Nargis and her friend walked away.

I was filled with joy, thankful for the precious opportunity the Lord had given me to share the gospel with a sweet Muslim young lady. I rejoiced as I thought to myself, "Nargis now knows."

Making Much of the Messiah to Mohammed

[Muslims'] religion might be sustained by scimitars[1], but Christians' religion must be maintained by love.

He who religiously obeys Mahomet may yet be doing grievous moral wrong; but it is never so with the disciple of Jesus: obedience to Jesus is holiness.

This book (the Bible) is more than a book—it is the mother of books, a mine of truth, a mountain of meaning. It was an ill-advised opinion which is imputed to the [Muslims] at the destruction of the Alexandrian Library, when they argued that everything that was good in it was already in the Koran, and therefore it might well be destroyed.

I have heard that an Englishman has professed himself a [Muslim] because he is charmed by the polygamy which the Arabian prophet allows his followers. No doubt the prospect of four wives would win converts who would not be attracted by spiritual considerations. If you preach a gospel which makes allowances for human nature, and treats sin as if it were a mistake rather than a crime, you will find willing hearers.

I have made it a College exercise with our brethren. I have said—We will read a chapter of the Koran. This is the [Muslim's] holy book. A man must have a strange mind who should mistake that rubbish for the utterances of inspiration.

---

[1] A scimitar is a short, curve-bladed sword, which broadens toward the point. In times past, this was a common weapon in Arab and other eastern countries.

When [Muhammad] would charm the world into the belief that he was the prophet of God, the heaven he pictured was not at all the heaven of holiness and spirituality. His was a heaven of unbridled sensualism, where all the passions were to be enjoyed without let or hindrance for endless years. Such the heaven that sinful men would like; therefore, such the heaven that Mahomet painted for them, and promised to them.
Charles Spurgeon

Editor's Note: Mohammed's earnest curiosity and difficulty understanding English led him to ask the same questions over and over again. Due to the repetitive nature of this conversation, it has been abridged for the sake of the reader. If you are interested in watching the full-length video of this conversation on YouTube, please visit https://www.youtube.com/watch?v=ad4AdGjPfU8.

It was a warm and clear July afternoon on the corner of 2nd Street SW and 7th Avenue SW in downtown Calgary, Alberta, Canada. I was in Calgary in 2015 for the annual Calgary Stampede Outreach, which was shepherded by Fairview Baptist Church[2] and the Calgary Peacemakers[3] evangelism team. The Calgary Stampede is known as the largest annual sporting event in Canada. This outreach is one of my favorite evangelist efforts for a number of reasons, not the least of which is that one of my best friends and fellow evangelists, Kevin St. John, leads the efforts.

The aforementioned street corner is one of our favorite "fishing holes." It is close to one of the rail stations, surrounded by businesses and restaurants of all kinds, and it sees a good deal of pedestrian traffic throughout the day. The sidewalk area at the northwest corner of the intersection is very large, which allows people to stop, gather, and listen to the open-air proclamation of the gospel.

---

[2] For more information about Fairview Baptist Church (Pastor Tim Stephens), visit the church's website at http://www.fairviewbaptistchurch.ca/.

[3] For more information about the Calgary Peacemakers evangelism team, visit the group's website at http://www.calgarypeacemakers.com/.

The summer of 2015 marked the third time I had participated in the Calgary Stampede Outreach. During the first two outreaches in which I participated, a Muslim man would stand nearby, sometimes for hours, quietly listening to the preaching. Due to providence (i.e. reasons unknown to me), I had not had an opportunity during those previous outreaches to engage the man in conversation. However, during the 2015 outreach, several members of our team spoke with this Muslim man, and I was blessed to be one of them.

After I had finished preaching one of my open-air sermons, I stood close to a nearby building in order to take a break and get out of the sun. At the opposite end of the building stood the Muslim man wearing his religion's traditional male headdress, the *taqiyah*. The *taqiyah*, commonly referred to as a "skull cap," is short and brimless. Muslim men wear the *taqiyah* to publicly display their respect for Muhammad, because they believe he wore one as well. The man turned and looked in my direction. Seeing me standing alone, he made his way toward me with a bright, warm smile. He spoke with a thick Middle-Eastern accent and his eyes were dark and very expressive. His name was Mohammed.

"What is atheism?" Mohammed asked.

Atheism? Of all the questions I anticipated this man asking me, this was not one of them.

"What is atheism?" Mohammed asked again.

"What is atheism? Atheism is the denial of the existence of God." I answered.

"Again?" Mohammed asked.

Mohammed would ask this question, well, again...*and again*. I never could determine if Mohammed asked me to repeat myself because he had difficulty understanding the English language, was deeply processing what he was hearing, or a combination of both.

"Those who claim to be atheists say that there is no god," I explained.

"Oh, okay."

"Now, the Bible teaches that every human being knows that God exists, but they suppress that truth by their unrighteousness."

"Again?"

"The Bible, in Romans 1:18, says that even though man knows that God exists, he suppresses, he pushes down that truth, by his unrighteousness. Because he loves himself, and because he loves his sin, he denies that someone has created him."

"Okay." Mohammed thought for a moment. "And they know?"

"Oh, they know. Every human being knows," I said.

Mohammed then asked if atheism was a religion.

At that moment I understood why Mohammed began our conversation with such an unexpected question. He had been listening to me preach. I often explain to those within the sound of my voice that atheism is one of the fastest growing religions in the world, and now I explained to Mohammed why I believe this is so.

"Yes, because the god of atheism is the god of self. The atheist denies God and puts himself in the place of God."

"Okay, so that is a religion?"

"Yes, it is. Atheists would deny it. They would say that they are not religious, but everyone is religious. Everybody worships something or someone."

"So, who do they worship?"

"They worship themselves."

"Okay. And they are called atheists?"

"Yes."

"That is new. That is a new religion."

"Well, no. Atheists have been around for many hundreds of years. In fact, everyone who denies Jesus Christ as Lord is denying the God they know exists."

"Okay. The new, uh, the new concept, when did it start?"

"I'm not sure exactly, but it's become very popular over the last 20, 30 years. But it's been around much longer that. So long as there have been people denying Jesus Christ as Lord, there have been people trying to create gods in their own imaginations. They come in many different forms and one of them is atheism."

"But it looks like the others are religion, right? But this looks new." Mohammed continued to try to grasp what I was saying to him.

"Well, no. It's not new because those who deny Jesus Christ as Lord set up for themselves false gods to worship instead of worshiping their Creator. Can I show you something?" I asked, as I opened my Bible. "I was just sharing this earlier today."

Whether paperback, genuine leather, calf skin, or (while I don't want to encourage it; don't hate me) on a phone, every Christian should have a Bible with him wherever he goes. He should have one in his car, at his work station, in his pocket. He should be ready at any moment to draw the Sword of the Spirit from its sheath and wield it with love for God and love for people.

"Bible?" Mohammed asked as he pointed to my Bible.

"Yes, sir."

"Bible?" Mohammed asked again. Mohammed had already spent an hour or two that afternoon surrounded by Bible-carrying, gospel-preaching, people-loving Christian men who patiently answered his questions. So, I do not believe Mohammed was surprised by my Bible. I believe he wanted to make sure it was, in fact, a Bible in my hands.

"Yes, sir. Yes. In the prophet Isaiah, in chapter 44, beginning in verse six..."

Using my finger so Mohammed could follow along, I read Isaiah 44:6-8 from the English Standard translation of the Word of God. "Thus says the Lord, the King of Israel and his Redeemer, the Lord of hosts: 'I am the first and I am the last; besides me there is no god. Who is like me? Let him proclaim it. Let him declare and set it before me, since I appointed an ancient people. Let them declare what is to come, and what will happen. Fear not, nor be afraid; have I not told you from of old and declared it? And you are my witnesses! Is there a God besides me? There is no Rock; I know not any.'

"The answer is, 'no,'" I said. "'*There is no Rock; I know not any.*' That's God speaking through the prophet Isaiah. Now we come to the New Testament, in the book of Revelation, in chapter 1. And this is Jesus speaking..."

"That was Old Testament?" Mohammed said with surprise.

"Yes. That was the Old Testament. This is the New Testament," I said, pointing in my Bible to Revelation 1. "This is Jesus speaking."

"Okay," Mohammed said, looking intently at the worn page of Scripture.

Once again, I read to Mohammed. "Fear not, I am the first and the last, and the living one. I died, and behold I am alive forevermore, and I have the keys of Death and Hades" (Revelation 1:17-18).

"The God who said in the Old Testament, 'I am the first and the last,' is the same. Jesus Christ said here, 'I am the first and the last,'" I explained. "And though He experienced death ('...and the living one. I died, and behold I am alive forevermore...'), He rose from the grave. So, the God of the Old Testament, our Creator, is one and the same. Jesus Christ, God in the flesh, said the very same thing. 'I am the first and the last and the living one.' In Isaiah 44, God says, 'I am the first and the last. There is none like me.'"

"This is interesting!" Mohammed exclaimed.

"Isn't it, though?"

I was excited. There I was, more than 1,500 miles from home, talking to a Muslim man who was likely much farther from home than I was. The Lord was allowing me to convey His great and eternal truths to a man enslaved to a false religion—one that deceives as many as 1.8 billion people in the world today. I was excited that this friendly Muslim man was excited about what He just saw and heard from the Word of God.

"This was before? This was before Jesus?" Mohammed asked, referring to Isaiah 44.

"Yes. This was written 700 years before Jesus was born."

"Okay. Old Testament?"

"Old Testament. The prophet Isaiah…"

"And this is written by the Creator, right?"

"Yes. *Exactly.* 'Thus says the LORD,'" I said with emphasis.

"This is by the Creator?" Mohammed asked again.

"Yes, yes. The Lord God, *our* Creator, spoke through His prophets. He spoke through Isaiah the prophet." I read portions of Isaiah 44 and Revelation 1 again.

"This is New Testament?"

"Yes, sir."

"When it was written?" Mohammed asked again.

"There's some speculation. Some believe it was written before 70 AD. Others believe it was written about 90 AD. It was written probably about 40-50 years after Jesus rose from the grave."

"Okay." Mohammed answered in a way indicating he understood.

"Jesus came to the Apostle John in a vision."

"Oh, not in the real?" Mohammed asked.

"Well, Jesus had already ascended back to heaven. So, He appears to John in a vision. See, this? It says…" I turned back to Revelation 1 and directed Mohammed to John's account of the vision, reading verses 1-3 aloud: "The revelation of Jesus Christ, which God gave him to show to his servants the things that must soon take place. He made it known by sending his angel to his servant John, who bore witness to the word of God and to the testimony of Jesus Christ, even to all that he saw. Blessed is the one who reads aloud the words of this prophecy, and blessed are those who hear, and who keep what is written in it, for the time is near.

"So, John receives this revelation…"

"But this judgment—this judgment is the same?" Mohammed interrupted to ask.

"It's the same. Jesus said this to the prophet and to the Apostle John. God—Jesus Christ, God in the flesh—spoke in both the Old Testament and the New Testament. And this shows us, my friend, that Jesus Christ is God. The same thing God spoke to the prophets in the Old Testament, He spoke to John in this vision, through His son Jesus Christ—God in the flesh."

As I shared with Mohammed, the thought hit me, "*I'm speaking with authority.*" Of course, I knew the authority was not my own, so I worshipped the One who had given me authority, even as I spoke to Mohammed. I had my Bible in my hands. I had an unbeliever, a member of a false religion, in front of me. It was God's powerful Word that was making an impact on this man. I knew that while questions could be asked *about* the Word, no argument could be made *against* the Word. I felt no haughtiness, no superiority over Mohammed, for we were both under the authority of God's Word. I was simply and nothing more than one of the King's heralds. So, I spoke to Mohammed with confidence, but my confidence was not my own. I was confident in the truth of Scripture and the power of the Author of Scripture. I was confident in the faithfulness of God and His promise that His Word never returns to Him void.

"Okay, so this was Jesus. This was after, uh..." Mohammed said as he processed the information.

"Yes, after. After Jesus died, three days later He rose from the grave. He spent 40 days..."

"With people?" Mohammed interrupted.

"Jesus rose bodily—not just His spirit, but His body as well. He rose from the dead and He spent 40 days with His disciples teaching them and fellowshipping with them."

"With a body?"

"Yes, in body. In fact, He said to his apostle Thomas who doubted—when Thomas saw Him, Jesus said, 'Put your finger into My hands; put your finger into My side': His hands, where the nails pierced His hands, when they nailed Him to the cross; the wound in His side from where the soldier pierced His heart to see if He was dead. Jesus said, 'Put your finger here. Put your finger here.' And Thomas dropped to his knees and said this. Mohammed, he said *this*: 'My Lord and my God.' And Jesus said these words to Thomas: 'Blessed are you, Thomas, because you have seen and believe. Blessed more are those who have not seen, but yet believe.' See, salvation through Christ, my friend, is through faith—through faith in what Jesus Christ did on the cross, faith in His resurrection, faith that God the Father accepted His sacrifice as an atonement for your sins."

Then Mohammed asked the most important question of all. "What is salvation?"

A Christian witness must always be ready to explain the gospel in terms a lost person can understand. Christians, particularly in the United States, often spend so much of their time nestled deep inside the American Evangelical hamster habitat that they just assume the rest of the world understands "Christianese."

"Salvation is receiving forgiveness from our sins, being made right and justified before God through the work of Jesus Christ on the cross," I answered.

"That is, repent?" Mohammed asked.

"Right. Repentance is turning from our sin, turning from any belief that denies Jesus as God, as Lord, and by faith putting our trust in Him alone for our salvation."

"Okay. So, salvation and repentance are the same?"

"Well, repentance is a fruit of salvation. Those whom God saves through faith in Jesus Christ will repent. They will turn from their sins and put their trust in Jesus Christ alone for their salvation. And, Mohammed, it is such good news because..."

"It is not the same thing?" Mohammed interrupted.

"When God saves someone, they will repent as a result of that," I explained.

"Oh, as a result. Ah." Mohammed understood.

"Yes. And the good news, Mohammed, is that you can be brought into right relationship with your Creator. You can have assurance of the forgiveness for your sins."

Our conversation then returned to Revelation 1, as Mohammed asked me again to identify the person (the Apostle John) to whom Jesus was speaking and to confirm that Jesus was in heaven when He gave John the vision. I tried to make it very clear to Mohammed that after Jesus died on the cross He rose bodily from the grave before ascending into heaven. Qur'an-believing Muslims deny the death, burial, and resurrection of Jesus Christ:

> That they said (in boast),
> "We killed Christ Jesus
> "The Son of Mary,
> "The Messenger of Allah" –
> But they killed him not,
> Nor crucified him,
> But so it was made
> To appear to them,
> And those who differ
> Therein are full of doubts,
> With no (certain) knowledge,
> But only conjecture to follow.
> For of a surety
> They killed him not –
> Nay, Allah raised him up
> Unto Himself; and Allah
> Is Exalted in Power, Wise –

And there is none
Of the People of the Book
But must believe in him
Before his death;
And on the Day of Judgment
He will be a witness
Against them (Surah 4:157-159).[4]

---

[4] This portion of text is copied as it is written and interpreted in what is regarded as the most reliable translation of the Qur'an (Abdullah Yusuf Ali, "The Meaning of the Glorious Qurán: Text, Translation and Commentary," *Islamic Bulletin*, accessed April 22, 2016, http://www.islamicbulletin.org/free_downloads/quran/quran_yusuf_ali2.pdf.). Ali's notes on this passage are as follows:

663: "The end of the life of Jesus on earth is as much involved in mystery as his birth, and indeed the greater part of his private life, except the three main years of his ministry. It is not profitable to discuss the many doubts and conjectures among the early Christian sects and among Muslim theologians. The Orthodox Christian Churches make it a cardinal point of their doctrine that his life was taken on the Cross, that he died and was buried, that on the third day he rose in the body with his wounds intact, and walked about and conversed, and ate with his disciples, and was afterwards taken up bodily to heaven. This is necessary for the theological doctrine of blood sacrifice and vicarious atonement for sins, which is rejected by Islam. But some of the early Christian sects did not believe that Christ was killed on the Cross. The Basilidans believed that someone else was substituted for him. The Docetae held that Christ never had a real physical or natural body, but only an apparent or phantom body, and that his Crucifixion was only apparent, not real. The Marcionite Gospel (about A.D. 138) denied that Jesus was born, and merely said that he appeared in human form. The Gospel of St. Barnabas supported the theory of substitution on the Cross. The Quranic teaching is that Christ was not crucified nor killed by the Jews, notwithstanding certain apparent circumstances which produced that illusion in the minds of some of his enemies; that disputations, doubts, and conjectures on such matters are vain; and that he was taken up to Allah (see next verse and note)."

664: "There is difference of opinion as to the exact interpretation of this verse. The words are: The Jews did not kill Jesus, but Allah raised him up (rafa'u) to Himself. One school holds that Jesus did not die the usual human death, but still lives in the body in heaven, which is the generally accepted Muslim view."

665: "Before his death: Interpreters are not agreed as to the exact meaning. Those who hold that Jesus did not die refer the pronoun 'his' to Jesus. They say that

"Jesus shed His innocent blood on the cross," I said. "He was nailed to a Roman cross and He died. He was taken down from that cross and He was buried in a tomb that belonged to a rich man."

"Okay. In the ground?"

"In a tomb. They rolled a large stone in front of the tomb and then that was customary in Israel."

"And he was buried?"

"He was buried. He was wrapped in burial clothes. His body was embalmed, covered in what some think was as many as 70 pounds of spices and ointments."

"But how many days?"

"Three days."

"Okay. And then?"

"Then, in three days He rose from the grave. The stone was rolled away and the women who followed Jesus rushed to the tomb because they were going to continue to anoint His body as part of the burial process. They looked inside the tomb and all they saw were the burial clothes of Jesus. They thought the soldiers had taken him; they thought someone had stolen His body. But angels appeared to them and said, 'Why do you seek Him here? He is alive, He is risen.' Then Jesus, in bodily form, appeared to these women and said to them, 'Go tell My disciples that I have risen and I am coming to see them.' And He did. He spent 40 days with His apostles, teaching them throughout all of the Scriptures what the Word of God says about Him. Then, after 40 days, He ascended into heaven, where now He sits at the right hand of power.

"Forty to 50 years later, towards the end of the Apostle John's life, Jesus appeared to John in this vision, in this revelation. This is where we find the exact same words that God said through the prophet Isaiah. Jesus Himself speaks of Himself. Isn't that amazing?"

Jesus is still living in the body and that he will appear just before the Final Day, after the coming of the Mahdi, when the world will be purified of sin and unbelief. There will be a final death before the final Resurrection, but all will have believed before that final death. Others think that 'his' is better referred to 'none of the People of the Book', and that the emphatic form 'must believe' (la-yu' minanna) denotes more a question of duty than of fact."

"Uh, good. And He only appeared to John?"

"Well, in this particular vision, yes, after He ascended to heaven. He rose from the grave and He spent 40 days on earth; He appeared to more than 500 people. Many of them went to their death testifying that they had seen Jesus Christ, the risen Lord."

"Okay, and he had 12 disciples?"

"He had 12 original disciples. Many other people followed Jesus, but He had chosen 12 to spread the message that He lived, He died, He was buried, and He rose from the grave so that sinners like you and me can receive forgiveness for our sins through faith in Him."

"They wrote the same message?"

"We have four gospels: Matthew, Mark, Luke, John. Mark was not a disciple, but Mark was a follower. We have the book of Acts that was also written by Luke who was a physician and a part of the Apostle Paul's team. And then we have several other letters—epistles—that were written by James (Jesus' brother), written by the apostle Paul, written by the apostle John."

"No contradictions?" Mohammed asked.

"No contradictions. From, from the beginning of Genesis to the end of Revelation, through all 66 books of the Bible, the message is the same: there is one God, man has fallen, man has sinned against their Creator. God provided only one way for man to be reconciled to Him and that is through faith in his Son, God in the flesh, Jesus Christ the Lord. The good news, Mohammed, is that you can receive forgiveness. You can receive salvation, but you must come to God on His terms. And He commands all men everywhere to repent, to turn from sin, and to put their trust in Jesus Christ alone for their salvation."

"What is the difference between Old and New Testament?" Mohammed asked.

"The Old Testament was written before Jesus came to earth. The New Testament was written after Jesus came to earth and after He died on the cross and rose from the grave."

"Okay. Jewish people, they are also part of the Old Testament?"

"Well, the Jewish people are in the New Testament as well. Jesus was Jewish. All of the apostles were Jewish. Many thousands of people who first came to faith in Christ were Jewish. But then (God's grace is so amazing), God saved a man named Saul of Tarsus who was a Hebrew, a Pharisee, who was trained by Gamaliel, one of the greatest Pharisees who ever lived. He was a persecutor of the followers of Jesus. And Jesus Christ appeared to him on the road to Damascus in a great light, and..."

"Jesus was Jewish?" Mohammed interrupted.

"Yes. He is a descendant of King David in the body, in His flesh, in His humanness. Jesus Christ is a descendant of King David."

"Okay," Mohammed said.

"God said of Judah that His scepter would never depart from the tribe of Judah. David was of the tribe of Judah. Jesus, King of kings and Lord of lords, is of the tribe of Judah. He's known in the Word of God, in the Old Testament, as the Lion of the tribe of Judah [Revelation 5:5]. Yes, Jesus Christ, my friend, is God in the flesh."

"In the Jewish religion, right? The Jewish religion, part of the Old Testament?" Mohammed asked.

"The problem is, the Jewish people rejected their Messiah. They deny their Savior, Jesus. So, while the Jewish people hold to the law of God (or try to), the law of Moses, and while they believe that a messiah will come, they deny Jesus as the Messiah. And they killed Him. But Jesus died so that people like you and me, Mohammed, can be set free."

"The Jewish people are waiting for a messiah?" Mohammed asked.

"The Jewish people are awaiting a messiah, at least those who still believe. Many Jewish people today, Mohammed, are atheists."

"Oh," Mohammed exclaimed.

Many of the religious Jewish people believe they are still waiting for a messiah to come. But Messiah has already come in the person of Jesus Christ—fully God and fully man and without sin. He shed His innocent blood on the cross and rose from the grave to set sinners free."

"And why did they kill Jesus?" Mohammed asked.

"They killed Jesus because He said He is God. Jesus said to the Pharisees (the Jewish religious leaders), 'Before Abraham was, I AM' [John 8:58]. Now, if you remember what Moses wrote, Moses talked about his encounter with God in the burning bush. Do you remember that?" I asked.

"Okay."

"Moses asked God, 'Who shall I say sent me?' And God said, 'I AM that I AM has sent you.' He identified Himself as 'I AM.' 'Yahweh.' 'I AM.' Jesus said to the Jewish leaders, 'Before Abraham was, I AM.' And they picked up stones to kill Him, because by saying 'I AM,' they knew that Jesus was saying He is God."

"And they deny it?" Mohammed asked.

"They deny it. Yes. And so do most of the people of the world, my friend. So, do most of the people of the world."

Mohammed gave every outward indication that he was Muslim, but he had not yet identified himself as such. While I was confident he was Muslim, I didn't want to make assumptions and risk unnecessarily offending him. So I asked, "Are you Muslim?"

"Yes."

"Okay. Correct me if I'm wrong, but the Muslim religion also denies that Jesus is God."

"Ah, yes. We believe Jesus was prophet," Mohammed explained.

"But He was more than a prophet," I said. "Let me show you."

I opened my Bible to the book of Hebrews

"In a letter written to the Hebrews (we're not sure who wrote the letter; many people believe it was the Apostle Paul, but no author is given in the letter, so we're not sure who actually wrote it) it says this: 'Long ago, at many times and in many ways, God spoke to our fathers by the prophets, but in these last days he has spoken to us by his Son, whom he appointed the heir of all things, through whom also he created the world. He is the radiance of the glory of God and the exact imprint of his nature, and he upholds the universe by the word of his power. After making purification for sins, he sat down at the right hand of the Majesty on high, having become as much superior to angels as the name he has inherited is more excellent than theirs [Hebrews 1:1-4].'

"Yes, God spoke through prophets, but in these last days he has spoken through His Son, Jesus Christ. He is more than a prophet. He is the exact imprint in human form of God Himself. He is God in the flesh. He was with the Father in creation and the Word of God says that all things were created by Him and through Him and for Him [Colossians 1:15-20]. Nothing has ever been made that was not made by our Creator, Jesus Christ. And God has given Him all authority on earth and in heaven and under the earth [Matthew 9:6-8; 28:18-20; Philippians 2:5-11; Ephesians 1:20-22]," I explained.

"Okay. There are groups in Christianity?" Mohammed asked, changing the subject.

I do not believe Mohammed changed subjects as frequently as he did because he did not want to deal with the information I was presenting to him. I really believe he was simply an inquisitive man who was hearing many things, some of which maybe for the first time.

"Yes. There are different groups in Christianity, just as there are different groups in Islam," I explained.

"Okay. How many?" Mohammed asked.

"I don't know how many."

"But the bigger?"

"There are what we call 'denominations.' Some of them are good. Some of them are bad. Some of them believe the Bible. Some of them preach the gospel that I'm sharing with you. Some of them declare Jesus as Lord. Others of them say they are Christian, but they deny the truth of God's Word and they deny Jesus Christ. So, a Christian is not one who belongs to a denomination or a particular church. A Christian who is one who has, by faith, turned from his sin and put his trust in Jesus Christ alone for his salvation. So long as the Bible is being taught and Christ is being worshiped, there are many different churches that are truly Christian churches. What makes them truly Christian is that the members of that church worship the Christ, worship Jesus Christ as Lord, as Creator, as King, as Savior. They believe the Word of God as the true and inerrant, infallible Word of God and they bring the gospel to the world," I asserted.

"So a big group is Roman Catholic?"

"Well, Roman Catholicism is not Christian."[5]

"Oh."

---

[5] See Appendix 4.

"Roman Catholicism is not Christianity. Most of the world thinks that Roman Catholicism is Christianity because Roman Catholics say they believe in Jesus. But they believe a different gospel. They believe a message that is not from Christ."

"So, what is the difference?"

"Here's the difference: The Bible says that it is by grace we are saved through faith and that not of ourselves. It is a gift from God, not as a result of works, so that no man may boast [Ephesians 2:8-9]. Roman Catholicism believes that it is faith in Jesus plus works. The Apostle Paul gave this very stern warning in his letter to the Galatians, to a church in a city called Galatia. Here in chapter 1, the Apostle Paul writes: 'I am astonished that you are so quickly deserting him who called you in the grace of Christ and are turning to a different gospel— not that there is another one, but there are some who trouble you and want to distort the gospel of Christ. But even if we or an angel from heaven should preach to you a gospel contrary [or different than] the one we preached to you, let him be accursed. As we have said before, so now I say again: If anyone is preaching to you a gospel contrary to the one you received, let him be accursed [Galatians 1:6-9].'

"The Roman Catholic Church is cursed of God because they have distorted the gospel. They preach a different gospel than what Jesus Himself and the apostles brought."

"And they don't believe in Jesus?"

"They believe in Jesus, but they believe that Jesus' sacrifice on the cross is not enough to save them. They believe they must also do good works and that they must be part of the Roman Catholic Church and that they must do penance for their sins. They don't trust Christ alone for their salvation as the Bible commands. They trust in Jesus and their ability to do good works."

"Okay," Mohammed said.

I sensed it was time to begin probing deeper into Mohammed's beliefs and gently confront him about some of the myriad issues with the false religion to which he subscribed.

"Isn't that true in Islam, as well?" I asked. "Aren't you required to do good works, obey the five pillars of Islam[6], in order to hope for mercy from God?"

---

[6] According to the "A Brief Illustrated Guide to Understanding Islam" website ("What Are the Five Pillars of Islam?," *A Brief Illustrated Guide to Understanding Islam*, accessed March 31, 2016, http://www.islam-guide.com/ch3-16.htm.): "The Five Pillars of Islam are the framework of the Muslim life. They are the testimony of faith, prayer, giving *zakat* (support of the needy), fasting during the month of Ramadan, and the pilgrimage to Makkah once in a lifetime for those who are able.

"1) The Testimony of Faith: The testimony of faith is saying with conviction, '*La ilaha illa Allah, Muhammadur rasoolu Allah.*' This saying means 'There is no true god (deity) but God (Allah), and Muhammad is the Messenger (Prophet) of God.' The first part, 'There is no true god but God,' means that none has the right to be worshipped but God alone, and that God has neither partner nor son. This testimony of faith is called the Shahada, a simple formula which should be said with conviction in order to convert to Islam (as explained previously on this page). The testimony of faith is the most important pillar of Islam.

"2) Prayer: Muslims perform five prayers a day. Each prayer does not take more than a few minutes to perform. Prayer in Islam is a direct link between the worshipper and God. There are no intermediaries between God and the worshipper.

"In prayer, a person feels inner happiness, peace, and comfort, and that God is pleased with him or her. The Prophet Muhammad said: {Bilal, call (the people) to prayer, let us be comforted by it.} Bilal was one of Muhammad's companions who was charged to call the people to prayers.

"Prayers are performed at dawn, noon, mid-afternoon, sunset, and night. A Muslim may pray almost anywhere, such as in fields, offices, factories, or universities.

"3) Giving *Zakat* (Support of the Needy): All things belong to God, and wealth is therefore held by human beings in trust. The original meaning of the word *zakat* is both 'purification' and 'growth.' Giving zakat means 'giving a specified percentage on certain properties to certain classes of needy people.' The percentage which is due on gold, silver, and cash funds that have reached the amount of about 85 grams of gold and held in possession for one lunar year is two and a half percent. Our possessions are purified by setting aside a small portion for those in need, and, like the pruning of plants, this cutting back balances and encourages new growth.

"A person may also give as much as he or she pleases as voluntary alms or charity.

"4) Fasting the Month of Ramadan: Every year in the month of Ramadan, all Muslims fast from dawn until sundown, abstaining from food, drink, and sexual relations.

"Yes."

"That's no different than the Roman Catholic Church, and that's a different gospel. Salvation is through faith in Christ alone."

"Okay. The Christians who follow the Bible are called..." Mohammed wondered.

"They are Christians. Those who believe the Bible is the Word of God and who believe in Jesus Christ alone for their salvation, they are Christians.

"So, Mohammed, do you know if your sins will be forgiven?" I asked.

"Uh, no," Mohammed matter-of-factly replied.

"You *can* know. The Bible says, 'These things have been written so that you may know that you have eternal life' [1 John 5:13]. My friend, you can know that you are forgiven for your sins against God, but you must come to God on His terms. And He commands you, my friend, He *commands* you to repent and to put your trust in Jesus Christ alone for your salvation."

"You said that Jesus has paid, has paid for your sins?" Mohammed asked.

"Although the fast is beneficial to health, it is regarded principally as a method of spiritual self-purification. By cutting oneself off from worldly comforts, even for a short time, a fasting person gains true sympathy with those who go hungry, as well as growth in his or her spiritual life.

"5) The Pilgrimage to Makkah: The annual pilgrimage (*Hajj*) to Makkah is an obligation once in a lifetime for those who are physically and financially able to perform it. About two million people go to Makkah each year from every corner of the globe. Although Makkah is always filled with visitors, the annual *Hajj* is performed in the twelfth month of the Islamic calendar. Male pilgrims wear special simple clothes which strip away distinctions of class and culture so that all stand equal before God.

"The rites of the Hajj include circling the Kaaba seven times and going seven times between the hillocks of Safa and Marwa, as Hagar did during her search for water. Then the pilgrims stand together in Arafa and ask God for what they wish and for His forgiveness, in what is often thought of as a preview of the Day of Judgment.

"The end of the Hajj is marked by a festival, Eid Al-Adha, which is celebrated with prayers. This, and Eid al-Fitr, a feast-day commemorating the end of Ramadan, are the two annual festivals of the Muslim calendar."

"Yes. Jesus took upon Himself the punishment I deserve for my sins against God. Let me put it to you this way..."

"Okay. Uh, listen, listen," Mohammed insisted.

"Sure."

"You said, you said Jesus has paid for your sins. Yes?"

"Yes."

"And you don't need to work anymore?

"No."

"Then why you go to church?

"I don't go to church to work. I go to church to worship."

"Huh?"

The idea of going to church to freely worship God seemed to perplex Mohammed.

"I don't go to church to work. I go to church to worship. Here's the beautiful thing, Mohammed: because God saved me, because He forgave me of my sins through what Jesus did on the cross, I now *want* to do what pleases Him—not to earn His love, not to earn His forgiveness, but because I am so thankful for the salvation that He freely gave to me through faith in His Son. So, I go to church to thank God for the love He has given me."

"Oh, to worship?"

"Yes. Yes. Yes," I replied.

"So, that is also work."

Like every false religion created in the minds of sinful men, Islam is a works-righteousness belief system. Like the Mormon, Jehovah's Witness, and Roman Catholic, the Muslim is taught that he must earn God's favor through good works.

"That's not work," I explained. "I don't earn anything for worshiping God. I don't earn anything, because Jesus already paid my debt. Let me show you. This is beautiful. The Apostle Paul wrote a letter to a church in Colossae." I quickly turned to Colossians in my Bible. "Almost there. Here we go. The Apostle Paul wrote this letter to a church in Colossae, and he says to them: 'See to it that no one takes you captive by philosophy and empty deceit, according to human tradition, according to the elemental spirits of the world, and not according to Christ. For in him [in Christ] the whole fullness of deity dwells bodily, and you have been filled in him, who is the head of all rule and authority. In him also you were circumcised with a circumcision made without hands, by putting off the body of the flesh, by the circumcision of Christ, having been buried with him in baptism, in which you were also raised with him through faith in the powerful working of God, who raised him from the dead. And you, who were dead in your trespasses and the uncircumcision of your flesh, God made alive together with him [Jesus, having raised him from the dead], having forgiven us all our trespasses [all our sins] by canceling the record of debt that stood against us with its legal demands. This he set aside, nailing it to the cross. He disarmed the rulers and authorities and put them to open shame, by triumphing over them in him [Colossians 2:8-15].'

"What God did through His Son Jesus Christ is this: the debt I owe to God, the debt you owe to God was nailed to that cross. God looked at the sacrifice of His Son as sufficient, as payment in full for the sins of those who would repent and believe in Jesus."

"Okay," Mohammed said.

"So, you can have your sins forgiven—not based on your righteousness, not based on your works, but based on the work of Christ on the cross. It would be like this: if you were standing before a judge in a courtroom, and you had broken the law, and the judge said, 'Mohammed, it's going to be a million-dollar fine or the rest of your life in prison,' could you pay that fine?" I asked.

"No."

"Neither could I," I replied. "Just as the judge is about to do what is right according to the law and send you away to prison forever because you could not pay the fine, somebody walks into the courtroom (someone you've never met). He walks up to the judge's bench, puts $1,000,000 on the judge's bench, and he says, 'Your Honor, I've sold everything. I've sacrificed everything. And because I love Mohammed, I'm going to pay his fine. You can let him go.'

"The judge looks at you and says, 'Mohammed, you are guilty of breaking the law and I have sentenced you to a fine you cannot pay. I would be just, I would be right to send you to prison. But I'm going to let you go, not because you are good (you broke the law), not because you could pay the fine (you couldn't). I'm going to let you go because this other person came into the courtroom and he paid the fine you owe.' Would that be good news?"

"Ha! Yes."

"What would you think of the man that paid your fine? What would you think of him?" I asked.

"Good!" Mohammed exclaimed.

"And that's what Jesus Christ did on the cross, my friend. He took upon Himself the punishment we deserve for our sins against God. He took it upon Himself even though He knew no sin. And He defeated sin and death when He rose from the grave. Now, Mohammed," I continued, "to receive that good gift, you must turn from your sin (repent) and put your trust in the One who paid the fine for sinners."

"Okay."

"I mean you no disrespect, but Muhammad could not pay your fine. In your religion, there is no one to pay your fine. But Christ did. So, turn to Christ, my friend, and live. Turn to Christ and receive forgiveness of your sin!"

"Uh, all Christians go to church for worship?" Mohammed asked.

My conversation with Mohammed had already been a long one, but I was fully invested. As men, Mohammed and I couldn't be more different. We were worlds apart in just about every conceivable way. By this point, we had known each other for all of half an hour. It was likely that I would never see Mohammed again. But I loved this man.

I continued to fight off the frustration of communicating the gospel to Mohammed, only to have him to return to a subject we had covered several minutes prior. I was in a fight, but not a fight with Mohammed. I was in a fight *for* Mohammed—*for his soul.*

"Yes, not to work; to worship," I explained. "Christians go to church to worship Christ and to learn through the teaching of His Word, the Bible. We do not go to church to work. We Christians have rest from work in Christ. We don't have to work to earn forgiveness. We don't have to work to earn God's love. It's given to us as a gift because of what Jesus did on the cross."

"So, you only do worship?" Mohammed asked.

"We do good works, too. As Christians we are called to do good works, but not to earn salvation."

"Okay."

"God has created us for good works. He has created us for that—good works to bring Him glory. We do not earn forgiveness. We do not earn love from God through our good works. We do good works to express our love *for Him* and our love for our fellow man."

"Okay. So, you do both things. You do both things: good works and worship."

"Yes, but we do not do good works for our salvation. That is a gift from God. We do good works as a form of worship."

"Okay, and explain more," Mohammed requested. "Like you said to me that it is not for forgiveness. You said that works are not forgiveness."

"We are forgiven freely. It is a free gift through our faith in Jesus Christ [Romans 6:23]. It is not through our works. Christians are not saved, we're not forgiven by our works. We're forgiven because of what Jesus did on the cross on our behalf. Because Jesus has saved us, He has changed our hearts. Now we want to do what pleases Him through worship and through good works, because we are thankful for the free gift of salvation He gave us. Does that make sense?"

"Yes," Mohammed answered. "This makes sense."

"Good. So, Mohammed, is there any reason why you would not repent and put your trust in Jesus Christ alone for your salvation? Why would you not receive such a wonderful gift?"

"Uh, uh." Mohammed wasn't sure what to say.

"Mohammed, do you believe what I'm telling you is true?" I asked.

"There are little differences."

"Do you mean there are differences between what I believe and what you believe?"

"Yes."

"Oh, yes. I know that. I know. And what I'm calling you to, my friend, is to repent of those differences, my friend. Jesus Christ is your only hope. Your only hope for forgiveness, your only hope for heaven, your only hope, my friend Mohammed, is Jesus Christ."

"In the beliefs, there are little differences," Mohammed said.

"Actually, Mohammed, they are big differences, because if you don't believe that Jesus Christ is God in the flesh, you are condemned by God. That's a big difference. They're not little differences, my friend. They are differences that span all of eternity. They are the difference between heaven and hell."

"Okay."

"They're big differences."

"Yes."

"And, my friend, you must repent and put your trust in Jesus Christ alone for your salvation, my friend. I want to see you in heaven. I want to see your sins forgiven. I want to worship our Creator together. But you must come to faith in Jesus Christ alone. Will you please think about these things? God bless you, my friend. Very good talking to you. God bless you. I'm going to do a little preaching."

But, I could tell Mohammed has at least one more question for me. "Do you have one more question?" I asked.

"Atheists: they have no evidence?"

"They have the same evidence of God's existence that you and I do. The difference is, my dear friend, you and the atheist deny the evidence that there is but one God and that He has sent His Son Jesus Christ to save sinners. So, if you do not want to be condemned, my dear friend Mohammed, turn to Christ and live."

"Thank you."

"God bless you, Mohammed."

And with that we said goodbye.

Mohammed stayed in the area until we finished our evangelism for the day. Even as I preached in the open air, my mind often returned to our conversation, and I prayed for him throughout the remainder of the day.

I have thought of Mohammed many times since that day, and I sincerely hope that we will meet again in heaven.

Appendices

Appendix 1: The Gospel According to Satan

American Evangelicalism's False Gospels

American Evangelicalism, as a religious system, is not Christian. It is a pool filled with the swill of strange fire, false teachers, and blasphemy. It is a river of spiritual refuse in which one should not bathe. It is a deadly stream of demonic theology and methodology from which no one should ever drink.

American Evangelicalism is not the Body of Christ. The true Church, the beautiful Bride of Christ, finds herself within American Evangelicalism. Entire biblical churches and remnants of true believers within bad, dying, or dead churches are lumped into that category and must wade through the muck and mire. While not yet perfected, fully sanctified, or glorified, the Bride of Christ is kept clean and healthy and is constantly being refined (most often by fire) by her Bridegroom Jesus Christ the Lord in the midst of American Evangelicalism's quasi-Christianity.

American Evangelicalism is Roman Catholicism in a Hawaiian shirt. It is Mormonism in Birkenstocks. It is Transcendentalism in a three-piece suit. It is Buddhism with bling. It is Spiritism for suburbanites. It is just about anything but Christian. Sadly, what flows like damaging flood waters over the banks of the American Evangelicalism River is not one false gospel but many false gospels. And every false gospel is a gospel according to Satan.

With the above in mind, I will strive to answer two questions: what and why? *What* common false gospels have found a home in American Evangelicalism? And, *why* must we publicly identify false gospels and their teachers? Paul's example in Scripture will help to explain why we must call the false teachers to repent and warn Christians and non-Christians alike to steer clear of (witting or unwitting) sons and daughters of the devil who are under God's anathema.

The What: False Gospels of American Evangelicalism
The False Gospel of Works Righteousness

Works righteousness is frequently taught in many American Evangelical churches. It's simply packaged and delivered in a way that is less obvious and, frankly, less honest than the methods employed by other false religious groups.

What does a works righteousness message sound like? A cursory look at some of the sermons and sermon series being preached in American Evangelical churches is rather telling. The following sermon title suggestions are taken from Outreach.com[1] under the heading "Changing Your Life":

- "Simple Steps to Change Your Marriage"
- "Simple Steps to Being a Better Parent"
- "Simple Steps to Getting Your Finances on Track"
- "Simple Steps to Eternity"

Under a series titled "Make Great Choices" are other suggestions:

- "Choices that Enhance Your Marriage"
- "Choose to Make Your Family Great"
- "Choices that Improve Your Finances"
- "The Choice that Changes Your Eternity"

Can you hear the works righteousness in the titles? Suggested steps and choices too often come before any call to repent and believe the gospel.

While I'm sure that many American Evangelical pastors who preach these kinds of sermons intend to help people, they only set the unconverted up for failure. The person in the pew hears about formulas for a better marriage, family, and finances. In their lost state, they try very hard to implement these formulas. They work, and they work, and they work. After all, the guy at the front of the church, sitting at the small table in front of the coffee shop set design, claimed that these five simple steps would work.

Sadly, these series too often end with a presentation of the life-enhancement gospel, which is no gospel at all. "Have you been trying

---

[1] "Sermon Theme Postcards," *Outreach, Inc.*, last modified 2016, accessed July 26, 2015, http://www.outreach.com/promo/sermon-series-examples.aspx.

to do the things I suggested but still find yourself struggling?" the pastor asks. "Could it be that you haven't chosen Jesus yet? Could it be you haven't yet taken the steps necessary to have a relationship with Jesus? Trust Jesus and you will find that it will get so much easier to have the marriage, the family, the financial stability, and the peace of mind and heart you've always wanted."

The lights dim. The worship leaders quietly make their way back to the stage as the pastor makes his final pitch and the chorus to a catchy tune plays softly in the background. "Come on," the pastor pleads with the audience. "What do you have to lose? You've tried everything else. Try Jesus."

Sadly, the unconverted sinner sitting in the pew wants a better life more than he wants to be reconciled to his Creator, so he says to himself, "Maybe Jesus is the missing piece. I'm doing everything else. I'm doing the best I can, but it's not enough. Something's missing."

Instead of realizing, through repentance and faith, that Jesus is all in all, he relegates the King of kings and the Lord of lords to the position of divine butler—the missing piece to the good life. With a tear in his eye, he finally gives in. He raises his hand when asked to by the pastor. He repeats the pastor's suggested prayer. He asks Jesus into his heart and he hopes for the best.

Then he continues to work. He doesn't work out his salvation with fear and trembling. He doesn't examine and test himself to see if he is in the faith. He doesn't repent of his sin. He just keeps working very hard with all the sincerity he can muster. But he still never seems to measure up. For the next 20 years, he struggles to love his wife, lead his family, have integrity at work, manage his money well, and make it to church on a regular basis. All the while he holds onto the hope he placed in his sinner's prayer and in his best efforts to live according to the Bible's teachings.

But when he dies, he is clothed only in his works righteousness, instead of the imputed righteousness of Christ. He hears the Lord say, "Depart from me, you worker of lawlessness. I never knew you."

As a side note, Outreach.com also offers rather revealing sermon suggestions for a series titled "Sorry We Were Jerks!":

- "Sorry for Being Hypocritical and Non-Relevant"

- "Sorry for Being Judgmental and Only Trying to Convert You"

Do you think a pastor preaching this series is going to preach the converting gospel of Jesus Christ? No, he will be relevant and non-judgmental. He will be a life coach and never a pastor.

In this respect, the narcissistic, self-help false gospel of works righteousness demonstrates that American Evangelicalism not only failed to cut the umbilical cord to Rome Catholicism, but actually had no real intention of ever leaving Rome in the first place.

The False Gospel of "Just Lovin' on People"

His name was Ethan, a young man in his early twenties from Arkansas. I met him, of all places, in the Chinook train station in Calgary, Alberta, Canada.

Kevin St. John (my brother in the faith) and I were heralding the gospel and reading Scripture on a very hot Saturday afternoon. When Ethan approached me, Kevin was preaching and I was distributing tracts and watching Kevin's six (his back). We had a table set up with Bibles and tracts on it. "So, have you guys been out here doing this all day?" Ethan asked.

"Yes we have."

"I'm a missionary," Ethan said. "I'm up here with a group of people. We were sent up here by Generation Send, a group in the Southern Baptist Convention."

"So, what's your mission?" I asked.

"Oh, we're here just to love on people."

"And what does that mean?"

"We're here to get to know people and to love them where they're at."

"And how are you presenting the gospel to people?" I asked.

"Oh. Well our leader told us, 'Don't you dare share the gospel with anyone until you know the color of their eyes.'"

I explained to Ethan, as gently as I could, that no one needed his friendship, that his ability to know the color of someone's eyes was not the power of God for salvation. I told Ethan that the people of Calgary didn't need his love. They needed Christ's love. I tried to encourage him to ignore what his leader had told him and, instead, hand out gospel tracts and communicate the gospel with people, whether or not he knew their eye color.

Ethan seemed to receive what I told him. Later in the afternoon, however, I saw Ethan with several young ladies, presumably members of his group. They were walking from a nearby mall to the train station. Each of them was carrying bags from expensive stores in the mall.

Ethan and the members of his group were not missionaries. They were "vacationaries." They weren't in Calgary to reach lost people with the gospel. They were in Calgary to "love on people" while taking a vacation. This kind of pseudo-evangelism encourages young people to be narcissistic on mommy and daddy's dime. American Evangelicalism's idea of loving people to Jesus is, in many ways, just a repackaging of the false social gospel.

Building houses in Mexico is not the gospel.

Building irrigation and water purification systems in Africa is not the gospel.

Volunteering at homeless shelters and soup kitchens is not the gospel.

The church's food and clothing pantries are not the gospel.

Political activism in Jesus' name is not the gospel.

Teaching English as a second language in a foreign country is not the gospel.

Neither are you, yourself, the gospel. Your love for people is not the gospel. Your service to people is not the gospel.

I am not saying that any of the above actions are wrong or unimportant. Christians should be engaged in acts of love and service. Build houses, irrigation systems, and water purification systems. Volunteer at homeless shelters and soup kitchens. Work at and/or supply food and clothing pantries. Teach English as a second language in a foreign land. But, do it all as a means to the most important end, the most loving end, the only eternal end. Do it all as you are making disciples, as you are preaching the gospel of Jesus Christ.

Without the gospel, all of your labor, no matter how well intended, is vanity and will have no eternal significance in the lives of the lost people you serve.

The False Gospel of "Synergism"

One more false gospel of which I want to make you aware is "synergism, a concept woven into the two false gospels already considered.

The GotQuestions.org website provides a clear explanation of "synergism" and the reasons it is unbiblical[2]:

> When we talk about monergism vs. synergism, theologically speaking, we're talking about who brings about our salvation. Monergism, which comes from a compound Greek word that means "to work alone," is the view that God alone effects our salvation. This view is held primarily by Calvinistic and Reformed traditions and is closely tied to what is known as the "doctrines of grace." Synergism, which also comes from a compound Greek word meaning "to work together," is the view that God works together with us in effecting salvation. While monergism is closely associated with John Calvin, synergism is associated with Jacob Arminius, and his views have greatly shaped the modern evangelical landscape. Calvin and Arminius aren't the creators of these views, but are the best-known proponents of Calvinism and Arminianism.
>
> While monergism claims that God is both a necessary and sufficient condition for our salvation, synergism will agree that God is a necessary condition, but will deny His sufficiency. Our free will plus God's activity is what makes it sufficient. Logically speaking, we should be able to see the flaw in the synergistic argument—that God doesn't actually save anyone. This places the responsibility for salvation on us, for it is we who have to make salvation real by placing our faith in Christ. If God doesn't actually save anyone, then it is possible that no one will be saved.

Synergism is cancer in the blood of American Evangelicalism. It rejects the sovereignty of God and instead makes man sovereign over salvation. Is it any wonder that so many pastors who buy the lie of synergism also water down the gospel to make it more palatable to

---

[2] "Monergism vs. synergism—which view is correct?", *Got Questions Ministries*, accessed July 27, 2015, http://www.gotquestions.org/monergism-vs-synergism.html.

the lost hater of God? Is it any wonder that so many synergistic American Evangelical churches put the "felt needs" of the lost before the worship of Christ through man-centered music, man-centered programs, and man-centered forms of outreach?

Synergistic Christians and churches believe God needs their help. After all, God needed their help to save them, so why wouldn't He need their help to save others? To the synergist, the gospel alone is not the power of God for salvation to all who believe. Instead, they believe the gospel, plus the believer's winsome personality, ability to be relevant, and efforts to serve, make the gospel desirable, make Jesus lovelier, and make salvation attractive.

Synergism and its blasphemous counterpart, decisional regeneration (i.e. altar calls, the sinner's prayer, etc.), are responsible for more false converts around the world than any other aspect of American Evangelicalism.

The Why: Publicly Identifying False Gospels and Their Teachers

> I am amazed that you are so quickly deserting Him who called you by the grace of Christ, for a different gospel; which is really not another; only there are some who are disturbing you and want to distort the gospel of Christ. But even if we, or an angel from heaven, should preach to you a gospel contrary to what we have preached to you, he is to be accursed! As we have said before, so I say again now, if any man is preaching to you a gospel contrary to what you received, he is to be accursed!
>
> For am I now seeking the favor of men, or of God? Or am I striving to please men? If I were still trying to please men, I would not be a bond-servant of Christ (Galatians 1:6-10).

Paul was astonished at how quickly the church in Galatia was turning from the truth of the gospel to the lies of the zeitgeist (the spirit of the age). The Greek word Paul uses to express his astonishment is *thaumazó*. The same word is used similarly in Luke 11:37-38: "Now when He had spoken, a Pharisee asked Him to have lunch with him; and He went in, and reclined at the table. When the Pharisee saw it, he was surprised that He had not first ceremonially washed before the meal." The Pharisees' astonishment no doubt included a sense of indignation because Jesus, a rabbi, made no effort to follow the ceremonial law of washing.

Paul's astonishment at the Galatians quick desertion was fueled by a sense of indignation. The rapidity with which the Galatians began to abandon the gospel bewildered him. Paul had never witnessed a church abandon the gospel. Paul's visceral reaction to what he was seeing in the Galatians was not unlike the disciples' reaction to seeing Jesus publicly engaged in conversation with a Samaritan woman (John 4:1-42).

In verse seven, Paul makes it clear that the gospel he preached to the Galatians was the only true gospel and that any other teaching presented as the gospel is no gospel at all. There is no room for argument or debate. Nowhere in his writings does Paul communicate a tolerance for the intellectual and theological cowardice found in so much of American Evangelicalism—this erroneous idea that one's own interpretation of Scripture is not to be challenged, questioned, or corrected. So many evangelicals echo the world when they say, "Your truth is your truth, and my truth is my truth."

Nonsense! The apostle Paul did not write to the Galatians to confirm that the gospel is open to anyone's interpretation or that the false gospels of the world should be given equal consideration with true gospel of Jesus Christ. Paul, like Jesus, was utterly intolerant of everything that was false.

Just as Jesus is the only way, the only truth, and the only life, His gospel (as revealed in Scripture) is the only gospel. Like Jesus and Paul, every Christian must be utterly intolerant of any false idea masquerading as the true gospel.

Paul finishes Galatians 1:7 with these words: "there are some who are disturbing you and want to distort the gospel of Christ." In his commentary on verse seven, Charles John Ellicott describes the troublemakers as "The Judaising party, with its restless factiousness and bigotry, causing schisms and divisions in the Church."[3]

---

[3] "Ellicot's Commentary for English Readers," *Bible Hub*, accessed July 27, 2015, http://biblehub.com/commentaries/galatians/1-7.htm.

Albert Barnes provides more detail in his commentary on the verse[4]:

"Though this is most manifestly another system, and not the gospel at all, yet there are some persons who are capable of giving trouble and of unsettling your minds, by making it plausible. They pretend that they have come direct front the apostles at Jerusalem; that they have received their instructions from them, and that they preach the true gospel as they teach it. They pretend that Paul was called into the office of an apostle after them; that he had never seen the Lord Jesus; that he had derived his information only from others; and thus they are able to present a plausible argument, and to unsettle the minds of the Galatians."

Barnes' comments bring to mind the New Apostolic Reformation, a cultish movement with false teachers and false gospel peddlers like Bill and Beni Johnson and Kris Vallotton of Bethel Redding, Mike Bickle of the International House of Prayer, Cindy Jacobs, Bob Jones (now deceased), Patricia King, Che Ahn, Dutch Sheets, and the man who started it all—C. Peter Wagner. These charlatans actually believe they are super apostles who have been specially anointed by God to be greater than the original apostles. Sadly, millions of people around the world lack the most basic levels of wisdom and discernment to see through their false teachings.

These false teachers work from a theological mixing bowl containing the dry ingredients of Word of Faith, Prosperity, and New Age Mysticism heresies, which are bound together by the wet ingredients of carny schemes, parlor tricks, and psychological manipulation. The result is a poisonous and deadly spiritual cake that the undiscerning and unsaved enjoy. Like the Judaizers who had infiltrated and influenced the church of Galatia, false teachers of the New Apostolic Reformation distort the gospel for their own sordid, narcissistic gain.

---

[4] "Barnes' Notes," *Bible Hub*, accessed July 27, 2015, http://biblehub.com/commentaries/barnes/galatians/1.htm.

The ESV translates the Greek word *metastrephó* as "distort." The NASB's translation is somewhat weak and doesn't provide the reader with a depth of understanding of this word. It is better translated as "pervert."

In Acts 2:20, Peter quotes Joel 2:28-32 during his Pentecost sermon and uses the same Greek word (*metastrephó*) to describe how "The sun shall be turned to darkness and the moon to blood, before the day of the Lord comes, the great and magnificent day."

In this verse, *metastrephó* is translated as the phrase "shall be turned." The heretical, bloodsucking false teachers of the New Apostolic Reformation and other similar movements are trying to turn the gloriously bright light of the true gospel into something dark and demonic, something that cannot breathe life into a single soul.

In Galatians 1:8-9, Paul uses repetition, a common Jewish literary device, to drive home his very important point: "But even if we, or an angel from heaven, should preach to you a gospel contrary to what we have preached to you, he is to be accursed! As we have said before, so I say again now, if any man is preaching to you a gospel contrary to what you received, he is to be accursed!" Twice, Paul warns the Galatians that those who propagate a false gospel—one contrary to the message Paul received directly from Jesus Christ—are accursed. They are anathema. Paul also uses the same word in 1 Corinthians 16:22. "If anyone does not love the Lord, he is to be accursed. Maranatha." Paul sees those who do not love Jesus as no different than those who tamper with the Word of God. They are to be pronounced spiritual outcasts. They are literally dead to the Spirit of Christ and are cursed of God.

Why is there such a harsh pronouncement on false teachers? It starts with love for the Lord and His Word, love for His people, and even love for the false teachers themselves. Galatians 1:10 says, "For am I now seeking the favor of men, or of God? Or am I striving to please men? If I were still trying to please men, I would not be a bond-servant of Christ."

Exposing and defeating the false gospels of Satan requires us to be willing to die to self, deny ourselves, take up our crosses, and follow Christ, no matter what the cost. To seek the approval of men over God is to love men more than God. To seek to please men at the expense of the gospel is to love men more than the gospel. Anyone in a pulpit or pew who seeks the approval of the lost at the expense of Christ and His gospel should not be thought of as a brother or sister in Christ.

Rick Warren and Luis Palau, who overtly seek the approval of the antichrist pope and Vatican City, should not be seen as our brothers in Christ. Joel Osteen, the invertebrate pastoral darling of Oprah Winfrey, should not be seen as our brother in Christ. Any pastor who welcomes homosexuals into his church without calling them to repentance and faith in Christ should not be seen as our brother in Christ. Homosexuals and other unsaved individuals are certainly welcome in my church, but they are welcomed to hear the Word of God and the glorious gospel of Jesus Christ, welcomed that they might come to repentance and faith and be numbered among those Paul speaks of in 1 Corinthians 6:9-11:

> Or do you not know that the unrighteous will not inherit the kingdom of God? Do not be deceived; neither fornicators, nor idolaters, nor adulterers, nor effeminate, nor homosexuals, nor thieves, nor the covetous, nor drunkards, nor revilers, nor swindlers, will inherit the kingdom of God. Such were some of you; but you were washed, but you were sanctified, but you were justified in the name of the Lord Jesus Christ and in the Spirit of our God.

The local congregations that truly represent the Bride of Christ do not welcome sinners into their midst so they can remain pleased and comfortable with their sin or continue to live in the delusion that God loves them just the way they are. No, sinners of every kind are welcomed into real churches so they can hear the glorious truth that God does not love them just the way they are (another one of American Evangelicalism's false gospels). Rather, He loves them in spite of who they are. He loves them so much that He will not leave them just as they are. Because of His great love for the sinners He has chosen from eternity past to save, He changes them! He makes them new creatures!

In 2 Corinthians 5:16-21, we read:

Therefore from now on we recognize no one according to the flesh; even though we have known Christ according to the flesh, yet now we know Him in this way no longer. Therefore if anyone is in Christ, he is a new creature; the old things passed away; behold, new things have come. Now all these things are from God, who reconciled us to Himself through Christ and gave us the ministry of reconciliation, namely, that God was in Christ reconciling the world to Himself, not counting their trespasses against them, and He has committed to us the word of reconciliation. Therefore, we are ambassadors for Christ, as though God were making an appeal through us; we beg you on behalf of Christ, be reconciled to God. He made Him who knew no sin to be sin on our behalf, so that we might become the righteousness of God in Him.

Conclusion

American Evangelicalism is rife with satanic gospels and antichrists. But the true Church, the true Bride of Christ, portions of which presently exist within the realm of American Evangelicalism, is beautiful. While not yet fully sanctified and not yet glorified, Satan and his false gospels have no hold on her. Satan will never be able to separate the Bride of Christ from the love of God, which is in Christ Jesus her Lord.

Therefore, the Bride of Christ, because of her love for the Bridegroom and His gospel, because of her love for the Word of God, because of her love for the lost, cannot remain silent. The false gospels that are welcomed and presently allowed to run loose through American Evangelical churches must be identified. And the propagandists, whether in the pulpit or the pew, must be exposed and called to repentance and faith in Jesus Christ.

Appendix 2: Starting an Abortuary[1] Ministry
By Patte Smith

The content of this chapter is taken from Patte Smith's blog article, "How to Begin to Witness at Killing Places."[2] It has been edited and reprinted here with Patte's consent. Patte was the first person to whom I turned when the thought entered my mind to minister outside of abortuaries.

~~~~~~~~~~~~

Jesus used the birth of my son, almost 38 years ago, to draw me to Himself. At 21 I was a godless girl. The Lord gave me a great gift. He allowed me to become a single mother to a beautiful boy at the age of 21.

When my husband Scott and I went off to seminary in Orlando in 1992, I found out that there were three abortuaries killing babies in the shadow of parachurch ministries, Bible colleges, and church steeples. I was horrified. Knowing personally what an incredible blessing it is to be given a child, and being convinced that it is the very time God can get a lost woman's attention, I wanted Jesus to use me to rescue the perishing.

At first I would stand and quietly pray outside the killing places. Then, I started shadowing a sidewalk counselor who would personally engage every abortion-bound mother in conversation, offering her love and help. Eventually, the Lord helped me to find my

---

[1] Author's Note: "Abortuary" is a slang term for an abortion clinic. I (Tony Miano) had never heard the term before I started using it, but I also know there is nothing new under the sun. However the word came into existence, I use "abortuary" because I believe it aptly describes what takes place inside the building: murder. Unborn children are summarily and cruelly put to death as those who should be expectant parents offer their babies as human sacrifices on the altar of convenience.

[2] Patte Smith, "How to Begin to Witness at a Killing Place," *Sanctuary Ministries*, last modified April 21, 2010, accessed January 26, 2016, http://sanctuaryministries.blogspot.com/2010/04/how-to-begin-to-witness-at-killing.html.

trembling voice and I began to speak to the lost mothers, too. One of the things I noticed was that pro-life ministries tended to speak in very humanistic, therapeutic language. Abortion-vulnerable and post-abortive mothers were called "victims." I became more and more uncomfortable with this unbiblical, man-centered approach, so I integrated God's law and His just demands to repent when I spoke with mothers. I also began to call out when the women were far away and even when they went inside the building.

It was very encouraging to me when I heard Ray Comfort's message on biblical evangelism, called *Hell's Best Kept Secret*, for the first time. Finally, another Christian was agreeing that the law is essential to helping sinners to see the terrible truth about their sin, the reality of their impending doom in hell, and their desperate need to repent and believe the gospel—to believe upon the Lord Jesus Christ.

We are honored to love the mothers and fathers and babies we meet, and are willing to do our best, by the grace and provision of God, to help them physically, emotionally, practically, and financially. But, the central focus of all our labor is to lift up the name of Jesus Christ in the field of blood and souls. We want to glorify the Lamb as well as visit the orphans in their affliction. We give the lost and their children the gospel of life and eternity.

Establish where and when abortions are taking place in your community. You'll need to call the killing place posing as someone who is interested in having an abortion.[3] Get the earliest and latest possible abortion appointment times on the day that you would like to minister.

The editorial staff of Forerunner.com provides the following suggested script:[4]

---

[3] Author's note: Before taking this step, you must reconcile in your own heart whether there are any circumstances in which it is not sinful to be untruthful. I recommend seeking your pastor's/elders' counsel and follow his/their lead. In the end, if you cannot personally reconcile the issue, then you should not follow this particular suggestion.

[4] "Behind the Scenes (Part 3) Call the Abortion Center for Information," *The Forerunner*, last modified December 14, 2011, accessed January 26, 2016, http://www.forerunner.com/impact/behind-the-scenes-part-3-call-the-abortion-center-for-information.

1. Call the 800 number of the killing place from a pay phone (on their dime). (Doesn't have to be a pay phone, but this prevents them from being able to ID you.) Be prepared to give the date of the first day of your last period. (For first trimester abortions count back two months from today. For second or third trimester, count back 4, 5, 6, 7 months, whatever stage of pregnancy you are trying to find out about.) A man can just as easily call and give his girlfriend or wife's last period.

2. Say: "I'd like to make an appointment for a termination/abortion/procedure on _____. What is the earliest and latest time I can come in?" Or if you want all the killing times in a given week (or two): "I'd like to make an appointment for a termination/abortion/procedure next week. I want to find the best possible time to come in. What is the earliest and latest time I can come in on Monday? Tuesday? Wednesday?" etc.

3. You can either say, "Okay. I'll figure it out and call you back" or ask any detailed question that you want to know about the actual "procedure."

4. You can also witness to the clinic worker by telling her that you feel guilty because you know that it's a baby and that you know you are killing your baby. You can say that it isn't your baby's fault that you had sex and the baby shouldn't be punished. You also wonder if you should think about adoption. You can ask her if they give any counseling about adoption. etc., etc., etc.

5. You can ask the clinic worker if there are any "Christians" outside who hold signs and will try and talk to you to change your mind. You can ask the worker what she thinks about those people. What are they like? Are they nice? Do they really help anyone? etc.

Arrive 45 minutes early and if possible, plan to stay at least 30 minutes after the last abortion time. Arriving early will allow you to get situated, pray, and then engage every abortion-bound mom and their companions. This will often allow you to engage the abortuary workers as well.

Procrastination is a big problem. Don't put it off. Get out there and spy out the land. Figure out where to park, where to stand, etc. If possible, try to stop everyone who is arriving as they pull into the parking lot and offer them your ministry packet. Of course, much of what you are able to do depends on the set up of the clinic itself. Hopefully you'll have good access to the mothers. There may be other pro-lifers out there and they can show you the lay of the land.

Visit your local Crisis Pregnancy Centers (CPCs). Before you go to the killing place, I'd highly recommend that you make an appointment and speak with the director of your local CPC. CPCs can be located by looking under Abortion Alternatives in the yellow pages. Let them give you a tour of the center and look through their ministry materials. Get their hours of operation and establish whether they perform ultrasounds on abortion-minded women. Ask if they can give you brochures for pregnant and abortion-minded women so that you can have these on hand or even include them in your ministry packet. Be sure to get the ones *for* pregnant women and *not* the ones they give to raise support from the church.

Ask the director about the ministry. Be sure to inquire about their message, whether they are faithful to use Scriptures and to share the biblical gospel. For example, you can ask, "Exactly what do you say to a woman who says she is going to have an abortion?" CPC counselors rarely, if ever, speak of God or use the words "wrong," "murder," "sin," "judgment," "wrath," "hell," and "repentance." Almost half of the women who abort today will already have murdered at least ONE child or *more* before you meet them at the killing place. Ask the director what they say to a woman who admits to having already had one or more abortions. The call to repentance is often left out of counseling or at least is compromised and diluted by many other humanistic, non-directive/non-judgmental types of counseling, as is often the case in the churches.

Explain to the CPC director how vital God's law and the call to repentance are in reaching the lost. Take time to give her some biblical evangelism materials, such as a CD with Ray Comfort's *Hell's Best*

Kept Secret and *True and False Conversion.*[5] These gospel tools may revolutionize the life and ministry of that women's center, bring many women to the saving knowledge of Christ, and save the lives of countless children.

As a side note, it is ideal if the center's brochures include the hours of operation and a map, showing exactly where the CPC is located.

While I appreciate these CPCs, they often have a "build it and they'll come" philosophy (similar to many American Evangelical churches). Studies have shown that 85% of many CPCs' business is *not* preventing abortion (unless they are located next to or across from a killing place). The vast majority of the women they serve are seeking pregnancy tests (whether they want their babies or not). They give out diapers, baby clothes, pregnancy clothes, and car seats. Women come for the free stuff. This is not bad in and of itself, but it is a fact that women's centers don't save the lives of many infants. All of this changes dramatically when the CPC purposely locates itself next to or across from a killing place and/or the counselors themselves go to the abortion clinic to call out to the women. I've seen this first hand and it is amazing proactive pro-life missionary labor! There is nothing that takes the place of Jesus' example of going to the lost.

If you go directly to an abortuary during abortion times, you *will* be involved in a direct- intervention ministry and will meet *all* of the aborting women (and men) face-to-face.

Here's a great book every Christian should have on his or her shelf. I highly recommend that you get the book *Pro-Life Answers to Pro-Choice Arguments* by Randy Alcorn. This comprehensive book is full of thought-provoking answers to the justifications that people make for killing children. It's wonderful!

Find adoption agencies in your area. Look under "adoption" in the yellow pages or do a Google search for Christian adoption agencies. Visit the director there as well. Ask if they are willing to help pregnant women, get their brochures for birth moms, and share

---

[5] *Hell's Best Kept Secret* and *True and False Conversion* are available on a single CD through Living Waters Publications
(http://store.livingwaters.com/audio/equipping/two-in-one.html).

Hell's Best Kept Secret and *True and False Conversion* with them, too. They will help you understand how adoption works. Remember, though, you do not have to become an expert on adoption. God has provided professionals to offer adoption counseling. Direct the women you counsel to the adoption agency. Be sure to ask about the process of open adoption. It's a wonderful way for the abortion-minded mom to be proactive in personally selecting the right couple for her baby and also keep communication open so that she can continue to know how her child is doing.

Your initial approach with abortive mothers and fathers is very important. Here's how you might begin to reach out to the people you meet at the killing place. We commonly use the Good Samaritan model to start with. Smile and wave the car over and say, "Hi, my name is _____ and I have a special ministry packet for you." If they draw near or roll down their window to receive your ministry materials, ask the woman and her companions, "What is the biggest reason (or #1 reason) why you feel like you just can't have this baby right now?" From there, offer her practical, emotional, and spiritual help. Be genuine. Give her Scriptures such as Jeremiah 1:5 ("Before I formed you in the womb I knew you...") and Psalm 127:3 ("...children are a gift of the Lord..."). Help her to see that her baby is designed, created, and sustained by God, just as she is. It is important that you are willing to LISTEN and to give of your time, talent, and treasure to love the individual mothers that you meet, as God gives you the grace. It is important to direct her to the nearest women's pregnancy help/resource center if she is looking for a free pregnancy test. It's almost always a good idea to mention adoption as a wonderful option as well. Bring the adoption brochures (from a local Christian adoption agency if possible) with you and consider placing them right in your ministry packet. We like to point abortion-bound women to the websites: www.birthmother.com and www.parentprofiles.com because many of them are able to peruse these sites from their phones, even while inside the waiting room of the abortuary.

As the Lord (and time) allows, move your conversation from the natural to the spiritual. Go straight to the law, focusing on the sixth commandment. (There is no need to take them through the Good Person Test because it will already have been established that the woman and/or man is murdering their baby. Very few people deny that abortion is "wrong" or "murder" and most readily admit that it is "sin" and that God does not want them to do it.) Since sexual immorality is such a serious and damnable sin, we often explain that fornication is also forbidden by God. Avoid referring to abortion (murder) as one of their "options." God does not allow for murder of an innocent person, so we shouldn't either. Let the mother (and her companions) know that God forbids the shedding of innocent blood, so it is not a "choice" she is permitted to choose. We do not offer the gospel's message of grace unless or until a person is humble and stops justifying their sin.

If you are at the abortion clinic as the mothers and fathers are leaving after they have murdered their child, how you engage them is as important as how you engaged them when they arrived. It's important that you have a biblical understanding of genuine repentance. Proverbs 28:17 says, "A man who is laden with the guilt of human blood will be a fugitive until death; let no one support him." Because of this scriptural truth, I don't recommend post-abortion ministries or retreats.[6]

Visual aids are an effective component of abortion clinic ministry. When we first began our ministry, we arrived on the sidewalk outside the killing place with nothing but ourselves, our love of Christ, and His gospel for our perishing neighbors. After Jesus commanded His disciples to go out and preach the Kingdom, He asked them in Luke 22:35, "When I sent you out without money belt and bag and sandals, you did not lack anything, did you?" (See also Matthew 10, Mark 6, and Luke 9-10.) We saw the Lord use us to save babies

---

[6] Author's Note: Men and women who have carried out the horrendous act of murdering an unborn child should be treated in a biblical manner. However, speaking the truth in love does not mean that murderers of children should be coddled. They should not be treated as victims. They are perpetrators of a violent act and, as Patte indicates, many abortive parents have aborted more than one child by the time you will meet them at an abortuary. Abortive parents do not need retreats to heal and reflect. They need God to cause them to be born again so that they can repent and believe the gospel. Without Christ, God will punish abortive parents as murderers. Their only hope for forgiveness and reconciliation with their Creator is to repent and believe the gospel.

from abortion. He used us to love their mothers through their pregnancies and to share the truth of Christ with them.

As the years have gone by, we have supplemented our witness with many wonderful visual tools: fetal models of babies through the gestation period and signs and posters (with photos of aborted babies, babies developing in the womb, adoptive families, scriptures, etc.). We who are reaching out to counsel the women do not carry a sign, as we have our hands full with ministry materials and fetal models. But, a few of the Christians who join us to pray and to witness do carry signs.

I believe graphic images of aborted babies are the law of God ("You shall not murder.") in picture form, and as we all know, a picture is worth a thousand words. I believe that the law of God is perfect, converting the soul, because that is what the Word of God declares (Psalm 19:7). I believe that the law brings the knowledge of sin, because the Bible tells us so (Romans 3:20). I believe that the law of God is a tutor that points us to Christ, because the Scriptures plainly teach it (Galatians 3:24). So, we are unapologetic about using these photos right where we minister, and we keep them close at hand, but we keep them a short distance from us as we give the aborting mothers our earnest gospel plea.

Don't wait! Go out to the killing place as soon as you can. The enemy does not want you to reach out to women there, and he will do everything in his power to fill you with fear and discourage you. We have seen flat tires, sickness, family troubles, haunting dreams, and a serious escalation of vitriol (even violence) from a world filled with unsaved people who want to come against those who plan to engage the lost at killing places. Your abortion-bound neighbors might appear to be giants, but the Lord is able to give you courage and confidence and His anointing and authority. Just go! Grab a friend if you can. It's always better to go out to the lost in twos.

As the years have gone by, I have become more convinced than ever that the abortuary (as a mission field) should be part of every Christian's life in one way or another. If Christians don't care enough to go where the babies are sacrificed, it tells aborting moms, dads, abortionists, and clinic workers that Christians just like to say they care that infants are murdered by abortion. If Christians really cared, their "love" would be a verb.

Missionary David Livingstone said, "Sympathy is no substitute for action." The lost are not impressed or reached or impacted by feelings, words, or even prayers of "intention." As a friend of mine likes to say, "You don't get points for intention." Our love for those who are perishing must have feet. We must engage and intervene on behalf of Christ and the children He has created and the lost mothers who are slaves to sin and under the judgment of God.

You might enlist friends at church by explaining that there is room for every kind of spiritual and natural gifting outside killing places. We need prayer warriors, evangelists, mercy-gifted women to walk through pregnancy with the moms, men who will befriend the fathers, folks who will offer practical help (like fixing cars, home repairs, financial planning/budgeting, help with babysitting, housekeeping tips, etc.), people who can design ministry materials, benefactors who will "adopt" a woman through her pregnancy to help with financial needs, people to organize church groups to pray (I called it Adopt-a-Clinic), people to videotape ministry efforts, and the list goes on and on.

Here's a bold suggestion. I suggest that you prayerfully consider going to meet with the abortion clinic staff. You or someone on your team could call the mill ahead of time and ask to speak with an administrator. Or, ask for an appointment with the administrator. Say that you are organizing a help/support team for women in crisis pregnancies and thought she would know more about them than anyone else. Ask her, "What is the number one need of women who are aborting?" Ask her how many women change their minds about aborting every week and why. Ask her what she thinks would be the most helpful, practical resource to provide for women who are pregnant. Ask her how she thinks you can best help pregnant teens. Ask her what adoption agencies or adoption attorneys she recommends. Educate her with what you know about adoption and the resources of local CPCs. Ask whatever else you can think of. See how much she will tell you about the "procedures." Share the gospel! Offer your own ministry as a support for women who just can't go through with the procedure. Jesus could use your bold and compassionate witness to the clinic worker to bring him or her to Christ! It has happened! Give clinic workers gospel tracts and pass along these two websites: www.clinicworker.com and www.turnstatesevidence.com.

~~~~~~~~~~~~~~~

If what you have read in this chapter has moved you to consider engaging in abortuary ministry, you can contact me at info@crossencountersmin.com, or you can contact Patte Smith at pattesmith@gmail.com. We would be happy to further assist you with encouragement and ministry counsel and point you to helpful resources such as abortion-related gospel tracts, websites, and other materials.

Appendix 3: Scriptures for Abortion Clinic Ministry

These verses are listed in the order they appear in the Bible.

Genesis 1:27
"God created man in His own image, in the image of God He created him; male and female He created them."

Psalm 2:11-12
"Worship the Lord with reverence and rejoice with trembling. Do homage to the Son, that He not become angry, and you perish in the way, for His wrath may soon be kindled. How blessed are all who take refuge in Him!

Psalm 22:9-10
"Yet You are He who brought me forth from the womb; You made me trust when upon my mother's breasts. Upon You I was cast from birth; You have been my God from my mother's womb."

Psalm 127:3
"Behold, children are a gift of the Lord, the fruit of the womb is a reward."

Psalm 139:13-16
"For You formed my inward parts; You wove me in my mother's womb. I will give thanks to You, for I am fearfully and wonderfully made; wonderful are Your works, and my soul knows it very well. My frame was not hidden from You, when I was made in secret, and skillfully wrought in the depths of the earth; Your eyes have seen my unformed substance; and in Your book were all written the days that were ordained for me, when as yet there was not one of them."

Proverbs 3:7

"Do not be wise in your own eyes; fear the Lord and turn away from evil."

Proverbs 3:27

"Do not withhold good from those to whom it is due, when it is in your power to do it."

Proverbs 6:16-19

"There are six things which the Lord hates, yes, seven which are an abomination to Him: haughty eyes, a lying tongue, and hands that shed innocent blood, a heart that devises wicked plans, feet that run rapidly to evil, a false witness who utters lies, and one who spreads strife among brothers."

Proverbs 10:23

"Doing wickedness is like sport to a fool, and so is wisdom to a man of understanding."

Proverbs 14:12

"There is a way which seems right to a man, but its end is the way of death."

Proverbs 15:3

"The eyes of the Lord are in every place, watching the evil and the good."

Proverbs 21:7

"The violence of the wicked will drag them away, because they refuse to act with justice."

Proverbs 28:14

"How blessed is the man who fears always, but he who hardens his heart will fall into calamity."

Ecclesiastes 12:13-14

"The conclusion, when all has been heard, is: fear God and keep His commandments, because this applies to every person. For God will bring every act to judgment, everything which is hidden, whether it is good or evil."

Isaiah 1:15

"So when you spread out your hands in prayer, I will hide My eyes from you; yes, even though you multiply prayers, I will not listen. Your hands are covered with blood."

Isaiah 1:18

"'Come now, and let us reason together,' says the Lord, 'Though your sins are as scarlet, they will be as white as snow; though they are red like crimson, they will be like wool.'"

Isaiah 5:20

"Woe to those who call evil good, and good evil; who substitute darkness for light and light for darkness; who substitute bitter for sweet and sweet for bitter!"

Luke 1:39-45

"Now at this time Mary arose and went in a hurry to the hill country, to a city of Judah, and entered the house of Zacharias and greeted Elizabeth. When Elizabeth heard Mary's greeting, the baby leaped in her womb; and Elizabeth was filled with the Holy Spirit. And she cried out with a loud voice and said, 'Blessed are you among women, and blessed is the fruit of your womb! And how has it happened to me, that the mother of my Lord would come to me? For behold, when the sound of your greeting reached my ears, the baby leaped in my womb for joy. And blessed is she who believed that there would be a fulfillment of what had been spoken to her by the Lord.'"

Luke 2:6-7

"While they were there, the days were completed for her to give birth. And she gave birth to her firstborn son; and she wrapped

Him in cloths, and laid Him in a manger, because there was no room for them in the inn."

John 3:35-36

"The Father loves the Son and has given all things into His hand. He who believes in the Son has eternal life; but he who does not obey the Son will not see life, but the wrath of God abides on him."

Hebrews 10:26-31

"For if we go on sinning willfully after receiving the knowledge of the truth, there no longer remains a sacrifice for sins, but a terrifying expectation of judgment and the fury of a fire which will consume the adversaries. Anyone who has set aside the Law of Moses dies without mercy on the testimony of two or three witnesses. How much severer punishment do you think he will deserve who has trampled under foot the Son of God, and has regarded as unclean the blood of the covenant by which he was sanctified, and has insulted the Spirit of grace? For we know Him who said, 'Vengeance is Mine, I will repay.' And again, 'The Lord will judge His people.' It is a terrifying thing to fall into the hands of the living God."

Revelation 20:11-15

"Then I saw a great white throne and Him who sat upon it, from whose presence earth and heaven fled away, and no place was found for them. And I saw the dead, the great and the small, standing before the throne, and books were opened; and another book was opened, which is the book of life; and the dead were judged from the things which were written in the books, according to their deeds. And the sea gave up the dead which were in it, and death and Hades gave up the dead which were in them; and they were judged, every one of them according to their deeds. Then death and Hades were thrown into the lake of fire. This is the second death, the lake of fire. And if anyone's name was not found written in the book of life, he was thrown into the lake of fire."

Revelation 21:8

"But for the cowardly and unbelieving and abominable and murderers and immoral persons and sorcerers and idolaters and all liars, their part will be in the lake that burns with fire and brimstone, which is the second death."

Appendix 4: Pastor Chuck O'Neal's[1] Roman Catholicism Notes

The False Sacrifice of Christ in the Mass
The Catechism of the Catholic Church says:

CCC-1323: "At the Last Supper, on the night he was betrayed, our Savior instituted the Eucharistic sacrifice of his Body and Blood. This he did in order to perpetuate the sacrifice of the cross throughout the ages until he should come again, and so to entrust to his beloved Spouse, the Church, a memorial of his death and resurrection: a sacrament of love, a sign of unity, a bond of charity, a Paschal banquet 'in which Christ is consumed, the mind is filled with grace, and a pledge of future glory is given to us.'"

CCC-1324: "The Eucharist is 'the source and summit of the Christian life.'"

CCC-1357: "...bread and wine which, by the power of the Holy Spirit and by the words of Christ, have become the body and blood of Christ. Christ is thus really and mysteriously made *present*."

CCC-1367: "The sacrifice of Christ and the sacrifice of the Eucharist are one single sacrifice: 'The victim is one and the same: the same now offers through the ministry of priests, who then offered himself on the cross; only the manner of offering is different.' In this divine sacrifice which is celebrated in the Mass, the same Christ who offered himself once in a bloody manner on the altar of the cross is contained and is offered in an unbloody manner."

CCC-1405: "Every time this mystery is celebrated, 'the work of our redemption is carried on'..."

But the Word of God says:
(Scriptures are taken from the New King James Version of the Bible; emphasis is Pastor Chuck O'Neal's.)

---

[1] Pastor Chuck O'Neal is the pastor of Beaverton Grace Bible Church, in Beaverton, Oregon (http://www.beavertongracebible.org). His notes regarding Roman Catholicism are reprinted here with his permission.

Hebrews 1:1-3 – Repeated Sacrifice vs. Purged Our Sins

"God, who at various times and in various ways spoke in time past to the fathers by the prophets, has in these last days spoken to us by His Son, whom He has appointed heir of all things, through whom also He made the worlds; who being the brightness of His glory and the express image of His person, and upholding all things by the word of His power, when He had by Himself purged our sins, sat down at the right hand of the Majesty on high…"

Hebrews 7:26-27 – Repeated Sacrifice vs. Does Not Need Daily

"For such a High Priest was fitting for us, who is holy, harmless, undefiled, separate from sinners, and has become higher than the heavens; who does not need daily, as those high priests, to offer up sacrifices…"

Hebrews 9:12 – Repeated Sacrifice vs. Once & Obtained Redemption

"Not with the blood of goats and calves, but with His own blood He entered the Most Holy Place once for all, having obtained eternal redemption."

Hebrews 9:22 – Non-bloody Sacrifice vs. Without Blood No Remission

"And according to the law almost all things are purified with blood, and without shedding of blood there is no remission."

Hebrews 9:24-28 – Repeated Sacrifice vs. Once & Put Away Sin

"For Christ has not entered the holy places made with hands, which are copies of the true, but into heaven itself, now to appear in the presence of God for us; not that He should offer Himself often, as the high priest enters the Most Holy Place every year with blood of another—He then would have had to suffer often since the foundation of the world; but now, once at the end of the ages, He has appeared to put away sin by the sacrifice of Himself. And as it is appointed for men to die once, but after this the judgment, so Christ was offered once to bear the sins of many. To those who eagerly wait for Him He will appear a second time, apart from sin, for salvation."

Hebrews 10:11-14 – Repeated Sacrifice vs. One Sacrifice Forever

"And every priest stands ministering daily and offering repeatedly the same sacrifices, which can never take away sins. But this Man [CHRIST], after He had offered one sacrifice for sins forever, sat down at the right hand of God, from that time waiting till

His enemies are made His footstool. For by <u>one offering</u> He has <u>perfected forever</u> those who are being sanctified."

1 Peter 3:18 – Repeated Sacrifice vs. Once (Peter's Words)

"For Christ also suffered once for sins, the just for the unjust, that He might bring us to God..."

John 19:30 – Repeated Sacrifice vs. It Is Finished!

"He said, 'It is finished!' And bowing His head, He gave up His spirit."

Romans 6:9-11 – Repeated Sacrifice vs. Dies No More!

"...knowing that Christ, having been raised from the dead, <u>dies no more</u>. Death no longer has dominion over Him. For the death that He died, He died to sin <u>once</u> for all; but the life that He lives, He lives to God. Likewise you also, reckon yourselves to be dead indeed to sin, but alive to God in Christ Jesus our Lord."

Revelation 1:17-18 – Repeated Sacrifice vs. Alive Forevermore!

"And when I saw Him, I fell at His feet as dead. But He laid His right hand on me, saying to me, 'Do not be afraid; I am the First and the Last. I am <u>He who lives</u>, and <u>was dead</u>, and <u>behold, I am alive forevermore</u>. Amen. And I have the keys of Hades and of Death.'"

The Idolatry of the Mass
The Catechism says:

CCC-1375: "It is by the conversion of the bread and wine into Christ's body and blood that Christ becomes present in this sacrament."

CCC-1377: "The Eucharist <u>presence of Christ</u> begins at the moment of the consecration and endures as long as the Eucharist species subsist."

CCC-1378: "*Worship of the Eucharist.* In the liturgy of the Mass we express our faith in the <u>real presence of Christ</u> under the species of bread and wine by, among other ways, genuflecting or <u>bowing</u> deeply as a sign of <u>adoration of the Lord</u>."

CCC-1183: "The tabernacle is to be situated 'in church in a most worthy place with the greatest of honor.' The dignity, placing, and security of the Eucharistic tabernacle should foster adoration before <u>the Lord really present</u> in the Blessed Sacrament of the altar."

But the Word of God says:

Commentary

Is Christ bodily transubstantiated out of heaven and into the wafer? Is the wafer worthy of worship? Does the wafer have the power of justification, the forgiveness of sin? No! Christ finished His work upon the cross, said, "It is finished," bowed His head, gave up His Spirit, and now sits at the right hand of the Father as the one Mediator between God and men! (See John 19:30; 1 Timothy 2:5; Hebrews 10:12.)

Is Christ in the cup? Is it literally the transubstantiated blood of the Lord Jesus Christ, the same as the blood that flowed down at the cross? Is it worthy of worship! Does it have the power to save? A thousand times no! And no matter how big the cup of Roman Catholic wine, or who prayed over it, there is no Christ therein or power therein to save!

Scripture

Exodus 20:4-5

"You shall not make for yourself a carved image—any likeness of anything that is in heaven above, or that is in the earth beneath, or that is in the water under the earth; you shall not bow down to them nor serve them. For I, the Lord your God, am a jealous God, visiting the iniquity of the fathers upon the children to the third and fourth generations of those who hate Me..."

Isaiah 42:8

"I am the Lord, that is My name; and My glory I will not give to another, nor My praise to carved images."

Hebrews 10:11-14 – Sat Down at the Right Hand of God

"And every priest stands ministering daily and offering repeatedly the same sacrifices, which can never take away sins. But this Man [CHRIST], after He had offered one sacrifice for sins forever, sat down at the right hand of God, from that time waiting till His enemies are made His footstool. For by one offering He has perfected forever those who are being sanctified."

Mark 13:21-23

"Then if anyone says to you, 'Look, here is the Christ!' or, 'Look, He is there!' do not believe it. For false christs and false prophets will rise and show signs and wonders to deceive, if possible,

even the elect. But take heed; see, I have told you all things beforehand."
Mark 13:26
    "Then they will see the Son of Man coming in the clouds with great power and glory."
Acts 1:10-11
    "And while they looked steadfastly toward heaven as He went up, behold, two men stood by them in white apparel, who also said, 'Men of Galilee, why do you stand gazing up into heaven? This same Jesus, who was taken up from you into heaven, will so come in like manner as you saw Him go into heaven.'"
Matthew 25:31-32
    "When the Son of Man comes in His glory, and all the holy angels with Him, then He will sit on the throne of His glory. All the nations will be gathered before Him, and He will separate them one from another, as a shepherd divides his sheep from the goats."

The Idolatrous Worship of Mary

The Catechism says:
Regarding Mary's so-called "saving office":
    CCC-969: "Taken up to heaven she did not lay aside this saving office but by her manifold intercession continues to bring us the gifts of eternal salvation . . . . Therefore the blessed Virgin is invoked in the church under the titles Advocate, Helper, Benefactress, and Mediatrix."

Commentary
    This is a denial and blasphemy of Christ! Christ alone is our Advocate and Mediator! Christ sent the Spirit to be our Helper. Mary is none of these things, nor is she the "Queen" of heaven as paragraph 966 blasphemously declares. Bowing before a statue of Mary and/or praying to her is idolatry.

But the Word of God says:
1 John 2:1 – Christ Is Our Singular Advocate
    "If anyone sins, we have an Advocate with the Father, Jesus Christ the righteous."
1 Timothy 2:5 – Christ Jesus Is Our Mediator

330 of gospel conversations

"There is one God and one Mediator between God and men, the Man Christ Jesus."

John 14:16-17 – The Spirit of God Is Our Helper

"I will pray the Father, and He will give you another Helper, that He may abide with you forever—the Spirit of truth."

John 16:7-8 – The Spirit of God Is Our Helper – Sin, Righteousness, Judgment

"Nevertheless, I tell you the truth. It is to your advantage that I go away; for if I do not go away, the Helper will not come to you; but if I depart, I will send Him to you. And when He has come, He will convict the world of sin, and of righteousness, and of judgment."

Roman Catholicism's Ecumenical Heresy
The Catechism says:
(Emphasis is Pastor Chuck O'Neal's.)

CCC-1129: "The Church affirms that <u>for believers</u> the sacraments of the New Covenant are necessary for salvation. 'Sacramental grace' is the grace of the Holy Spirit, given by Christ and proper to each sacrament."

What does the Catholic Church teach regarding nonbelievers? "Good" people go to heaven without Christ or the Church:

CCC-846-847: "Outside the [Roman Catholic] Church <u>there is no</u> salvation," and yet in direct contradiction, the paragraph goes on to say:

> This affirmation is not aimed at those who, through no fault of their own, do not know Christ and his Church: Those who, through no fault of their own, do not know the Gospel of Christ or his Church, but who nevertheless seek God with a sincere heart, and, moved by grace, try in their actions to do his will as they know it through the dictates of their conscience - those too may achieve eternal salvation.

What does the Catholic Church teach regarding Muslims who deny the deity of Christ and His death, burial, and resurrection? "Good" Muslims go to Heaven without Christ or the Church:

CCC-841: *"The Church's relationship with the Muslims.* 'The plan of salvation also includes those who acknowledge the Creator, in the first place amongst whom are the Muslims; these profess to hold the faith of Abraham, and together with us they adore the one, merciful God, mankind's judge on the last day.'"

Commentary

According to Pope Francis and the Catholic Church, all you have to do to go to heaven is be a "good" pagan or a "good" idol worshiping Muslim. This is a blasphemy of Christ! This is the very definition of a "broad road" false gospel. The Catholic gospel is a gospel that the Bible knows nothing of.

But the Word of God says:

Matthew 7:13-14

"Enter by the narrow gate [CHRIST ALONE]; for wide is the gate and broad is the way that leads to destruction, and there are many who go in by it [ROME'S ECUMENICAL WAY]. Because narrow is the gate and difficult is the way which leads to life, and there are few who find it."

John 3:16 – Rome Can't Even Get John 3:16 Right!

"For God so loved the world that He gave His only begotten Son, that whoever believes in Him should not perish but have everlasting life."

John 3:18

"He who believes in Him is not condemned; but he who does not believe is condemned already, because he has not believed in the name of the only begotten Son of God."

John 3:36

"He who believes in the Son has everlasting life; and he who does not believe the Son shall not see life, but the wrath of God abides on him."

John 14:6

"Jesus said to him, 'I am the way, the truth, and the life. No one comes to the Father except through Me.'"

Revelation 21:8

"But the cowardly, unbelieving, abominable, murderers, sexually immoral, sorcerers, idolaters, and all liars shall have their part in the lake which burns with fire and brimstone, which is the second death."

Roman Catholicism's Baptism Heresy

The Catechism says:

CCC-1263: "By Baptism <u>all sins are forgiven</u>, original sin and all personal sins, as well as <u>all punishment for sin</u>."

CCC-1265: "Baptism <u>not only purifies from all sins</u>, but also makes the neophyte 'a new creature,' an <u>adopted son of God</u>, who has become a '<u>partaker of the divine nature</u>,' member of Christ and co-heir with him, and a temple of the Holy Spirit."

CCC-1213: "Through Baptism we are <u>freed from sin and reborn</u> as sons of God; we <u>become members of Christ, and are incorporated into the Church</u>..."

But the Word of God says:

1 Peter 1:18-19 – Water vs. Blood of Jesus

"Knowing that you were not redeemed with corruptible things, like silver or gold, from your aimless conduct received by tradition from your fathers, but with the precious <u>blood</u> of Christ, as of a lamb without blemish and without spot."

Revelation 5:9 – Water vs. Blood of Jesus

"You were slain, and have redeemed us to God by Your <u>blood</u> out of every tribe and tongue and people and nation."

Colossians 1:13-14 – Water vs. Blood of Jesus

"He has delivered us from the power of darkness and conveyed us into the kingdom of the Son of His love, in whom we have redemption through His <u>blood</u>, the forgiveness of sins."

1 John 1:7 – Water vs. Blood of Jesus

"The <u>blood</u> of Jesus Christ His Son cleanses us from all sin."

1 Corinthians 1:17-19 – Catholic Baptism vs. Not Sent to Baptize, but to Preach

"Christ did <u>not send me to baptize</u> [if baptismal regeneration were true, Paul would not say this], <u>but to preach the gospel</u>, not with wisdom of words, lest the cross of Christ should be made of no effect. For the <u>message of the cross</u> is foolishness to those who are perishing, but to us who are being saved it is the power of God."

Titus 3:5 – Catholic Baptism vs. Holy Spirit

"Not by works of righteousness which we have done, but according to His mercy He saved us, through the washing of regeneration and renewing of the Holy Spirit."
Ephesians 2:8-10 – Catholic Baptism vs. Grace and Faith That Is Not of Ourselves

"By grace you have been saved through faith, and that not of yourselves; it is the gift of God, not of works, lest anyone should boast. For we are His workmanship, created in Christ Jesus for good works, which God prepared beforehand that we should walk in them."

Tony Miano

A retired, 20-year law enforcement veteran, Tony Miano began preaching the gospel on the streets in 2005. He has communicated the gospel to thousands of people throughout the United States and other parts of the world, on street corners, on university campuses, outside abortuaries, inside malls, at bus and train stations, and anywhere else people gather. Tony is a frequent conference speaker and is often called on by churches to assist in their local evangelistic efforts. "Cross Encounters" is Tony's third book. Tony and Mahria have been married since 1985. Together, they have three adult daughters.

CPSIA information can be obtained
at www.ICGtesting.com
Printed in the USA
BVHW051928070522
636269BV00008B/151